THE
HOME
BUYER'S
KIT

THIRD EDITION

► **WORKING WITH AGENTS**

► **FINDING YOUR DREAM HOME**

► **FINANCING YOUR PURCHASE**

► **MAKING THE BEST DEAL**

EDITH LANK
Award-winning real estate columnist, Los Angeles Times Syndicate

**Real Estate
Education Company**
a division of Dearborn Financial Publishing, Inc.

While a great deal of care has been taken to provide accurate and current information, the ideas, suggestions, general principles and conclusions presented in this text are subject to local, state and federal laws and regulations, court cases, and any revisions of same. The reader is thus urged to consult legal counsel regarding any points of law—this publication should not be used as a substitute for competent legal advice.

Publisher: Anita A. Constant
Acquisitions Editor: Christine Litavsky
Associate Editor: Karen A. Christensen
Managing Editor: Jack L. Kiburz
Editorial Assistant: Stephanie Schmidt
Interior and Cover Design: S. Laird Jenkins Corporation

Published by Real Estate Education Company,
a division of Dearborn Financial Publishing, Inc.

Printed in the United States of America

96   10 9   8   7   6   5   4   3

Library of Congress Cataloging-in-Publication Data
Lank, Edith.
    The homebuyer's kit / Edith Lank. — 3rd ed.
        p.   cm.
    Includes index.
    1. House buying.   I. Title.   II. Title: Homebuyer's kit.
HD1379.L326 1994
643'.12—dc20   94-22977
                                                      CIP

Praise for the Previous Editions:

"If you are selling your home, Lank's *The Homeseller's Kit* is must reading. Lank's years of experience and knowledge are there for the taking."

—*Tri-City Herald*

"Whether you are selling your home or buying one, this book will answer most of your questions. The author is Edith Lank, an experienced real estate writer and teacher who knows her subject very well. . . . her valuable insight into how agents operate make the book well worth studying. . . . This is an excellent book for sellers and buyers who want to know what to expect. It is simple, nontechnical and easy-to-read, with insights that give the reader the confidence to sell a home."

—Robert Bruss, Syndicated Real Estate Columnist

"Lank, national real estate columnist and author, tells how to sell a home for the most money. . . . She offers advice on how much to ask, how to prepare the house for sale, when to use an agent and how to judge a buyer's capability to afford your house. She also covers recent law regarding home selling (Fair Housing and human rights laws), FHA/VA mortgage regulations, tax-saving strategies, charts, tables and checklists."

—*St. Petersburg (FL) Times*

"*The Homeseller's Kit* and *The Homebuyer's Kit* provide as thorough a coverage of the homebuying/selling process as you are likely to find. Lank is a veteran real estate practitioner whose writing reflects her knowledge of life in the real estate trenches."

—*The Real Estate Professional* (rated *The Homeseller's Kit* one of the 10 best-selling real estate books in the United States)

Contents

Preface

When our son and daughter-in-law called long-distance to say they were starting to look for their first home, I sat down at the typewriter and sent them ten closely typed pages of advice—everything I'd learned that could help first-time buyers—drawn from my experience in selling houses, teaching real estate at the college level and answering thousand of queries that pour in every year to my syndicated newspaper column, and radio and TV shows:

- How do we start to buy a house?
- How much house can we afford?
- Should we wait to save up more down payment?
- Which mortgage plan is best?
- Where do you find a good agent?
- Do we need a lawyer?

When I got up the courage to ask my daughter-in-law over the phone a few weeks later if the letter was helpful, she answered, "Terrific! I've already lent it to three people at my office. Edith, make it into a book."

Dannie, here it is.

Buying a home, particularly your first one, is an adventure, like a trip to a foreign country. First off, there's the language problem—the natives use words like *easement, margin* and *amortization* so fast you can't follow them. And they have strange customs as well. Is it polite to ask questions? Should you tip the driver?

It always helps to have a guidebook for the trip—here it is. Bon voyage, and have fun on your journey!

If you'd like to send me a postcard about your adventures, do write me at 240 Hemingway Drive, Rochester, NY 14620 or send e-mail to lank@sjfc.edu.

CHAPTER ONE

Starting Your Homebuying

Dick and Jane had fun in their house in the suburbs with Father (who carried a briefcase), Mother (who wore an apron) and Baby Sally (who laughed at funny Spot and Puff). You just knew they owned that home and that Father was paying off the mortgage as quickly as he could.

First-graders don't spend much time with that fictional family anymore. Neither do real estate agents—too much has changed. Mother may be out there building a career; more than half of today's mortgages involve two earners. Baby Sally may be among the missing; household size has shrunk. Neighbors may look different; one homebuyer in four is single, and unrelated persons are buying houses together.

Recent surveys by the U.S. League of Savings Institutions and the National Association of REALTORS® have documented the trends of the 1990s. Only 44 percent of homebuying households are made up of married couples with dependents. Unmarried couples, with or without dependents, now form a measurable segment of the homebuying population. As the 21st century approaches, older homebuyers make up an increasing share of the market, affecting the design of new housing and creating "trickle-down" opportunities for younger homebuyers in the form of the larger homes they leave behind.

Real estate finance has also changed. Where Grandpa was offered a simple mortgage at a standard, fixed interest rate, today's buyer can choose among hundreds of innovative plans, each designed to meet the borrower's particular financial needs.

The desire to retreat from the pressures of an increasingly crowded society, inflation, tax considerations, the need for self-expression: all enter into the decision to buy a home. When you own your own home you can play the stereo at midnight, keep a dog (keep two dogs!), plant a garden, drive nails into the walls wherever you want and use your own washer and dryer. And the portion of your monthly mortgage payment that goes to reduce the principal debt acts as automatic, forced savings.

What Must You Have in Order To Buy?

It takes just three things to buy a house: some cash, dependable income and good credit. And if you're lacking any of these three, no need to despair. Home ownership is still possible: there are techniques for overcoming each problem.

Just be sure to level with the real estate agent you work with about your financial problems. A competent agent can recommend appropriate financing strategy for your particular situation.

Shelter Two Ways: Income Tax

Deductions

In the 1990s home ownership offers one of the few remaining tax shelters. Property taxes on one's home and even on vacation property are completely deductible. Interest paid on up to $1 million in loans to acquire or improve a home (or two homes) is deductible—and that more than covers most of us. If the value of one's property rises over the years, additional borrowing of up to $100,000 in equity loans, refinancing or second mortgages also qualifies for federal tax deduction.

For homeowners in a 28 percent tax bracket, this means that Uncle Sam is making almost 28 percent of their monthly payment, with deductible property taxes and interest forming almost the whole of the payment in the first few years of the loan. Uncle's contribution shows up in the form of lower income tax owed or unexpected income tax refunds. Using the formula in Figure 1.1 will give you a rough idea of how much you could afford to spend on monthly mortgage payments. The calculation does not include further possible savings on state income taxes.

Deferrals

In addition, any profit you make when you sell your own primary residence qualifies for several delightful income tax breaks. If you replace your home with another of equal or greater value within two years (before or after the sale of the first), tax on your profit is postponed indefinitely. (If you buy a less expensive replacement, some of your profit is immediately taxable, the rest qualifies for rollover postponement.)

You can repeat this process any number of times, piling up untaxed profits on a string of homes, and then, any time you are 55 or older, you can take advantage of a one-time chance (you choose when to use it) to sell your long-time home and take up to $125,000 profit free of any federal income tax ever. And that exclusion can include untaxed profit on previous homes.

How Equity Builds

Besides the tax saving, in most areas you can expect some increase in the value of your home: an additional return on your investment, known as *equity* buildup. Price trends in real estate vary with locality; brokers can estimate what might happen in your area over the next few years.

FIGURE 1.1

Rent versus Mortgage Payment

This calculation arbitrarily assumes that 10 percent of your mythical mortgage payment would cover home-owner's insurance and principal repayment, with the rest going for deductible interest and property taxes. It also assumes your top tax bracket (known to accountants as your *marginal tax rate*) is 28 percent. If your tax bracket is higher, your tax savings will be correspondingly higher.

A. Your present rent $_____
B. Multiply by 1.32   × 1.32
C. Equivalent monthly
   mortgage payment $_____

The result (line C) is a rough estimate of the amount you could spend for monthly mortgage payment (principal, interest, property taxes and homeowner's insurance) without being out any more money at the end of the income tax year than you are with your present rental.

Equity represents the amount you'd have if you sold your home and paid off the *liens* (financial claims) against it—usually the mortgage. If you buy a $120,000 house with $25,000 down and a $95,000 mortgage, your equity the day after you move in is $25,000. Equity is the money you have invested in the house—it's like money in the bank.

If the house goes up in value by 5 percent in the next year, and your debt is paid down (*amortized*) by a paltry $1,900 that first year, your equity has grown to $32,900 (market value, $126,000, less remaining debt, $93,100).

Equity buildup assumes, of course, that the value of real estate rises. Can you count on prices rising in your area?

BUYER'S TIP

Financial advantages of buying your own home include

- Income tax deductions for property taxes and mortgage interest

- Prospect of increase in value over the years

Not since the 1930s have real estate prices varied so much from one area to another as they do now. At any given time, one part of the country sees rising values while another is hit by unfavorable economic factors. The real estate market is cyclical: A drop in prices eventually attracts new industries and turns into recovery. At one point the farm states are badly hit, but prices are skyrocketing on the East and West coasts; then the Midwest sees steady growth and increase in values while the coasts experience what stock analysts would call a "correction."

Overall, the United States experiences gradual growth in real estate prices every year, at least matching general inflation. Many experts believe that the major problems affecting certain areas—factors such as unemployment, drought, fluctuations in farm prices or the price of oil—have already been discounted, with the severe drops behind us. And in hard-hit areas, it's great to be a buyer. It's like buying stock when the market has bottomed out; recovery is almost certain.

There are better and worse times to sell one's home, but it's almost always a good time to buy.

If You Wait

Young people's first attempts at house-hunting often trigger bewildering—and misguided—advice from parents and grandparents who remember what things used to be like.

"You must not be looking carefully. Some broker's taking you for a ride. Why, we only paid $9,500 for this house, right after your father came back from the war," says a mother stunned by the prices her son reports in a Sunday phone call.

"Somebody's telling you all wrong, saying you should buy with such a small down payment. You tell that husband of yours to wait a few years until you've saved up some more money," says a grandparent with painful memories of the Great Depression.

The solid old-fashioned virtues of denial and thrift, however, no longer reward the homebuyer. The old traditions have some drawbacks. For young people in some areas, the house they want to buy keeps going up in price faster than they can accumulate a larger down payment. Meanwhile, they lose out in tax benefits, and their rent is probably raised too.

BUYER'S TIP

To prepare for your purchase:

- Start reading classified ads in the real estate section of your newspaper and visit open houses on the weekends—all this even though you're not ready to buy yet.

- If you're a veteran, send for your VA certificate of entitlement, just in case you end up wanting a VA mortgage.

- Contact a credit bureau and request an inexpensive (sometimes free) report on yourself, just to make sure that no mistakes will turn up.

- Sock away extra cash; you'll be motivated to skip a vacation or a movie when you have a short-term goal like accumulating money for a down payment and closing costs.

- *Don't buy anything on credit.* This is not the time to take on another car payment, buy a boat, or even apply for an additional credit card.

- If someone is making you a large cash gift toward your purchase, try to get it into your own savings account months before you apply for a mortgage loan.

If you can't find your dream house or can't afford it today, your best bet is to buy whatever you can, as soon as you can, however you can. Then start building your savings. When you finally locate the perfect house, you'll have something to trade in on the deal: a house in the same market area that's kept pace with whatever is happening in real estate values.

CHAPTER
TWO

You and the Broker

As you begin your house hunting, it helps to keep straight the various terms for real estate licensees.

Agent is a general term for anyone empowered to act for another. Most agents you meet have been hired by the seller and have special fiduciary duties to the seller (more on that important point later).

Broker is a legal term for someone licensed by the state to negotiate real estate transactions and to charge (usually the seller) for services.

Salesperson is the term for the holder of an entry-level license; allowed to assist a broker who is legally responsible for the salesperson's activities. (In some areas the word "agent" may be used for a salesperson, as opposed to a broker). A salesperson may not operate without supervision and may collect fees only from the sponsoring broker as a share of commissions earned by the salesperson's efforts.

REALTOR® is a trademark designation (properly capitalized, like Xerox or Frigidaire or Coke) for a broker (in some areas a salesperson) who belongs to a private organization called the local Association, or Board, of REALTORS®, a state board of REALTORS® and the National Association of REALTORS®. REALTORS® subscribe to a code of ethics that goes beyond state license law and usually sponsor a local multiple-listing system, which offers access to houses listed for sale by many different firms.

REALTOR-*Associate*® is the term used by some boards of REALTORS® for salespersons associated with member brokers.

So as you start your search for the best agent, should you prefer a salesperson or a broker? There's something to be said for each. In general, you can expect a broker to have had more education and experience. On the other hand, some long-time salespersons remain at that status simply because they prefer not to go into business for themselves. And you could run into a well-trained, highly motivated newcomer with the time and enthusiasm to do a first-class job for you.

Does the Broker Work for You?

So you think you're looking for "your" broker! In recent years, a Federal Trade Commission study found that most buyers believed the agent who helped them buy a house was their agent, putting their interests first. Many sellers also thought so, and, regrettably, so did many brokers.

It just ain't so.

Law of Agency

The Law of Agency clearly sets out the broker's duties to the *principal* (also known as the *client*), the one who retains and (usually) pays the agent. These *fiduciary* duties are complex, but they boil down to one thing: The agent must put the principal's interest first, above anyone else's, including the agent's own interest. Among the specific duties involved are the following:

- Obedience to the principal's instructions unless they are illegal. (Examples of instructions an agent would not obey: "Don't show the house to any Lithuanians." "Keep quiet about the broken furnace.")
- Loyalty to the principal, which strictly interpreted (it sometimes isn't) includes obtaining the highest possible price for the property and never suggesting any offer under the listed price.

- Confidentiality, which prohibits the agent from sharing with you details of the seller's financial or family situation, unless of course the seller has authorized such action to encourage offers. Whether the seller has received previous offers, and for how much, is also confidential information.
- Notice, a duty that obliges the agent to forward to the principal (seller) any fact that it would be in the seller's interest to know, whether or not the seller knows enough to inquire. *This one is of vital importance for you to understand.*

BUYER'S TIP

When house-hunting, keep in mind that an agent is *obligated* to tell the seller anything known about you that could benefit the seller.

So Where Do You Stand?

Unless you specifically hire your own buyer's broker to represent you (more on that later), none of these duties is owed to you.

"Yes," you say, "I know those are the duties of the listing agent. But I'm dealing with a different firm that cooperates through the multiple-listing system. My broker is the selling agent, and that's different."

No, it isn't. Both firms are agents for the seller. The second one, the one you're working with (let's not say "your agent") is a subagent of the first firm and of the seller. You are merely a third party in that relationship, a customer rather than a client.

It can be scary to realize this, but things aren't as bad as they seem.

First, the law does require the broker to be honest, straightforward and trustworthy with third parties. Your questions will receive honest answers, although sometimes an honest answer might be, "I am not allowed to tell you whether the seller is facing foreclosure; I must keep financial information confidential."

Besides answering your questions honestly, agents and sellers have an obligation to volunteer information about any serious (material) hidden defects you aren't able to see for yourself. State laws differ, though, on whether they must also tell you about past problems that don't technically affect the real estate, such as suicide or murder on the premises, illness of the seller and the like.

Second, you will receive a great deal of service (see list in the next chapter) paid for by the seller, because without this service to buyers, the property might never be sold.

And finally, you can take heart from the fact that, as a practical matter, many brokers end up violating their duty to the seller. A good agent empathizes with you, wants you to find what you want at a price you can afford and may emotionally adopt you. If brokers didn't to some extent identify with the buyer, not much real estate would get sold!

How To Protect Yourself

If the agent is duty-bound to put the seller's interest first (and there's only one first place), how should this affect your relationship with the broker?

First, realize that no confidentiality is owed to you. It's practical to reveal your financial situation if you expect to get effective service, but you may want to keep some information to yourself. The broker who knows that you would pay more "if we have to" is, strictly speaking, obliged to convey that information to the seller. Saying "but don't tell the seller that" won't help because the agent does not have any special obligation of obedience to you. Never reveal the highest price you are willing to pay to a seller's agent. Assume that whatever you say will be (or at least should be) transmitted to the seller.

Take advantage of the fact that you must receive honest answers to your questions. In a few states you are entitled to a seller's written disclosure of defects, but elsewhere, "Are you aware of any defects in this house?" is a good all-purpose query to ask of both seller and broker, preferably in front of witnesses.

Buyers' Brokers

What's to stop you from retaining your own broker, someone obligated to put your interests first and legally bound to help you obtain the property at the lowest possible price?

> ## 🏠 BUYER'S TIP
>
> In dealing with a seller's agent:
>
> - *Do not* reveal the highest price you are willing to pay on a particular property
>
> - *Do* ask whether the seller or agent knows of any defects in the property

Nothing.

If you want to find an agent who operates as a *buyer's broker,* call a few of the largest real estate firms in town and speak with the managing broker. If that company does not offer the service, it may know which ones do. Often a lawyer who is active in real estate can give you the names of buyers' brokers.

How are such brokers compensated?

The buyer's broker may ask for a nominal retainer to compensate for time invested; sometimes the retainer applies against eventual commission due or even against the purchase price of the property bought. If no property is bought within the contracted time, the retainer may be forfeited.

Occasionally, the buyer pays the usual share (perhaps half) of the commission that the seller originally promised to pay to a selling broker. In return, the seller may reduce the sale price by that amount, because the seller will be paying only half a full commission to the listing broker.

In theory, the buyer who specifically hires a broker should pay for the service. In real life, though, it usually works out that the seller pays the originally agreed-upon commission, part of which goes to the buyer's broker.

Why would the seller be willing to do that?

To help get the house sold.

Buyers, first-timers especially, don't have much spare cash lying around when the sale closes. Just to make the deal work, sellers are often willing to furnish the commission in that fashion.

Proponents of the system like it because it sets up an adversarial situation similar to that in which the parties retain two different attorneys.

Sellers and buyers each have a broker clearly working for them alone, without the conflicts of interest that arise under the more traditional system.

If you hire your own broker, you can expect to sign a contract in which you promise that during a specified period of time you will not house-hunt with anyone else, and that if you buy any property within that time in any fashion, your broker will be entitled to a fee.

The system can work well unless you find yourself tied to an agent who does not, in the end, suit your needs. But it's well to remember that the old-fashioned method, in which you would deal entirely with sellers' brokers, has been around for years, and can also bring satisfactory results.

Discount Brokers

Some sellers, willing to perform part of the brokerage work themselves, list their property with *discount brokers,* who offer a seller limited services for a reduced commission. You need to understand this relationship because if you run into one, you as a buyer will also be expected to do part of the work by yourself. Most often, the broker saves time by making appointments but sending you to view houses on your own. You may be offered less help with mortgage financing. Because discount brokers usually belong to a multiple-listing system, however, you can probably view their listed homes through other brokers, who can provide you with more service if that is what you want.

For Sale by Owner

Sellers who handle their own property are known as *FSBOs* (fizz-bo, "For Sale By Owner"). Some do it for the satisfaction of tackling an unaccustomed job, but they're not doing it just to pass on the saved commission to you. They usually plan to sell at fair market value and pocket the commission as extra profit in return for their efforts.

You will have extra work when you buy directly from an owner. Unless you retain your own broker, you'll have to negotiate face to face, seek extra attorney input into the written contract, explore financing options on your own and ride herd on your own mortgage application process. It may be extra important to have your own building inspector look the property over before you commit to buying.

There are two situations in which you might want to deal directly with a FSBO:

- The property is unique, and you feel strongly attracted to it.
- The place has been underpriced by a FSBO who chose to do without the services of an appraiser as well. In that situation, be prepared to act promptly; some investors lie in wait for unwary FSBOs and jump as soon as underpriced property hits the market.

It is generally a waste of energy to start your house hunting with FSBOs. Until you have a good grasp of prices in the area and the entire home buying process, it's difficult to deal with homeowners who often have an exaggerated idea of a home's value and who don't know how to proceed. Wait until you, at least, know what you're doing.

CHAPTER
T H R E E

Choosing an Agent

You will meet agents by answering advertisements, calling the phone numbers on lawn signs and visiting open houses. Best of all, perhaps, is a name suggested by a relative or friend who has had a good experience—but only if the agent in question specializes in the area or type of house you want.

In a strange town, you can write to the local chamber of commerce asking for maps and information; you will probably hear from several brokerage firms interested in working with out-of-towners. If you study the local newspapers, you will discover which agents are active in the areas you like.

If you don't hire a buyers' broker and you deal with sellers' agents, you might be tempted to play the field, thinking that you'll get many people out there looking for your dream house. In reality, though, the buyer who works with many brokers is working with no one. The first time an agent calls to tell you about a house that just came on the market and hears, "As a matter of fact, we saw that one with someone else this morning," your name is crossed off the list. In the absence of a legal relationship, most successful transactions flow from informal cooperation between buyer and broker. If you plan to use sellers' brokers, when you find a good one stick with him or her.

Tests To Apply

A few tests to apply when judging a sellers' broker:

- *Does the agent return phone calls promptly?* This simple question is a good screening device, whether you're looking for a broker, lawyer or plumber.
- *Does the agent explain things so you can understand them?* This attribute is especially important for first-time buyers. If you can find an agent who is a born teacher, you're in luck. (In fact, many brokers are former teachers.)
- *Does the agent seem ready to invest time in you?* Where the broker is holding open a house that's on the market, for example, does he or she just wave you through, asking as you leave whether you're interested in the house and letting it go at that? You want someone who, if not busy with other prospects, shows you the house in a professional manner, asks questions about your needs and wants and offers to sit down to discuss other places on the market if you're not interested in this one.
- *Does the broker suggest an initial session in the office, rather than simply meeting you at the house you called about?* To get good service, you need a financial analysis and discussion of your whole situation.
- *Does the agent ask questions about your finances soon after meeting you?* This may not be good manners in ordinary society, but it's the mark of an efficient broker who aims to give you good service.
- *Does the broker explain up front that he or she is acting as a sellers' agent?* In most states, this information must be given you in writing upon first contact.
- *Do the first houses suggested show that the broker has been listening and understands your wants and needs?* If you're shown houses with the wrong number of bedrooms or clearly out of your price range, forget it.

- *Does the agent seem conversant with local conditions?* Does he or she have maps of the area, handouts about schools, museums, property tax rates and the like?

The worksheet in Figure 3.1 can help you evaluate brokers.

Once you find a broker with whom you feel comfortable, one who inspires confidence, stick with him or her. Tell your broker about other firms' ads that interest you, even about FSBOs, so that the agent can investigate and report back to you. Ask for advice before visiting open houses on your own. And if you have the agent's home phone number, don't hesitate to use it. Real estate agents are accustomed to evening and weekend calls. Service is the only thing they have to sell, and they welcome any sign that you intend to utilize it.

FIGURE 3.1

✎ Worksheet for Evaluating Brokers

YES or NO	Agent 1	Agent 2	Agent 3
Returns phone calls			
Follows up on contact			
Uses office interview			
Understands your needs			
Runs financial analysis			
Uses interview sheet			
Explains things well			
Suggests financing methods			
Uses multiple-listing system			
Cooperates with other agents			
Knows the community			
Inspires confidence			

🏠 BUYER'S TIP

Look for an agent who

- Inspires confidence, is knowledgeable and has a professional manner

- Takes time to find out your needs and wants

- Discusses your current financial situation and suggests appropriate financing

- Knows about local conditions, such as schools and public transportation

- Extends your search through the multiple listing system and other agents

---

Using a Lawyer

Customs in real estate vary tremendously from one area to another. In some locations you may be told that no one uses a lawyer and that the legal work is handled by special escrow or title companies. The law does not require that you have legal counsel.

It is, nevertheless, usually foolish to proceed without professional help—your own attorney, entirely on your side. Lawyers are useful not so much for getting you out of trouble as for heading off trouble before it starts.

Your attorney can make sure that the sales contract protects your interests, intervene if problems arise before closing and review final figures to make sure that you get proper credit at settlement time.

Finding the Right Lawyer

Lawyers specialize, just as physicians do. You wouldn't go to a gynecologist for a sprained knee; neither do you want to end up with a corporate lawyer or a trial attorney for your house purchase. (In small towns, of course, most lawyers are generalists who handle real estate among many other matters.)

You can find a specialist in several ways:

- Ask your real estate broker to suggest (not recommend) two or three names.
- Ask a bank what firm handles its real estate work.
- Call a large law firm and ask which partner specializes in real estate.

Call an attorney's office early on and explain that you're starting to house-hunt. Don't hesitate to inquire about what the service is likely to cost. If you don't feel comfortable with what you hear, shop around.

Your lawyer will suggest the right time for further contact. If you have financial problems (judgments, etc.) that need clearing up, you may want legal input immediately. Otherwise you may not need to contact the lawyer again until you are ready to make a written offer to purchase a specific property.

What the Agent Does for You

The average person assumes that a real estate agent's job is to help you find a house, but that's only the tip of the iceberg. The typical broker will spend more time bringing you into agreement with the seller and, most important, helping you arrange to finance your purchase.

You can expect some services even if, as is most usual, you are using the seller's broker:

- *Analysis of your financial situation.* Don't be offended by what appear to be personal questions. A good agent asks them at the beginning because a lending institution will ask them later. During a first conversation, the broker is already forming a strategy for financing your purchase, based on the various mortgage options outlined in Chapter 7. Just don't reveal the top price you're prepared to pay.
- *Education in basic real estate principles.* Brokers expect to spend extra time with first-time homebuyers. You have a right to insist that every step be explained so that you feel comfortable with it.

- *Recommendation of a specific price range.* Without those parameters, all of you—sellers, agent and yourself—are just spinning your wheels.

- *Orientation to a new community.* If you are moving to another town, send for the local newspaper, read the ads and write to a couple of real estate firms that handle property in the area and in the price range you might be interested in. You may receive long-distance phone calls, maps and offers to meet your plane or arrange motel reservations or baby-sitting. Seeing the town with a broker as your chauffeur is one of the best ways to learn about neighborhoods, schools, shopping and the like.

- *Information about different locations.* The agent will not answer questions or volunteer information touching on any of the classes protected under human rights law—ethnic or racial composition of neighborhoods, for example. But a broker may answer your questions about the location of vegetarian restaurants and health clubs, give you factual information on per-pupil expenditure in various school districts or pinpoint on a map the organizations or religious institutions you are particularly interested in.

- *Screening of listings.* The agent will show you any house that's on the market and must be careful not to limit your choice by the use of subtle steering based on racial, religious or other forbidden criteria. Keep in mind, though, that a good agent is a skilled matchmaker, who listens instead of talking and then helps you narrow down available listings, thus making efficient use of your time.

- *Showing of property.* The agent will set up appointments for house inspections and (unless a discount broker) will accompany you. During the tours, don't be afraid to ask questions. The agent will have at hand a wealth of data on each house you see, including lot size, property taxes and assessment figures, age of the house, square footage, heating system and the like.

- *Estimation of ownership costs.* When you are seriously interested in a specific house, your agent will sit down to help you figure out how you could buy it and what it would cost you each month.

- *Contract negotiation.* The agent will prepare either a binding purchase contract or (in some areas) a preliminary memorandum of agreed terms. Differences between what you want and what the seller wants are negotiated by the broker until you and the seller reach what is known as a *meeting of the minds.*
- *Liaison with your attorney,* if you are using one. The broker works closely with the attorney from the moment you make your first written offer to purchase.
- *Financing expertise,* probably the most important and certainly the most time-consuming of the agent's activities. A skilled agent keeps in close touch with local lending institutions and helps you find the one that best suits you among hundreds of different mortgage plans.
- *Mortgage application assistance.* In many localities, the agent expects to make an appointment for you with a lending institution, help you prepare for the application interview, perhaps accompany you. While you're waiting for loan approval, the agent will keep in touch with the lender to straighten out any hitches that may develop.
- *Settlement.* Local customs vary, but in many areas the broker attends the closing session, and in a few places actually effects the transfer of title.

CHAPTER
F O U R

What Can You Spend for Your Home?

Back in the days when pork chops were a nickel apiece and people paid cash for their cars, an old rule of thumb said that you could spend up to two-and-a-half times your annual income for a house. If you made $5,000 (good money in those days), you could look at houses costing $12,500 (and that bought a lot).

That old guideline can still work if interest rates are around 10 percent, you can put 20 percent down, and you have few other debts. If rates were as low as 8 percent, you could plan on buying a house costing three times your income.

But otherwise it's not that simple any more. Most buyers finance with mortgages these days, and interest rates fluctuate in a way that would have been unthinkable in bygone days. Current thinking concentrates on monthly costs of ownership as they compare with income and debts.

Income is not the only criterion. Equally important in today's debt-driven society is the amount of your other obligations. Each lending institution and each mortgage plan has its own guidelines. Sometimes you are marked down for any long-standing debt that has more than six months to run, sometimes only for those with a full year or more to go. Outstanding student loans, life insurance payments or child support may affect your allowable mortgage payment— or they may not.

 **BUYER'S TIP**

If you are planning to finance a home purchase with a mortgage, don't finance major purchases, such as a new car, with loans that will reduce the amount of the mortgage for which you qualify.

First List Your Income

When making your estimate, include all the income of everyone who will be an owner of the house (see Figure 4.1). It's been many years since lenders refused to consider a wife's income toward mortgage qualification. Unmarried persons may pool their income to buy a house together, just as a married couple can. If you are self-employed, average your past two years' income from that source. Do not include one-time events like inheritances, insurance settlements and capital gains.

Next, list your monthly debt payments. Most lenders don't care about debts that will be paid off within six months (in some cases, 10 or 12 months), so omit those with less than six months to go. List actual monthly payments in a format like the one shown in Figure 4.2.

FIGURE 4.1

✎ Listing Your Income

	Owner 1	Owner 2
Salary (gross)		
Self-employment income		
Second job		
Dividends		
Interest		
Pension		
Social Security		
Rental income		
Child support, alimony (if under court order)		
Other		

Total _____ A _____ B

Total Income (A + B) = $_____

FIGURE 4.2

Listing Your Monthly Payments

	Owner 1	Owner 2
Car payment		
Furniture loan		
Appliances		
Boat or RV loan		
Revolving credit		
Student loan		
Other		
Total	_____ A	_____ B
Total (A + B) = $	_____	

Qualifying Ratios

Lenders figure your allowable mortgage payment many different ways. Some calculations even take into account your particular income tax payment and number of dependents. In general, though, you will hear about lending institutions' *qualifying ratios*. A typical ratio might be 28/36 or (more generous in the amount you could borrow) 29/41.

The first figure is the percentage of your gross monthly income the lender will allow as a maximum monthly payment. With a 28/36 ratio, you would be allowed to spend 28 percent of your monthly gross income on mortgage payment. This is roughly "a week's income for a month's payment" because a month contains an average of 4.3 weeks.

FIGURE 4.3

✎ **Maximum Monthly Payment (A)**

Using 28%:

Your monthly gross income $_____

Multiply by 28%   × 0.28

Maximum monthly payment $_____ (A)

Using a 28/36 ratio, a buyer with monthly gross income of $4,000 would be allowed up to $1,120 for monthly mortgage payment. You can perform the calculation for yourself.

The calculation in Figure 4.3 uses a ratio of 28/36. Local brokers can tell you if other ratios are currently in use.

Lenders figure the allowable payment two different ways, however, and the second calculation (shown in Figure 4.4) takes into account your other current debts. The second figure in the ratio (36%) seems to allow a higher percentage of monthly income for a mortgage payment, but that's because it must also cover other monthly debt payments.

FIGURE 4.4

✎ **Maximum Monthly Payment (B)**

Your monthly gross income $_____

Multiply by 36%   × 0.36

Maximum monthly debt service $_____

Subtract present payments   −_____

Available for monthly payment $_____ (B)

The same buyer, with a monthly gross income of $4,000, might have $400 in present debt payments. Applying the ratio (36%) yields $1,440 a month available for debt service. Subtracting present monthly payments of $400 qualifies the borrower for up to $1,040 in mortgage costs.

Lenders figure both ways and then take whichever figure is lower, more conservative. (That's why you don't want to go into debt for a new car while you're house-hunting.)

Whichever is the lower amount, A or B, is a rough estimate of the figure lenders will use for your maximum permissible monthly payment, PITI.

How Much Will This Carry?

The term PITI refers to the four standard components of a monthly mortgage payment: *principal, interest, taxes* and *insurance*. With most mortgage plans, the lender collects each month not only the first two items, but also one-twelfth of your yearly property taxes and one-twelfth of your homeowner's insurance premium. Those tax and insurance bills go directly to the lender, who will pay them with your money, put aside in a separate *escrow* or trust account. Lenders are concerned about those particular bills being met, to protect the security for their loan.

In the example given above, where $1,040 was the maximum PITI payment because the borrower had substantial other debts, how much could this buy? For starters, for how much of a mortgage loan could the borrower qualify?

The answer is not simple.

Property taxes and insurance figures differ from one house to another. Interest rates differ from one mortgage plan to another. And, of course, the amount of cash available for down payment will make a difference. It's relatively simple to make the calculation when a particular house is already in mind. Nevertheless, you can get a rough estimate at this point.

You'll need information (available from any agent) on average property tax bills in the price range and neighborhood you're aiming at. Homeowner's insurance is a simpler matter, since the whole calculation

FIGURE 4.5

> ### How Much for Debt Service?
>
> | | |
> |---|---|
> | Your maximum monthly payment (from last worksheets) | $_____ |
> | Subtract monthly property tax (from agent's estimate) | −_____ |
> | Subtract typical insurance | −_____30_____ |
> | Principal and Interest Payment | $_____ |

is a rough estimate anyway; $30 a month might be used. A wrong estimate won't make much difference here.

Assuming that property taxes average $2,400 a year in the neighborhood under consideration, the calculation on mortgage payment would run: $1,040 maximum payment, less $200 a month for taxes, less $30 a month for insurance, leaves $810 a month for principal and interest. Run the calculation for yourself in Figure 4.5, using the lower of the two final figures from your earlier calculations.

The next question: how much will that borrow? Again, the answer depends on several factors: mortgage plan chosen, interest rate, term (number of years the loan is to run). Assuming a 30-year fixed-rate mortgage and interest rates around 10 percent, the calculation comes from Appendix A. Locate 10 percent interest, for 30 years; the figure 8.78 indicates that each $1,000 borrowed will cost $8.78 a month. How many thousands will $810 carry? Divide $810 by $8.78. The result, 92.26, rounded off, indicates that $92,300 is the maximum mortgage for which the buyers qualify (see Figure 4.6).

So what price range should our hypothetical buyers look in? If they have $30,000 available for a down payment and can borrow $92,300, they can buy houses in the $122,000 range. For practical purposes, they could look anywhere under $135,000, because one never knows what

FIGURE 4.6

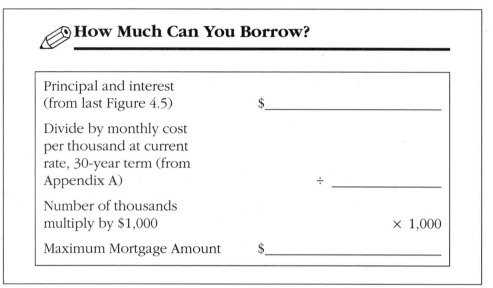

How Much Can You Borrow?

Principal and interest (from last Figure 4.5)	$_____
Divide by monthly cost per thousand at current rate, 30-year term (from Appendix A)	÷ _____
Number of thousands multiply by $1,000	× 1,000
Maximum Mortgage Amount	$_____

FIGURE 4.7

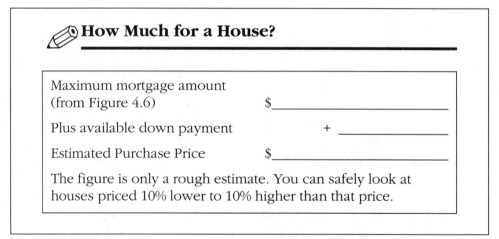

How Much for a House?

Maximum mortgage amount (from Figure 4.6)	$_____
Plus available down payment	+ _____
Estimated Purchase Price	$_____

The figure is only a rough estimate. You can safely look at houses priced 10% lower to 10% higher than that price.

sellers will take, and the whole calculation is rough anyway, until exact property taxes and interest rates are known (see Figure 4.7).

One caution: now that you've done all this work, don't be surprised if a skilled agent, working with knowledge of current ratios, interest rates and property taxes, comes up with a different recommendation!

CHAPTER

FIVE

Costs of Home Ownership

The monthly mortgage payment is, of course, the largest cost of home ownership for most people. If you buy at a time when interest rates are relatively low, you will probably opt for a fixed-rate mortgage. In that case, you can calculate at the start exactly what you'll pay each month for principal and interest for perhaps 15, 25 or 30 years.

When interest rates climb, more borrowers choose adjustable rate mortgages. If you know the lifetime cap or ceiling on your interest rate, you can calculate the worst case right at the beginning—the highest monthly charge you could ever have if interest rates shot through the roof some time during the term of your loan. These mortgage types are discussed in greater detail in Chapter 7.

The next two items in the standard PITI payment are taxes and insurance, which can be handled in one of two ways. You may meet those bills on your own, or—more likely—the lending institution will handle them for you.

Escrowing Taxes and Insurance

If your home were ever seized and sold for unpaid back taxes, the lending institution would be left with no security for its mortgage. If the house burned to the ground, only the vacant lot would remain as security. So your lender has a direct interest in seeing that you pay your taxes and insurance premiums on time.

With most mortgages, including all VA and FHA loans, an *escrow account* (reserve, impound, trust account) is set up for you by the lender. Each month, along with your principal and interest payment, you send one-twelfth of your anticipated property tax and homeowner's insurance cost. As the bills come due, they are sent to your lender, who pays them on your behalf.

Your lender is allowed to keep not only enough to pay the next bill due, but also a two-month surplus as a precaution. In less than half the states, you are entitled to interest on your escrow account.

You will receive regular reports, monthly or at the end of the year, on the status of the escrow account, which is, after all, your own money. At regular intervals, usually yearly, the account will be analyzed and your payment adjusted, up or down, depending on whether the account shows a surplus or deficit.

This adjustment can be a surprise to the homeowner with a fixed-interest mortgage, who expected monthly payments to remain at exactly the same amount for the full term of the loan. It is, of course, taxes and insurance costs that change, not—with a fixed-interest loan—the underlying principal and interest portion of the payment.

About Insurance

The *mortgagee* (lender) will require that you keep *hazard insurance* (fire and similar risks) on the property in an amount sufficient to cover the loan. As a prudent homeowner, you will want wider coverage, and for a larger amount.

Rebuilding after a fire, even partially, can sometimes cost more than your original purchase price. And you need personal protection for risks that don't concern your lender—liability for a guest who is hurt on your property, for example.

Your best bet is a *homeowner's policy,* which puts many kinds of insurance together in a package. The least expensive, called basic or HO (homeowner's)-1, covers fire, windstorm, explosion, smoke, glass breakage and other perils, including three very important ones: theft, vandalism and liability.

More expensive is the broad form, HO-2, which adds several more items, largely connected with plumbing, heating and electrical systems. *Comprehensive insurance* (all-risk) covers even more items and is considered a luxury item. HO-6 is used for condominiums and cooperatives. State regulations dictate the specific coverage in the various policies.

If you are presently renting, give serious consideration to *renter's insurance.* Your landlord's policy does not cover your possessions. Though you may feel you own little of value, you might be hard put to replace your stereo set, VCR and TV at the least. Renter's insurance is relatively inexpensive.

Besides asking what is covered by the policy you buy, it's important to find out what is *not* covered (earthquakes, floods, pop bottles dropped from airplanes). If you have a valuable collection or expensive jewelry, you may want to pay an additional premium for riders covering those items.

An insurance agent may represent one company or may be an independent broker who places your policy with any one of several companies. Most important, perhaps, is that the agent be able to explain things so that you understand exactly what kind of protection you are buying.

BUYER'S TIP

When buying homeowner's insurance, you should consider

- Insuring for full replacement cost
- Increasing the deductible to reduce premium payments

Replacement versus Depreciated Value

Suppose your ten-year-old roof is damaged by fire so badly that it must be completely rebuilt. How much is fair for the insurance company to pay you?

You now have a brand-new roof instead of the old one, which was halfway through its useful life. It could be argued that you are entitled to only half the cost of a roof. On the other hand, you couldn't buy a half-used roof; you had to spend the money now for a completely new one. Through no fault of your own, you had an expense you hadn't counted on.

So it's important to inquire whether the policy will pay full replacement cost, which should be your goal. Sometimes the answer depends on the dollar amount of your coverage; sometimes an inexpensive rider ensures replacement value.

One way to economize on insurance cost is to opt for a larger deductible. This is the portion of your loss you agree to pay yourself. You wouldn't want the bother of filing claims for $150 losses in any event, and you're not buying insurance as a money-making proposition. Agreeing to handle a larger amount of any loss on your own can cut premiums considerably.

About Taxes

In some areas, property taxes remain the same when ownership of a house is transferred, so you can be sure that the tax bill the seller received last year will be the one you receive next year, except for any community-wide increases. In other areas, the *assessment* (valuation of the house for tax purposes) changes to reflect your purchase price. Next year's taxes would be based on that figure. It's a simple matter to inquire which system is followed in the areas you are considering.

Make sure that you know the *true tax* figure on any house you are considering buying. The present owner may have some tax abatement; various possibilities, which differ from one state to another, include senior citizens' discount, veterans' tax exemption and preferential treatment for religious organizations.

On the other hand, the seller's tax figure may be higher than the true tax figure. In some localities, for example, unpaid water bills are added to the tax bill. On rare occasions a seller who neglects property could have costs for grass-cutting and even repairs by the city added to the tax bill.

Find out whether taxes in your state are paid in advance, for the coming fiscal year, or in arrears, at the end of the tax year. If you are considering a brand-new house, remember that present taxes are probably based on the value of the vacant lot; the exact amount you will be paying may or may not be established at the time you buy.

Other Costs

Find out whether trash collection is included in taxes and whether there is any extra charge for services such as sidewalk snowplowing. Inquire about sewer and water charges. Ask the sellers about their utility and fuel bills for the past year or, better yet, for two years back.

Some authorities recommend setting aside two or three percent of the purchase price for annual maintenance. It's impossible, of course, to set any rule, since the age and present condition of houses vary so widely.

Include in your calculation of monthly costs the price of basic telephone service and, for most households, cable TV; those figures may vary from one locality to another. Compare costs on homes you may be considering (see Figure 5.1).

Repairs versus Improvements

Improvements are just that—permanent additions that increase the value of your home. Every homeowner should keep a permanent file detailing all expenses for improvements, including bills, checks and receipts. The Internal Revenue Service considers your cost basis for the house to include not only original purchase price but also money spent on improvements.

Repairs and redecorating are not considered improvements. Patching the roof is a repair; installing a complete new one counts as an improvement. Repainting your living room doesn't count; painting a new wing does. Other improvements include fences, driveway paving, new furnace, new wiring, wall-to-wall carpeting, finishing a basement and adding new rooms or bathrooms.

FIGURE 5.1

🖉 Monthly Costs of Home Ownership

	Present Rental	House 1	House 2	House 3
Address				
Principal & interest				
(Rent)				
Property taxes (½)				
Insurance (½)				
Trash collection				
Water, sewer				
Heating and cooling				
Electricity				
Basic telephone				
Cable TV				
Reserve for repairs				
Total				

Risk of Overimproving

Few improvements increase the resale value of your property by the amount you spend on them; buyers may like the idea of a finished basement but seldom want to pay anything extra for it. Depending on the location of the property and neighborhood price levels and expectations, an in-ground swimming pool may add value or may actually be a detriment when time to sell comes. Make improvements for your own satisfaction, not necessarily as investments.

It is financially unwise to overimprove a house beyond its neighbors. When you decide to sell such a house, it's almost impossible to recoup your investment. A given street will support only a given price range; after that, buyers with more to spend want to live on a more prestigious street. As you house-hunt, keep in mind that any planning for alterations and additions is risky if it will make yours the most expensive house on the street.

On the other hand, you may pick up a bargain from owners who have put too much money into their home and can't get it out.

CHAPTER

SIX

What Sort of Home?

You may be sure of the kind of home you want now, but think about the future as you begin your search. Unless you are willing to move every few years, try to anticipate some of the changes that may lie in your future.

Nature-loving newlyweds may come into the agent's office asking for "an old house—we don't care if it's rundown because we can do some work on it, but it has to be in the country on five acres." (There's something mystic about five acres; no one ever requests four acres or six and a half.)

The agent faces a problem immediately, because it can be difficult to find financing for a rundown house. And a few years later the couple may come back to the office, having found themselves isolated with two infants and nary a babysitter in sight.

"Please," they say, "this time show us something in the middle of a tract full of toddler playmates and teenage girls."

Ideas about housing design can change also. The couple with the toddlers will be delighted with a family room open to the kitchen so that the tots can be supervised while the cooking's going on. But ten years later the parents will be longing for a family room located down a flight of stairs, around a corner and with a soundproof door.

Every house is a compromise. Before you start looking, accept that you will eventually give up something you now consider important: the mature trees, the open fireplace, the guest room. You'll fall in love with one special house and suddenly decide you can live without a sunny backyard after all (see Figures 6.1 and 6.2).

FIGURE 6.1

What Matters Most to You?

Before you start your house-hunting, consider which factors are most important to you. Rate on a scale of 1 to 10, from unimportant to very important:

Proximity to work	____	Storage space	____
Quality of schools	____	Room for hobby	____
Condition of house	____	Room for entertaining	____
Age of house	____	Fireplace	____
Ease of maintenance	____	Landscaping, view	____
Garage	____	Mature trees	____
Two-car garage	____	Light and sunshine	____
Number of bedrooms	____	Sidewalks	____
More than one bath	____	Outdoor play space	____
Powder room	____	Large lot	____
Large kitchen	____	Deck, patio	____
Separate dining room	____	Other	____
Family room	____		

FIGURE 6.2

✏ Your Personal Profile

Analyzing the ratings in Figure 6.1, establish your own priorities: factors that are essential, those on which you will compromise if necessary and those that don't matter at all.

Absolute Musts	Nice To Have	Don't Matter

Consider Traffic Patterns

Keep in mind a few basics about floor plans as you inspect houses. Stand in the entrance and try to imagine yourself going about the daily routine. Consider, for example, a hypothetical trip home with bags of groceries. Where will you park? Will you have to carry the load up stairs? Must you go through the living room? Is there a handy counter near the refrigerator for unloading?

If you have an infant, you sleep with your door open, and you want to stay within earshot. In a year or two, though, you will value a private, quiet bedroom. Check whether the master bedroom is separated from the others by a zone of closets, hall or baths. (The best floor plans incorporate such buffers for all bedrooms.)

If the front door opens directly into the living room, a house in the North will eventually need a small enclosed foyer to shield the thermostat from icy blasts. Then imagine yourselves in midsummer, eating out on the enclosed porch or patio. Will it be easy to serve from the kitchen, without risking spills on the living room carpet en route?

Check the kitchen for sufficient counter and cupboard space. Double-check for a place to put things down, not only next to the refrigerator but also at the stove and sink. Even if you are resigned to a small Pullman kitchen and plan to eat in the dining room, look for enough space in the kitchen for a high chair, or a stool for a chatty guest.

Give a house extra points if you don't have to go through the living room to reach other areas. A dead-end living room makes for relaxation and tends to stay neat. Look for the convenience of an outside entrance to the basement and a small outside door to the garage.

An engineer's inspection can help you evaluate condition, which is particularly valuable with an older home. But you are the only one who can judge whether a floor plan fits your lifestyle.

See Figure 6.3 for an illustration of common home architectural styles.

A Brand-New House

Buying a house that's newly built, you need to be concerned about a warranty for faults that may show up during the first year. The possibilities of negotiating on price with a builder or developer are limited; their price is based on cost and, except in hardship situations, is not usually too flexible. It may be possible, though, to dicker for extras that otherwise involve add-on prices.

In many areas, you may not know what property taxes will be levied on new construction; a talk with the assessor's office is in order.

It's important to get all promises in writing; if possible, have your attorney arrange for part of the purchase price to be held in escrow, pending the builder's attention to small matters that may come up during your first few months' occupancy.

Having a house custom-built to one's own specifications is a favorite daydream for many people. The chance to pick the right lot, site the house as you want and create an environment that reflects your taste and personality is a seductive thought.

FIGURE 6.3 Architectural Styles

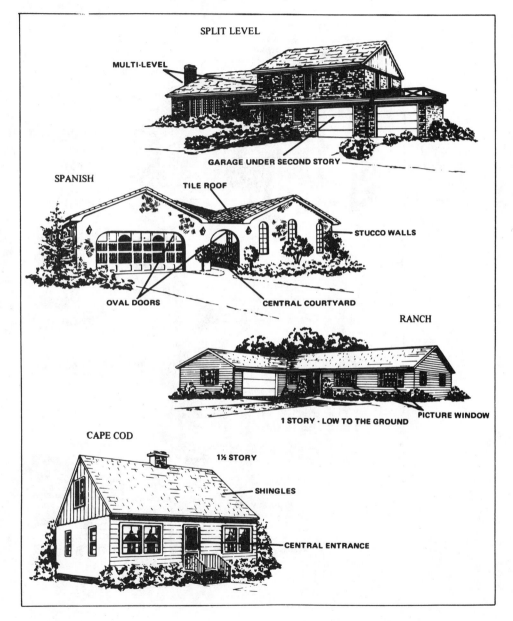

SPLIT LEVEL

MULTI-LEVEL

GARAGE UNDER SECOND STORY

SPANISH

TILE ROOF

STUCCO WALLS

OVAL DOORS

CENTRAL COURTYARD

RANCH

1 STORY - LOW TO THE GROUND

PICTURE WINDOW

CAPE COD

1½ STORY

SHINGLES

CENTRAL ENTRANCE

FIGURE 6.3 *(continued)*

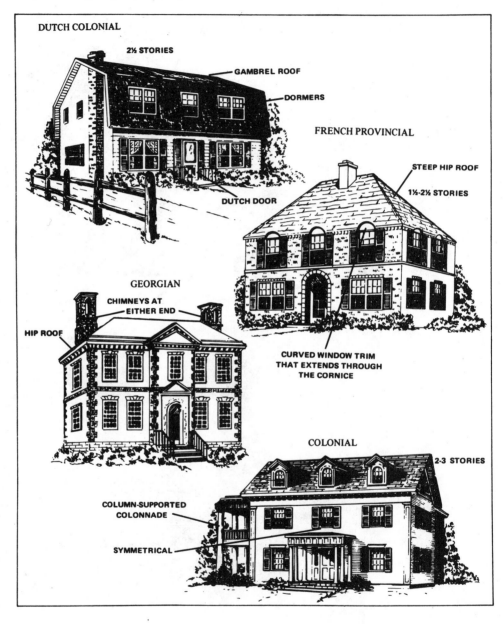

BUYER'S TIP

If you are purchasing a newly constructed home

- Get a builder's warranty for faults that may appear in the first year
- Check with the assessor's office about the amount of property taxes to be levied

---

Before you enter such an undertaking, however, be aware that:

- Everything will take longer than expected.
- Everything will cost more than expected.
- The weather will turn uncooperative.
- Changing your mind about anything as you go along will be amazingly expensive.
- Your marriage will be strained by constant decisions and different points of view.
- Even with the best contractor foreman, large amounts of your own time and attention will be required.

Owning an Apartment

In areas where land is at a premium, cooperatives, townhouses and condominium apartments may be attractive alternatives to more expensive housing. Many empty-nesters and busy young professionals also enjoy the absence of outside chores. Such apartments combine the advantages of homeowning with the convenience of apartment living. The Internal Revenue Service treats co-ops and condos exactly as it does single family houses.

Cooperatives

The cooperative is the oldest form of ownership, found mainly in New York City, Chicago and a few other areas. The owner of a co-op does not own any real estate. Rather, the buyer receives two things: shares in a corporation that owns the entire building and a proprietary lease for the particular living unit being bought.

These shares and the lease are classified not as real estate but as personal property. They may be borrowed against, however, to assist with the purchase, and the IRS will treat the loan as if it were a mortgage. The owner of a co-op does not owe any property tax on the individual living unit. Instead, the monthly payment includes a share of taxes paid by the cooperative on the entire building. It also includes a share of the cooperative's payment on the one large mortgage on the entire building, as well as the usual maintenance costs.

Tenant-owners in a cooperative building depend on each other for financial stability. For that reason, most co-ops require that prospective buyers be approved by the board of directors.

Because a large part of the monthly charge goes toward property taxes and interest on the underlying mortgage, the prospective buyer can expect a certain percentage of that expenditure to be income tax deductible at the end of the year. If you are interested in a cooperative, you will be told what percent of the monthly charge is deductible. Inquire also about the dollar amount of liability you will be taking on for your share of the existing mortgage on the whole building. This will be in addition to any loan you place to buy your shares.

Condominiums

The term *condominium* describes a form of ownership, rather than—as is usually assumed—an apartment. The buyer of a condominium receives a deed and owns real estate, just as a single house would be owned. In the case of a condominium, the buyer receives complete title to the interior of the apartment ("from the plaster in") and also to a percentage of the *common elements*—the land itself, staircases, sidewalks, swimming pool, driveways, lawns, elevators, roofs and heating systems.

The condominium is classified as real estate, and the buyer may place a mortgage on the property and will receive an individual tax bill for the one unit. In addition, monthly fees are levied to pay for outside maintenance, repairs, landscaping or snow removal, recreation facilities and the like.

Townhouse ownership is a hybrid form of condominium and/or cooperative and can take many forms. Typically, the unit owner has *fee simple* (complete) ownership of the living space and the land below it, with some form of group ownership of common areas. The individual may or may not own a small patio or front area and may or may not own the roof above the unit.

What To Check: Condos and Co-ops

Before buying either type of apartment, you should be furnished with a daunting amount of material to read. Look it over carefully. Enlist the aid of an accountant and/or attorney to review the material. You are particularly interested in four things:

1. The financial health of the organization you will be joining. Does it have substantial reserves put aside to cover major renovations and replacements?
2. The condition of the building(s). Is it likely to need new roof, elevators, boiler or windows, for which you would bear a share of responsibility?
3. The covenants, conditions and regulations you must promise to observe. Could you rent out your apartment, install awnings, paint your front door red, have a roommate under the age of 55 or eventually sell the unit on the open market?
4. The percentage of owner-occupancy. Traditionally, more homeowners and fewer tenants is the preferred situation.

Use the checklist in Figure 6.4 to rate the units you are considering.

Mobile Homes

In many parts of the country, particularly in the South and West, mobile homes are a way of life for a large proportion of the population. One attraction is lower initial cost, as compared with a completely furnished single home. One problem is finding the lot on which you can put your mobile home; some communities are zoned against them.

Many mobile homes, therefore, are placed on rented land; they are classified as personal property rather than real estate.

FIGURE 6.4

Checklist for Judging Condos (Co-ops)

	#1	#2	#3
Address			
Condo or co-op			
Square footage			
Number bedrooms			
Garage			
Fireplace, extras			
Price			
Monthly charges			
Percent deductible			
Financial stability			
Reserves			
On a scale of 1-10:			
Floor plan, layout			
Condition			
Kitchen			
Bath			
View, windows			

Choosing the mobile home community into which you buy may be more important than picking the individual home itself. Talk with occupants of the development; find out how cooperative and well-staffed the management is. Although the home is yours, to some extent you will be a tenant, and a fairly captive one, because mobile homes are not very mobile, and you are not likely to move yours to another location.

Give some consideration to buying a used mobile home. Brand-new ones in some areas depreciate in value like brand-new automobiles. You may pick up a bargain on a used one and stand a better chance of recouping your investment or even—in a choice development—seeing some profit when you turn around and sell in the future.

CHAPTER
SEVEN

Financing Your Home Purchase

Did you ever wish you could take the final exam in a course just for fun at the first session, to see how much you knew before you started? Right now, go ahead and try the following quiz, prepared by the Mortgage Bankers Association of America.

If you score 10 or higher, the Mortgage Bankers Association says that you are "an informed consumer with a head start on shopping for the mortgage that is right for you."

If you score less than 10—fine. It proves that you will profit by reading on.

✓ Finance Pop Quiz

1 According to most mortgage lenders, you could qualify for a mortgage amount of about four times your gross annual salary.
   True   False

2. What is the maximum amount that homeowners may borrow to purchase and/or improve a first and/or second home, and take full federal income tax deduction for the interest?
   A. $100,000.
   B. $1 million.
   C. $500,000.
   D. There is no limit.

3. A 15-year fixed-rate mortgage saves you nearly 60 percent of the total interest costs over the life of the loan when compared to a 30-year fixed-rate mortgage.
   True   False

4. Mortgage lenders refer to a homeowner's monthly payment as "PITI" because:
   A. Homeowners should be pitied because of their monthly payments.
   B. It includes principal, interest, taxes and insurance payments.
   C. "Piti" is French for "mortgage payment."
   D. PITI is short for "Pay It on Time In full."

5. A *jumbo* loan is:
   A. A mortgage that is really too big for you to afford.
   B. A loan that you pay monthly for a time and then pay one "jumbo" payment on the remaining principal.
   C. A mortgage that is larger than the limits set by the Federal National Mortgage Association (Fannie Mae) and the Federal Home Loan Mortgage Corporation (Freddie Mac).
   D. A loan to buy a house with more than four bedrooms.

6. A *buydown* refers to:
   A. A discount on the home price so you can afford it.
   B. A discount on the loan's interest rate during the first years of the loan to make financing easier to qualify for.

Source: Reprinted by permission of the Mortgage Bankers Association of America.

C. The purchase of a home in a southern resort area.

D. Buying a cheaper house than you live in now; also called a *trade-down*.

7. Typical closing costs can range from:
   A. 1–3% of the loan amount.
   B. 3–8% of the loan amount.
   C. 8–10% of the loan amount.
   D. 10–15% of the loan amount.

8. A biweekly mortgage (a loan on which you pay half the monthly payment amount every two weeks) shortens the life of a 30-year loan by:
   A. About 10 years.
   B. About 5 years.
   C. About 15 years.
   D. It doesn't shorten the life of the loan; it just decreases interest costs.

9. A *convertible* mortgage is one that:
   A. Allows you to buy a car with the house.
   B. Allows the homeowner to decrease the loan's interest rate without refinancing the mortgage.
   C. Can be used like a giant credit card.
   D. Allows you to make an adjustable rate mortgage into a fixed-rate mortgage.

10. Lenders normally recommend refinancing a mortgage if:
    A. The market rate is two or more percentage points below the rate on the loan.
    B. The homeowner has no equity in the property.
    C. The homeowner doesn't want to pay any taxes.
    D. The homeowner has a "convertible" mortgage.

11. Mortgages backed by the Federal Housing Administration (FHA) require what size down payment?
    A. 0% (nothing down).
    B. About 4–5% of the loan amount.
    C. About 10–20% of the loan amount.
    D. More than 20% of the loan amount.

12. When discussing *points,* your lender means:
    A. The things you really like about your new house.
    B. Prepaid interest; each point equals 1 percent of the loan amount.
    C. A rating system used by lenders to qualify applicants.
    D. The number of traffic violations that show up on your credit report.

13. What is a *deed of trust?*
    A. Money you receive before you have actually qualified for the loan.
    B. A special document waiving your right of rescission.
    C. A document used in place of a mortgage in some states.
    D. A special mortgage you can get if the lender knows you.

14. A VA loan is:
    A. A long-term, low- or no-down-payment loan guaranteed by the Department of Veterans Affairs.
    B. A loan on a home sold at a discount because it has been "Vacant and Abandoned."
    C. A loan on which the homebuyer pays a one percent premium.
    D. A loan for an animal hospital funded by the Veterinarians of America.

15. A *title search:*
    A. Examines the homebuyer's background to see if he or she is descended from royalty.
    B. Examines municipal records to determine the legal ownership of a property.
    C. Looks for books in the public library that tell about housing finance.
    D. Verifies property's past owners.

Answers: 1. False;   2. B;   3. True;   4. B;   5. C;   6. B;
            7. B;   8. A;   9. D;   10. A;   11. B;   12. B;
            13. C;   14. A;   15. B.

Broker Plans Strategy

Within the first few minutes of conversation, an agent probably begins, almost unconsciously, to plan a strategy for financing your loan. Those seemingly impertinent questions about your salary, cash on hand and present debts are important in helping you find the right way to manage your purchase.

Buying for All Cash

A purchase for all cash is, of course, the simplest and quickest method. It is also the most welcome to a seller and, in a normal open market sale, should be worth a concession on price.

You may run into an unusual situation that calls for immediate action—a seller facing foreclosure, for example. Sometimes when a divorce or death in a family occurs, owners are ready to accept a bargain price in return for quick cash. If you are in a position to take advantage of such an opportunity, resist the temptation to act without legal advice. You may need to sign an immediate purchase offer promising prompt settlement, but your own lawyer should ensure that the offer protects you properly.

Without the protection of a mortgage lender's investigation, you need assurance that you are receiving clear, trouble-free title, that taxes are paid to date, that the seller has the right to transfer the property to you and that you aren't taking over old financial claims along with the real estate.

In such emergency situations, the buyer often must accept the physical condition of the property "as is." You may want to bring in a building inspection engineer before your purchase contract becomes firm so that you know what you are getting into.

Buying with Nothing Down

You've seen those hot-shot speakers on cable TV. Can you really buy real estate with nothing down?

Yes, indeed.

There are several ways. And they're no secret. You don't need to send $299 for the books and tapes. Any good real estate broker knows the techniques and can tell you whether a particular plan fits your circumstances.

Veterans can place VA loans with nothing down and do it on houses valued to $184,000, if they qualify to carry the payments. If the seller agreed, a VA loan could even be placed with the seller paying all the buyer's closing costs.

For those with limited income who want to live in rural areas, the Farmers Home Administration makes no-down-payment loans on modest properties, discussed further in this chapter. Monthly payments with Farmers Home can be subsidized depending on family income, as low as 1 percent interest.

Then—particularly with income property, where the owner doesn't need to get the money out right away—you can always look for a seller who will turn the property over to you and finance your purchase, take back a mortgage—and if you look really good, perhaps do it with nothing down.

Picking a Mortgage

For the usual purchase, a smorgasbord of mortgage types is spread out for your consideration. At any time, perhaps 200 different plans will be available in the typical community. Dozens of terms describe particular mortgages: FHA, VA, assumable, purchase-money, second, package, balloon, portfolio, conventional, PMI, convertible, ARM. Your agent contemplates this dazzling array, trying to fit your needs with current offerings (lenders call them product—"We have some great new product this week" means "We've come up with yet another financing twist").

To ask, "Which is the best mortgage plan?" is like walking into a pharmacy and asking, "Which is your best medicine?" Choosing the right loan involves taking into consideration the following:

- Proposed down payment
- Your income and future prospects
- The seller's finances
- Current trend in rates
- Type and condition of the property
- Costs and fees

When you're offered a loan at a particularly favorable rate, inquire about closing costs. Certain costs are standard: appraisal of the property, credit check on yourself, other legitimate charges. But some lenders inflate their profit with fake junk fees or garbage fees, which might be listed as "underwriting fee," "document processing charge," "commitment fee" and the like.

Mortgagor and Mortgagee

To speak of "getting" a mortgage, by the way, is inaccurate. A *mortgage* is a financial claim against your real estate. You give that to a lending institution, along with a bond or note, which is a personal promise to repay. In return, the lender gives you money—cash. You do the mortgaging; you are the *mortgagor*. The lender takes your mortgage, holds your mortgage, and is the *mortgagee*.

Some who have trouble with the two terms find it helpful to remember that "borrower" has two "o"s in it, and so does "mortgagor." "Lender" and "mortgagee" have two "e"s each.

In some states, including California, a slightly different legal system uses a *deed of trust* instead of a mortgage. If your state is one of these, for practical purposes you can consider "deed of trust" and "mortgage" to be interchangeable terms.

Portfolio Loans

In looking for the right mortgage plan, it helps to understand the difference between portfolio loans and those intended for the secondary market.

Years ago, banks took part of their depositors' savings, lent it out on mortgages, collected monthly payments and, when enough money was returned, made more loans. This procedure is the exception these days. The bank that uses such a system is said to be making *portfolio* or *nonconforming loans,* keeping the mortgages as assets in its own portfolio.

Fannie Mae and Freddie Mac

Most other mortgages, these days, are bundled into large packages and sold to big investors in what is known as the *secondary market*.

Among the buyers are large insurance companies, banks and pension funds and, most important, organizations specifically set up to warehouse mortgages, like the *Federal National Mortgage Association* (Fannie Mae).

Borrowers may not know that their mortgages have been sold if the original lender retains the servicing—collecting payments, handling paperwork and forwarding the money. In other cases, particularly when the buyer of the packaged mortgages is another bank, borrowers may be instructed to send their payments directly to the new mortgagee. Many borrowers feel betrayed when they find they are dealing with out-of-state institutions instead of their friendly local bank, but the system allows lenders to recoup their investment immediately and to channel more mortgage money back into the community.

Lenders are required to notify you, before commitment, how likely your loan is to be sold on the secondary market.

When Fannie Mae, which owns perhaps one mortgage in 20 in this country, announces that it will buy packages of certain types of loans, lenders around the country quickly bring their mortgage plans into compliance. Other national standards are set by the *Government National Mortgage Association* (Ginnie Mae) and the *Federal Home Loan Mortgage Corporation* (Freddie Mac).

BUYER'S TIP

When choosing a mortgage to suit your financial situation, find out about

- The amount of down payment required

- Not only the interest rate, but also the adjusted percentage rate (APR)

- Standard closing costs, to protect yourself against fees added by the lender to inflate profits

- The possibility that your mortgage will be resold by the local lender on the secondary market

All of this can affect your search for the perfect mortgage. When you find that most lenders have identical upper limits on the amount they'll lend or analyze your income in the same way, they are probably planning to package your loan and sell it and are conforming to the requirements of the secondary market.

If you have an unusual situation (complicated self-employment income, for example, or the desire to pay your own property taxes and insurance instead of through the lender's escrow account, or a 200-year-old house that doesn't meet today's standards), find out which local lenders are currently making portfolio loans. On these they can be more flexible, making exceptions to their usual rules, subject only to state laws and their own judgment. Portfolio loans are sometimes called *nonconforming,* because they are not tailored to the requirements of the secondary market, or *jumbo* loans if they are for larger amounts than the secondary market will buy.

The process of analyzing a mortgage application, looking over the paperwork exhibits (appraisal and/or inspection of the property, verification of employment, credit report, etc.) and making a decision about furnishing the loan, is known as *underwriting*.

Your Mortgage Lender

Don't be surprised if your mortgage lender turns out to be something different from the traditional "bank"—savings bank, commercial bank, or savings and loan institution. While those entities are still very much in the mortgage business, new players are active as well.

Mortgage bankers (mortgage companies) are in business solely to make (originate) mortgage loans and handle the ensuing monthly paperwork (servicing). Unlike traditional banks, they take no depositors' savings and offer no checking accounts. They are active in the secondary market, selling packages of mortgages and turning the proceeds over to make more loans. Mortgage banking firms have become a large part of the lending scene in the past decade or so.

Mortgage brokers, on the other hand, make no loans at all. Their role is to bring borrowers and lenders together. If you have an unusual situation or special needs, they can be particularly useful, because they may keep current with the offerings of many different lenders.

Credit unions are often overlooked in the search for the right lender. If you belong to one, mention this fact to the broker with whom you are working, and investigate for yourself whether your credit union offers mortgage loans. In some instances, favorable terms are available.

So What Are Points?

As with everything else, there are good points and bad points. Bad points are the ones you pay; good points are the ones someone else pays. They are charged by lending institutions as extra upfront, one-time lump-sum interest, when a new loan is placed.

Each point is 1 percent of a new loan being placed. If you buy a house for $150,000 and borrow $120,000, one point would equal $1,200 (not $1,500). Two points would be $2,400. The term is sometimes used interchangeably with percent, as in "You'll have a two-point cap," which means that you'd have a 2-percent cap.

Points are usually paid at final settlement when the loan is actually made or, occasionally, at the time of mortgage application (in which case, find out whether they are refundable if the loan does not go through).

Sometimes you can pay extra points in return for special favors—a *lock-in* guarantees that you'll receive the rate in effect when you apply for the loan, no matter what has happened to rates in the meantime (but what if rates go down before your closing?). Or you may be charged extra for an extension if you don't close within a given period after the bank commits to making the loan.

When rates are fluctuating rapidly, some borrowers have been known to make mortgage application at two different lenders: one with rate locked in, and one without. For whichever loan isn't eventually chosen, the wheeler-dealer will forfeit an application fee, usually several hundred dollars to cover at least an appraisal and credit report. If widespread, the practice would pose a great nuisance to lenders, but it could give the applicant a chance to choose the more favorable loan at the last minute.

Points may be paid by either buyer or seller, depending on their agreement. Points paid by you as the buyer of your own residence are income tax deductible as interest, in the year they are paid. Points you pay to purchase income property must be amortized (deducted bit by bit over the years) along with other costs of placing an investor's loan.

Points paid by the seller are one of the expenses of selling, and reduce the seller's capital gain on the sale. The buyer, however, is allowed to take points paid by either party as an income tax deduction for interest expense for that year.

Annual Percentage Rate

Which is better, a 9 percent, fixed-rate loan for 30 years with payment of 1 point plus a half-percent origination fee, or an adjustable-rate mortgage for 20 years, currently at 6 percent, with 4 points up front?

It's like comparing apples and oranges.

First, of course, you must decide whether you have a gambler's instinct and will enjoy following interest rates and taking a chance on next year's payment being higher or lower. If rates are currently at the lower end of their inevitable cycle, you might prefer a fixed-rate loan (see Figure 7.1).

But trying to compare rates on such different mortgage plans, with varying closing costs, is (as your algebra teacher used to say) like working with those apples and oranges.

To aid the consumer, lenders are required to quote you an *annual percentage rate* (APR), which takes into account points and certain closing costs.

Suppose you do pay 6 percent, but with 4 extra points in a lump sum at closing. Clearly, your rate is really more than 6 percent. It's not 6 plus 4, because you pay those 4 points only once, not every year. But it's more than 6. How much more? That's the APR. Not all lenders calculate it in the same fashion, but it is useful for comparison shopping.

Conventional Mortgages

Loans agreed upon between you and the lender, without any government intervention except for state banking regulations, are known as *conventional mortgages*. Because banking theory holds that it is unsafe to lend more than 80 percent of the value of the property, the standard conventional loan requires 20 percent down. With a 20 percent down payment, you have an 80 percent *loan-to-value ratio* (LVR).

FIGURE 7.1

✏ Checklist for Comparing Fixed-Rate Mortgages

	Loan 1	Loan 2	Loan 3	Loan 4
Lending institution				
Phone number				
Application cost				
Interest rate				
Points				
Term (years)				
Monthly payment (P&I)				
Loan-to-value ratio (required down payment)				
Private mortgage insurance?				
Monthly cost				
Qualifying ratio				
Prepayment penalty				
Buydown?				
Lock-in?				
Biweekly?				

If you are putting less down than that on a conventional loan, you will be asked to carry *private mortgage insurance* (PMI). This insurance, for which you pay a small premium, has nothing to do with life or health insurance. Instead, it protects the lending institution in case the loan goes sour and the property can't be sold for enough to cover the debt. Because this lowers the lender's risk, you can sometimes borrow with as little as 5 percent down (95 percent LVR).

Rarely offered is the mortgage plan known as *lo-doc,* low-documentation, no-documentation or "express" loan. If you are making a large down payment (usually 25 percent or more), the lender may waive most of its usual paperwork for verifying income or employment.

Understanding Adjustable Rate Mortgages

Until the early 1980s, almost all mortgages were fixed-rate, with the borrower knowing in advance exactly what the monthly payment would run for principal and interest over the full 25 or 30 years of a loan.

As interest rates began to skyrocket and finally hit 18 percent, lenders found themselves locked into unprofitable long-term commitments to keep their money lent out at rates like 5, 6 and 7 percent. This led to serious problems for lending institutions, and many were reluctant to make any further fixed-interest loans.

What emerged was the *adjustable rate mortgage* (ARM). The ARM shifts the risk of changing interest rates to the borrower, who also stands to benefit if rates drop during the period of the loan. It is often chosen when interest rates are high; when rates drop, many borrowers prefer to lock in long-term, fixed-rate loans. Those who plan to remain in a house for only a short time may opt for an adjustable that starts low and won't be adjusted for three or even five years.

To choose wisely, the borrower must shop around, asking about the details of each ARM loan to find the one best suited to his or her own situation (see Figure 7.2).

Judging adjustable rate mortgages requires understanding of a whole new vocabulary.

Index. The interest rate on your loan may go up or down, following the trend for interest rates across the country.

To keep things fair, your lender must key the changes to some national indicator of current rates. The index must be outside the control of your lender, and it should be a figure you can check for yourself, as published in the business sections of newspapers.

The most commonly chosen indices are the rates at which investors will currently lend money to the government through purchase of United States Treasury notes and bills. The index used for your ARM loan might be the rate on sales of one-year, three-year or five-year Treasury obligations. ("One-year T-bills . . .")

Another index might be the average mortgage interest rate across the country for the preceding six months (Federal Home Loan Bank Board Cost of Funds). This index changes more slowly than, for example, the

FIGURE 7.2

Checklist for Comparing Adjustable Rate Mortgages (ARMs)

	Loan 1	Loan 2	Loan 3	Loan 4	Loan 5
Lender					
Phone number					
Term (years)					
Adjustment period					
Index					
Margin					
Initial rate					
Today's true rate					
Points					
Adjustment cap					
Lifetime ceiling					
Application fee					
Loan-to-value ratio					
Qualifying ratio					
Buydown (yes or no)					
Negative amortization (yes or no)					
Convertibility					
When, at what cost?					
Assumability					
At what cost?					

one-year T-bill. It could work for or against you, depending on the general direction of rates.

Margin. If Treasury bills are the chosen index, and they are selling at 6 percent interest, your lender will not make mortgage loans at that rate. Rather, you will pay a specific percentage above the index.

If you are offered a 2 percent margin, you would pay 8 percent. If at the time of interest adjustment, Treasury bills had gone to 7 percent, a 2 percent margin would set your mortgage rate at 9 percent. If they had dropped to 5.5 percent, your interest would drop to 7.5 percent.

Cap. The word is used in two ways. First, your loan agreement may set, for example, a 2 percent *cap* (limit) on any upward adjustment. If interest rates (as reflected by your index) had gone up 3 percent by the time of adjustment, your rate could be raised only 2 percent.

When choosing an ARM, ask what happens in the above example. Is the extra 1 percent saved to be used for "catch-up" at the next adjustment, even though interest rates might have remained level? Or will you have negative amortization (see below)?

The second use of the word is synonymous with *ceiling*.

Ceiling. A ceiling (sometimes also called a lifetime cap) is an interest rate beyond which your loan can never go. Typically, you may be offered a five-point ceiling. This means that if your loan starts at 8 percent, it can never go beyond 13 percent, no matter what happens to national interest rates. A ceiling allows you to calculate your worst case.

Worst Case. If your 30-year adjustable loan for $85,000 now costs $510 a month for principal and interest at 6 percent, and if your ceiling is 5 percent, the worst that could ever happen is that your interest rate would go to 11 percent. You can and should calculate in advance what that could cost you—$809 a month.

Negative Amortization. Regular amortization involves gradually paying off the principal borrowed, through part of your monthly payments. If, however, your monthly payments aren't enough to cover even the interest due, negative amortization is a possibility.

Suppose that interest on your loan should total $700 a month. For some reason, however, your monthly payment is set at $650. The shortfall, $50 a month, may be added to the amount you have borrowed. At the end of the year you'd owe not less, but about $600 more, than when you started.

Negative amortization could result from an artificially low initial interest rate, or it could follow a hike in rates larger than your cap allows the lender to impose.

Not all mortgage plans include the possibility of negative amortization. Sometimes the lender agrees to absorb any shortfalls. But ask if it is a possibility, and in what fashion, before choosing a specific ARM.

Floor. Different ARM plans may or may not set a cap on decreases in your rate, either at each adjustment period or over the whole life of the loan. With a floor, you could calculate the best case for your loan—your lowest possible payment if interest falls deeply during the life of the loan.

Convertibility. If your mortgage offers this attractive feature, you have the best of both worlds. You can choose to convert your adjustable rate mortgage to a fixed-rate loan if you'd like.

With some plans, you can seize any favorable time (when fixed rates are generally low) during the life of the mortgage; more commonly, you can make the choice on certain anniversaries of the loan. Cash outlay for the conversion is low compared with the costs of placing a completely new mortgage; 1 point, or 1 percent of the loan, is typical. Be sure to inquire what it would be. You may, however, pay a slightly higher interest rate all along, in return for the option.

Initial Interest Rate. With most ARM loans, the rate during the first year, or the first adjustment period, is set artificially low to induce the borrower to enter into the agreement—a "teaser" or "come-on" rate. Buyers who plan to be in a house for only a few years may be delighted with such arrangements, especially if no interest adjustment is planned for three years. Other borrowers, however, may end up with negative amortization and payment shock.

The prudent borrower asks, "If you were not offering this initially lower rate, what would my true interest be today? If things remained exactly the same, what rate (and what dollar amount) would I be paying after the first adjustment period?"

Payment Shock. The borrower who starts out with an artificially low rate may easily carry initial payments.

Suppose, however, that the rate eventually rises to the full ceiling allowed. Result: a bad attack of payment shock, leading in some cases to foreclosure and loss of the property. After many bad experiences, most lenders require borrowers to qualify to carry the payments at next year's rate, even if this year's is low.

Adjustment Period. This is the length of time between interest rate adjustments. Typically made at the end of each year, adjustments might also be made as often as every six months or as infrequently as every three or five years.

With some loans, interest rates may be adjusted although monthly payments are not. This could result in negative amortization or, if rates had gone down while payments didn't, in faster reduction of the principal owed.

Principal. This is the amount you borrowed; the amount still remaining on the debt at any given time.

Buydown. Extra, upfront, lump-sum payment of interest may bring down the interest rate charged on a loan. In some cases, the lower rate lasts for the whole life of the loan. In a 3-2-1 buydown, however, interest is reduced 3 percent for the first year of the loan, 2 percent the next year, 1 percent the third year. After that, interest reaches normal levels.

Any plan offering a lower interest rate in return for more upfront points is, in effect, a buydown.

30 or 15 Years

Thirty-year mortgage loans have been losing some popularity to 20-year and even 15-year mortgages. Monthly payments on a 15-year loan can run about 20 percent higher than on the same loan figured on a 30-year basis. You would need about 20 percent more income to qualify for the shorter loan. On the other hand, you'd make payments only half as long and cut your total interest cost considerably.

The 15-year mortgage operates like enforced saving, because it requires you to pay off the debt faster. It may be appropriate if, for example, your children will be starting college in 15 years, at a time when you'd like to have your house free and clear.

It does tie up your money, however. If you have the discipline, there's nothing to stop you from putting that extra money, each month, into your own investment plan, where you can tap it as needed and where it will earn extra interest.

From an income-tax point of view, paying off a mortgage early is more or less a wash, because the money you use to pay it off could otherwise be earning taxable interest elsewhere. Make your decision on how large a mortgage, and how fast a payoff, from the point of view of your particular financial situation. Income tax considerations should not enter into that particular decision.

Biweekly Mortgages

Some mortgage plans involve biweekly mortgage payments: half a monthly payment is automatically deducted from your checking or savings account every two weeks. This plan not only adds up to the equivalent of 13 payments instead of 12 each year; it also reflects faster payoff of principal with a corresponding saving in interest, and could cut the length of a 30-year mortgage to less than 22 years.

FHA Mortgages

The Federal Housing Authority (FHA), an agency of the Department of Housing and Urban Development (HUD), was established to help homeowners buy with low down payments. Lenders can safely make loans of up to 97 percent of the value of property, because the FHA insures them against loss in case of foreclosure.

If FHA loans are used in your area, they can be a fine way to go. The money comes not from the government but from local lenders, so if none in your locality is handling FHA mortgages, you're out of luck. The loans are not intended for expensive property, but upper limits in high-price areas are raised from time to time. In 1994, the maximum FHA loan was raised to $151,725; in low-cost counties it remained at $67,500.

For inexpensive property (under $50,000), down payment can be as low as 3 percent; in any case, it runs less than 5 percent. FHA loans may be placed on one-family to four-family dwellings and are intended for owner-occupants.

Insurance premiums (to protect the lender in case of default) are due in a lump sum at closing and can run up to 2.25 percent of the loan. Because most FHA buyers don't have extra cash at closing, the mortgage insurance premium (MIP) can be added to the amount of the mortgage loan. If you pay off your FHA mortgage within the first few years, a portion of your MIP is returned. In addition to the one-time MIP, borrowers pay one-half percent of the outstanding balance each year. The number of years this extra premium is charged depends on the size of the down payment; minimum-down loans require the extra charge over the longest period.

The FHA bases its loans on the value found by authorized FHA appraisers and sometimes requires certain repairs (items concerned with the preservation of the property and with health and safety) before the loan will be granted.

In addition to the standard FHA program, #203-b, others are available in certain areas. FHA 203-k, for example, lends money to cover both the cost of a home needing rehabilitation and the money needed for repairs.

Your real estate broker will know whether any or all of these programs are available in your community—or you can sit down with the yellow pages open to "Mortgages" and spend a couple of hours calling around yourself.

The outstanding feature that has made FHA loans particularly desirable in the past is their assumability by the person to whom you might sell your property in the future. New regulations, however, limit this advantage; see the discussion on assumability below.

For a comparison of various mortgage plans, including conventional, FHA and VA options, see Figure 7.3.

VA Is for Veterans

The most attractive benefit of VA loans is the possibility of no down payment. Beyond that, the loans are assumable (with the restrictions listed below in the discussion of assumptions).

As with FHA mortgages, the money comes from a local lender; the Department of Veterans Affairs' (VA) contribution is to guarantee the

FIGURE 7.3

✏️ Cost Comparisons of Different Mortgage Loans

	Conventional				Adjustable Rate	FHA 203B	VA
	Fixed 30-Year	Fixed 15-Year	Buydown	Bi-Weekly			
Minimum Down	Some Plans 5% Down					3%–5%	0%
Mortgage Insurance	If Less than 20% Down					Upfront, Some Yearly	No
Maximum Loan	"Jumbo" Loans Sometimes Available					Moderate, Varies by Area	$184,000
Easier Qualifying	Somewhat		Yes		Yes	Yes	Yes
Faster Payoff		Yes		Yes			
Monthly Payment	Level	Level	Lower, Rises	Level	Lower, Can Rise or Fall	Level	Level
Assumability						Yes	Yes
Comments				Automatic Withdrawal from Checking		Repairs Sometimes Required	

loan at no cost to the veteran. While FHA loans require low down payments, VA loans may be made for the entire appraised value of the property (100 percent LVR)—nothing down. In 1994, the VA guaranteed loans as high as $184,000.

To qualify, the veteran must have the following:

- A discharge "other than dishonorable" and either
- 180 days' active (not reserve) duty between September 16, 1940 and September 7, 1980, or
- 90 days' service during a war (the Korean, Viet Nam and Persian Gulf conflicts are considered wars), or
- Six years' service in the National Guard.

For those enlisting for the first time after September 7, 1980, two years' service is required. In-service VA mortgages are also possible.

VA loans may be used for one-family to four-family houses, owner-occupied only. Eligibility for such mortgages does not expire. If one's first VA loan is paid off and the property sold, full eligibility is regained.

At closing, a funding fee is paid directly to the VA.

Farmers Home Administration (FmHA)

In rural areas, direct mortgage loans can sometimes be obtained from the Farmers Home Administration (FmHA, Department of Agriculture). If your income falls within specific limits (fairly low, depending on family size), you can buy a modest home on no more than one acre, with interest payments tailored to your income.

The program is intended for those who cannot obtain financing elsewhere. The money is allotted to local offices quarterly. At any given time, some offices will have money available; others will have waiting lists. The FmHA processes mortgage applications before you've found a house, then notifies you as money becomes available.

Assumable Mortgages

An *assumable mortgage* is one that can remain with the property when it is sold. This results in considerable savings for the next buyer; no outlay for the costs associated with placing a new mortgage—items like appraisal of the property, mortgage tax, etc.

A high assumable mortgage, or one at a low interest rate, is therefore worth a premium, and contributes extra value to property on the market.

FHA loans made before December 1, 1986, and VA loans made before March 1, 1988 are completely—freely—assumable. This means that you, or anyone the seller chooses, can take the loan along with the real estate, just as it stands. Neither you nor the house need pass any evaluation by the lending institution, which has no say in the matter. Closing costs are negligible, interest rates will not change and the transaction can be closed and settled as soon as the parties wish.

In areas where prices have risen, of course, these older loans represent only part of the value of the property. You must pay the seller the rest of the purchase price in cash, unless you can persuade the owner to take back financing. The seller who does that agrees to hold a second mortgage for part of the purchase price, or even—in rare instances—for the entire missing amount (nothing down!).

You'd have to look pretty good financially before a seller would enter into such an arrangement, because even though you take over the payments on the loan and ownership of the property, the seller retains liability for that FHA or VA debt if anything goes wrong.

BUYER'S TIP

The advantages of an assumable mortgage may include

- No points
- No change in interest rate
- Low closing costs

Newer FHA and VA loans are classified as "assumable with bank approval." To take over the newer FHA mortgages, the next borrower must prove qualification (income and credit) to the lending institution's satisfaction. Once that's done, if payments are made promptly, the original borrower retains liability for only five years. With new VA mortgages, the person assuming the loan (who need not be a veteran) must qualify with the lender before an assumption. A charge of no more than $500 may be made for the paperwork.

Besides FHA and VAs, many adjustable rate mortgages also have assumability features, which allow for considerable savings on closing costs. ARM mortgages differ; most stipulate that the new borrower must qualify with the lender and that the interest rate may be adjusted upon assumption. Some charge is made for the privilege; one point might be typical.

Private Mortgages

Private mortgages typically come from one of two sources. A seller may agree to hold financing, lending you money on a first mortgage, or, if the property already has one, on a second (typically shorter-term) loan. Or a family member may agree to lend you part of the purchase price. It is prudent to keep things on a business-like basis, offering the property as security for a regular mortgage.

Family members may offer low-interest or no-interest loans, but the Internal Revenue Service takes a dim view of them. It likes to see a private mortgage loan made at either the 9 percent or the *applicable federal rate,* an index published monthly by the government, which follows current trends in interest rates. If the mortgage rate does not meet that standard, the IRS will *impute* the interest and tax the lender as if it had been received anyway.

Land Contracts and Lease Options

A *land contract* is a type of layaway installment plan for buying a house. Typically it is sought by a buyer who does not have enough down payment to qualify for a bank loan or to persuade the seller to turn over title (ownership). You move in, make monthly payments to the seller and take care of taxes, insurance and repairs exactly as if you owned the place. But title does not transfer to you until a specified time, perhaps when you make the final payment. With some land contracts, you receive title when you have made enough payments to constitute 20 percent equity.

Equity is defined as the amount the owner "has in" the property—roughly, market value minus mortgages owed.

A *lease-option* differs from a land contract in that you are not bound to buy the property. Instead, you move in as a tenant and typically pay a flat amount in return for an option—the right to purchase at a given price within a given time (one year, two years)—if you so choose. If you choose not to buy, you simply remain as a tenant for the duration of the lease. Who pays for what expenses, and whether any of your rent goes toward the purchase price, are negotiable items.

Any land contract or lease-option requires extra-careful consultation with your own attorney before you sign anything. Such contracts can vary considerably in their provisions, and you must have someone on your side making sure your interests are protected. Either type of contract should be recorded—entered in the public records to notify the world at large of your rights in the property.

Balloon Mortgages

Suppose an 80-year-old seller is ready to take back a $100,000 mortgage on the house you are buying from him. It might be because the house could not meet bank standards and he is unable to do the necessary repairs, it could be because he'd prefer regular monthly income to realizing a lump sum, or it could be because you have unusual circumstances (just starting your own business) that don't let you qualify for a bank loan.

At that age, he doesn't like the idea of making a 30-year loan (not realizing that he could simply leave the remainder of the mortgage to his heirs). He will be comfortable only if he can count on seeing all his money within ten years.

But if you pay at the proper rate for a 10-year loan, your monthly payments will be more than you can handle. So you offer the seller a *balloon* mortgage. Your payments will be calculated, principal and interest, as if you were paying on a 30-year schedule. But at the end of ten years, whatever you still owe will be immediately all due and payable.

Because during the early years of a loan most of the monthly payment goes for interest, you will not reduce the principal much over those ten years. You will still owe about 90 percent of the original loan (see Appendix B). That final balloon payment will be a big one.

How will you meet it? The expectation is that your finances will have straightened out, you will have built up equity (the money you've paid off plus any increase in value), the house will have been repaired, and you can place a mortgage with a regular lending institution at that point. Or the old gentleman may still be in good health and so dependent on your prompt and regular checks that he agrees to renew the loan.

Building Your Own Home

Financing new construction is easiest if you are working with a large builder, who may finance the construction or may help you arrange a building loan that later converts to a mortgage. If you are buying your own building lot, you will find banks reluctant to lend on vacant land. You'll have to buy for cash or persuade the seller to hold a mortgage.

Once the land is paid for, you can count it toward equity to help qualify for another loan. Building loans are most readily obtained after you have taken all the necessary steps to have your plans and lot approved by local authorities, and if you are working through a recognized contractor. Do-it-yourselfers, particularly those on a shoestring, may find it very difficult to obtain financing.

House-Hunting

When a young couple walks into a REALTOR®'s office carrying a clipboard, the agent knows that one of them is an engineer. It seems to go with the training. Taking notes is a good way for you to approach your house-hunting, too. Another good way to look at real estate is without any children along, so that you can concentrate.

Inspecting houses is a tiring and confusing process. If you look at more than four in a morning or afternoon, you'll end up with your head in a whirl. Lying in bed that night, you'll try vainly to remember whether it was the brick ranch or the Victorian that backed up to the expressway. You'll be totally unable to recall which place had the purple kitchen. It can be helpful to take along a Polaroid or video camera (often an agent has one or can borrow one from the office).

Ask the agent for data on each property, and take it back with you. To concentrate fully on the house, wait to take your notes until you have finished, possibly when you are back in the car. Jot down your impressions right on the computer printouts or copies of the listing sheets for the houses you inspect.

If you then note the things you disliked about the place or which features really appeal to you, sorting them out later becomes easier. Figure 8.1 is a sample worksheet with space for rating various features of a home from 1 to 10. A rating of "1" is the lowest.

FIGURE 8.1

✏ Comparing Houses

Address	Price	Lot Size	Construc-tion	Roof	Driveway	Land-scaping	Square Feet	No. Bedrooms	No. Baths
275 Isabell	110,000	School Near	2-story Wood	New shingle	Gravel	Big Trees	1,550	3 1-small	1 1/2
		6	5	8	2	4		4	4
27W245 Patricia Ln. Winfield	125,900	Nice Open High	Ranch Brick	10 yrs. old shingle	B.T.	Good	1,900	3	3
		9	9	5	6	8		6	8
135 Marianne Pl. Carol Stream	129,900	Sloping Lot	Ranch Wood	9 yrs. old shingle	B.T.	Fair	2,000	3	2
		5	4	6	6	5		6	6

FIGURE 8.1 *(continued)*

Dining Room	Kitchen	Deck, Patio	Garage	Heat, AC	Fireplace	Basement	Plumbing Electricity	Water	General Appeal	Total Rating
Dining / Living	Old cabinets	breeze-way	1-car	Window AC Gas	None	Dry unfinished	OK	City	Older home in fair shape	
4	3	6	3	5	1	4	6	6		71
Yes	Small D.W.	yes	2-car	Central AC Gas	In L.R. Wood Stove	Finished	OK	OK City	Nice house, good view	
5	5	8	6	6	9	8	6	6		110
Yes	Good D.W.	screened porch	2-car	Central AC Gas	None	Finished	OK	City	Very pleasant house	
5	6	8	6	6	6	7	6	6		94

You may want to mark up a street map of the area, locating the houses you view and also noting schools, religious institutions, shopping areas and other amenities.

Where Are the Bargains?

Yes, bargains are out there, and after you've been looking a while, you'll be able to spot them.

As you park across the street from the house on Robin Circle, your agent says apologetically, "Now, I want to warn you: there are a lot of kids in this house, school's out and it doesn't show too well." Without moving from the car, you can see an old pickup truck in the driveway, a shaggy lawn, rusted toys on the front walk, old flyers moldering under the shrubs and a torn screen door.

A disaster?

No, an opportunity.

When you locate such a house, if it has had decent maintenance (as opposed to housekeeping), then you have stumbled upon a bargain. Houses that have been rented out sometimes fall into this category.

Most buyers cannot see past sloppiness. Perhaps without even knowing why, they say that "the place doesn't have good vibes." As a result, the house on Robin Circle may stay on the market for months and may eventually sell for as much as 10 percent under true market value.

Conversely, as you walk into a spotless house, try to ignore the smell of gingerbread wafting through the place, your own favorite music playing softly and the flowers on the designer coffee table. Of course such a house has probably had fine care, and it could be a pleasure to move into. Still, when the sellers move out, they will take the coffee table, the CD player, those great speakers and the gingerbread pan. You will be left with just three things: the location, the floor plan and the condition.

If those factors—apart from surface appeal—seem right to you, don't hesitate to put in your offer for such a house. It will sell quickly. If it's also been underpriced, emergency action is indicated, as described in the next chapter. More commonly, a house that shows well commands a premium.

BUYER'S TIP

When house-hunting, it is best to

- Take notes or photographs to record details

- Get detailed descriptions from the agent's listing sheet

- Mark features such as schools, parks or shopping centers on a map

- Keep in mind the difference between good (or poor) maintenance and housekeeping

- Focus on location, layout and basic condition of the property

---

When it comes to decorating and housekeeping, try to ignore the sizzle; concentrate on the steak. Pay attention to location, layout and basic condition. Location can't be changed, floor plan can be altered only at some expense, but the last factor—condition—can be remedied. Just be sure, if there's a problem, that you know what you're getting into. An engineering report can tell you exactly what to expect.

More Bargain Situations

Bargains can also be found where sellers are under pressure. The seller's broker won't—or shouldn't—reveal that the house is near foreclosure or the seller is going bankrupt. But you can see this for yourself sometimes—for example, if it's a divorce situation, or if she's on the new job in Chicago and he's here alone with three kids and big long-distance phone bills. Such sellers may be ready to deal and ready to trade a price concession for a quick sale.

Where the owner has died, an executor is sometimes amenable to any reasonable offer in return for a prompt, trouble-free winding up of the estate. An older person, suspicious of workers and short on cash, may not want to bring a long-time home up to standards required by a lending institution; sometimes a broker can help you work out a mutually beneficial arrangement to solve that impasse.

Above all, the way to buy a bargain is to buy promptly. The buying public is a sensitive judge of value. A house that is mistakenly underpriced will be snapped up quickly. For that reason, it's sensible to invest some time in learning the market and helpful to locate a broker in whose advice you have confidence.

Location, Location, Location

Before you are very far into your house-hunting, someone will tell you the oldest real estate joke (almost the only real estate joke) that the three most important factors in the value of a house are (1) location, (2) location and (3) location.

It's true, too. A house costing $600,000 in Beverly Hills might sell, on a comparable lot in the suburbs of Peoria, for $100,000. Never in the history of this country have locational differences been so marked. Closer to home, you know yourself that a modest home in the most expensive suburb is worth much more than the identical house in an inner-city neighborhood.

From a buyer's point of view, there are two ways of looking at this locational preference, which appraisers call *situs*. The classic advice is to buy the modest house on a more expensive street. Such a house is easy to resell, and its value will hold up well, for there are always buyers eager for the prestige of that particular neighborhood. And remodeling or adding to it is possible because alterations won't push it out of the price range for that area.

On the other hand, the most luxurious house on the street won't ever repay the owner for the money invested. No matter how elegant it may be, buyers with money to spend will aim at another, fancier neighborhood.

In one way, then, an overimproved house represents an opportunity for the buyer who wants lots of space and luxury features and isn't worried about resale value. If you think that you will live in the house for a long time and if you like the area, you may be able to pick up a great deal for your money.

Where, then, are the bargains?

- Sloppy houses, otherwise well maintained
- Family situations of stress: divorce, death, illness
- Property overimproved for its neighborhood
- The modest house on a prestigious street

That last is, perhaps, not so much a bargain as it is a classic good investment.

Choosing a Neighborhood

If you are moving across town, you probably know what area suits your lifestyle best. Coming to a new community, however, requires research. Real estate brokers must, by the nature of their work, help you narrow your choices if you are ever to settle on one house. Rigorously regulated by human rights law, however, brokers hesitate to characterize neighborhoods or give you opinions on school systems. If any of their assumptions are based on the forbidden factors—race, color, religion, country of origin, age, disability, sex—they could face charges of illegal *steering* (using subtle means to ensure that you end up where they think you should).

Brokers can, however, furnish solid data, and a good agent will have it available: per-pupil expenditure in various school systems, number of graduates going on to four-year colleges and the like.

One good way to learn about a new community is to subscribe to its local newspaper. Read it carefully for a few weeks, and you'll begin to get a feeling for neighborhoods. In the end, you will have to decide yourself which areas you want to consider.

Looking Over an Older Home

In general, houses built since World War II are more or less modern. In these, you can pretty much count on copper plumbing, adequate electric service and a furnace that is at least compact. Houses more than 20 years old, however, require extra-careful inspection. You won't inspect in detail every house you see, but when you're seriously considering making an offer on one, go over it carefully.

Start with the outside of the house. Does it have easy-care features—built-in sprinklers in a dry climate or self-storing storm windows up north? How soon might the place need a coat of paint?

Examine the roof; binoculars can be of help here. Look for missing or curled shingles, patched spots or a dried-up, crinkled appearance. Moss growing on the roof indicates a moisture problem. And if in midwinter every other roof on the street bears a load of snow while this one is clean, you are looking at a house with inadequate insulation.

BUYER'S TIP

Before you make an offer, inspect carefully, looking for

- Features that indicate ease of maintenance
- Adequate insulation and good condition of the roof
- Signs of termites
- Unobstructed gutters and attached downspouts

In termite areas (Southeast, Southwest), look for mud tubes where wooden parts of porch or foundation adjoin the ground. Poke exposed wood to see if it is solid.

Downspouts should be firmly attached. Gutters lose points if they have little trees growing out of them. If they need only repainting, that's a minor matter, but gutters with holes in them will need replacing. See Figure 8.2 for a diagram showing the location of all the various physical components of a house.

Electric Service

Within the house, remember that many homes built around the turn of the century didn't originally have any electric service. If the initial installation hasn't been updated, it can be inadequate for anything beyond the light bulbs, refrigerator and flatiron it was originally

FIGURE 8.2   House Diagram

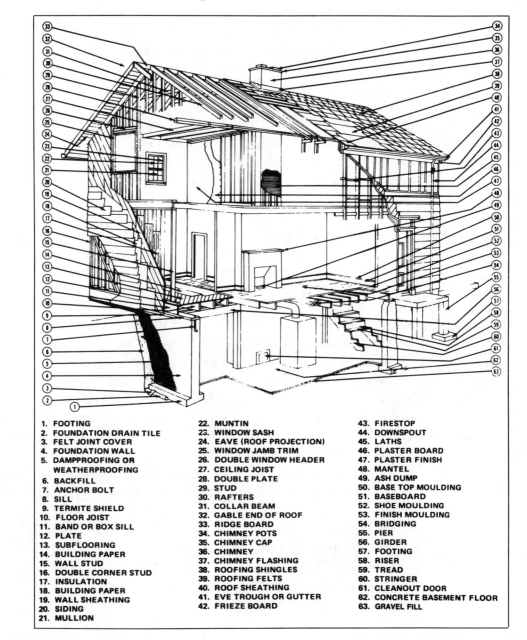

1. FOOTING
2. FOUNDATION DRAIN TILE
3. FELT JOINT COVER
4. FOUNDATION WALL
5. DAMPPROOFING OR WEATHERPROOFING
6. BACKFILL
7. ANCHOR BOLT
8. SILL
9. TERMITE SHIELD
10. FLOOR JOIST
11. BAND OR BOX SILL
12. PLATE
13. SUBFLOORING
14. BUILDING PAPER
15. WALL STUD
16. DOUBLE CORNER STUD
17. INSULATION
18. BUILDING PAPER
19. WALL SHEATHING
20. SIDING
21. MULLION
22. MUNTIN
23. WINDOW SASH
24. EAVE (ROOF PROJECTION)
25. WINDOW JAMB TRIM
26. DOUBLE WINDOW HEADER
27. CEILING JOIST
28. DOUBLE PLATE
29. STUD
30. RAFTERS
31. COLLAR BEAM
32. GABLE END OF ROOF
33. RIDGE BOARD
34. CHIMNEY POTS
35. CHIMNEY CAP
36. CHIMNEY
37. CHIMNEY FLASHING
38. ROOFING SHINGLES
39. ROOFING FELTS
40. ROOF SHEATHING
41. EVE TROUGH OR GUTTER
42. FRIEZE BOARD
43. FIRESTOP
44. DOWNSPOUT
45. LATHS
46. PLASTER BOARD
47. PLASTER FINISH
48. MANTEL
49. ASH DUMP
50. BASE TOP MOULDING
51. BASEBOARD
52. SHOE MOULDING
53. FINISH MOULDING
54. BRIDGING
55. PIER
56. GIRDER
57. FOOTING
58. RISER
59. TREAD
60. STRINGER
61. CLEANOUT DOOR
62. CONCRETE BASEMENT FLOOR
63. GRAVEL FILL

designed for. The proliferation of appliances these days calls for plenty of outlets. You want 100-amp service at minimum; 220 amps for electric stoves, some clothes dryers and air conditioners. Look for an outlet every 12 feet on a long wall so that any six-foot cord can be plugged in without using an extension cord. Small rooms should have at least one outlet on each wall.

Upstairs, be alert for any tangle of extension cords, which can signal inadequate outlets. Downstairs, examine the fuse box. If you find circuit breakers, you will know that the service has been modernized. But there is nothing wrong with having an old-fashioned fuse system, if it is extensive enough and was carefully installed.

Look Over the Plumbing

More expensive to remedy than inadequate wiring is faulty plumbing. You hope to find all the old galvanized pipes replaced with copper. Galvanized pipe suffers from corrosion and eventually develops hardening of the arteries as deposits build up on the inside until they impede the flow of water. This happens first with the horizontal hot water lines, so check by starting outward from the water heater.

What you don't want to see is a patch job, where a single emergency was solved by putting a length of copper pipe into old galvanized tubing. Such a joint signals a serious chemical reaction ahead. Eventually someone will have to rip out the whole line and replace it with copper, and that someone might be you.

If the house has modernized kitchen and baths, it's likely that the whole plumbing system was updated when they were installed. If you're in doubt, ask.

If there is a well, you'll want proof of water quality and flow. If there is a septic system, ask questions about legal installation and past performance. (If sewers are available but not utilized, the FHA will refuse to insure a mortgage.)

Basement Water

In some areas, buyers are understandably worried about a basement that might develop a running stream during spring thaws or summer storms. One quick way to judge is to see how much junk people store directly on a basement floor. Piles of very old newspapers may mean a packrat style—and a dry basement.

To see if a basement has flooded, inspect the bottom of the furnace and the water heater. Rust, or a newly painted neat strip across the bottom few inches, calls for an explanation. If a one-time flood (which can happen in the best of families) occurred while the furnace was hot, the firebox may be cracked.

Small amounts of dampness on basement walls, though, are almost standard in some localities.

Pay little attention to the condition of the water heater. Even the most meticulous householder will use one down to the very end, so it isn't much of a clue to how the rest of the house has been maintained. And it is more of an appliance than a structural part of the house. Replacing it would not be a drastic enough expense to influence your decision on whether or not to buy.

Insulation

If an older house in a cold climate hasn't been adequately insulated, you will certainly do it yourself immediately. The best place for insulation is under the attic floor. Look for holes in the stair risers that were drilled for blown-in insulation and then plugged. Try to find out how many inches were installed. Some old jobs were very good indeed; others don't meet modern standards.

Another simple installation with a fine payback is band insulation around the top of the basement wall, where the foundation meets the floor joists.

If a house in a northern state doesn't have good storm windows and screens, it probably doesn't have much else, for this is one of the first comfort items people buy. You don't need fancy metal self-storing ones. A well-kept wooden set means that the place is owned by someone who doesn't mind climbing ladders to replace them spring and fall, and you'll have to do the same. Properly fitting old-fashioned wooden storm windows can be even better than new metal ones.

If the house lacks insulation or storm windows, inquire, when you come to the time of the mortgage application, about whether you may include the cost of energy-savers in your mortgage.

Don't pay more just because the house has sidewall insulation. It's nice, of course, but it doesn't have the payback of that thick layer under the attic floor.

Toxins and Termites

In some northern areas, termites are just about unheard-of, but you might run into carpenter ants. Look for small piles of fine sawdust below ceiling beams. To check for soft spots, prod floor joists that are exposed in the cellar.

High-Voltage Lines. Scientists are still debating the effect of electromagnetic radiation, particularly on children. Some early studies indicate increased rates of cancer in those who live close to high-voltage lines. There's not yet a dependable guideline in this matter; emissions are easily tested, however.

Radon. One toxic substance you can't see for yourself is radon, a colorless, odorless gas that seeps into houses from the earth itself. The Environmental Protection Agency (EPA) considers it second only to cigarette smoke as a cause of lung cancer. "It's like exposing your family to hundreds of chest X-rays a year," says the EPA. The agency estimates that one house in five has unacceptable levels of radon. Testing can be unreliable unless carefully done, best by a professional. Simply using a test kit can yield false results if windows are kept open during the test, which takes several days. Some areas are at higher risk than others.

Fortunately, curing a radon problem is relatively simple and inexpensive, usually with specific ventilation in foundation and basement.

Lead. High levels of lead in children have been shown to affect mental and physical development. Lead paint is no longer used, but for its loans the FHA requires that anyone considering a house built before 1978 receive a written information sheet about it. Chipping paint is particularly dangerous. As with asbestos, removing lead paint can release dangerous amounts of the substance; sometimes the best solution is to cover it. If it is to be removed, safety precautions must be taken.

Lead is also found in drinking water because of its use in soldering materials. Simple tests can be done, preferably on early-morning samples. Lead in water decreases when you let the tap run for a couple of minutes, especially if you haven't used the faucet for a few hours.

Asbestos. This fireproof mineral was widely used before about 1975 in all sorts of building materials, from insulation to floor tiles. Its tiny fibers can cause lung cancer. Where it is intact and not deteriorating, it poses little or no danger. The most common problem may be heavy insulation wrapped around heat ducts from an old-fashioned furnace. Removing it releases the fibers; sometimes the problem is best solved by encasing it.

Building Inspection Engineers

In many communities, home inspection services by a licensed engineer are available. (See the *yellow pages* under "Building Inspectors.") Those who belong to the American Society of Home Inspectors (ASHI) have met specific standards of education and experience.

You can hire an inspector before or after you make the offer on the house; the next chapter has information on how to make your purchase offer dependent upon a satisfactory report. You may be charged a few hundred dollars, depending on travel time.

Try to accompany your inspector with a tape recorder. You'll learn many interesting things about the house that wouldn't be in a written report. The engineer can't tell you what the house is worth or give you advice on whether to buy it. Instead, you'll hear things like "That roof looks as if it has another five years or so on it. If you had to replace it today, it might cost . . ." Making the final decision is up to you.

Ask specifically whether there are indications that the house needs a specialist's inspection for a toxic substance.

Check Taxes

Make certain that you know the true tax figure, as explained in Chapter 5, for every house you are considering. Find out whether tax assessment would be changed and how much taxes would be if you bought at a given figure.

Valiant efforts are made to keep taxes equitable, but the process is a constant challenge. Your agent can tell you what system is used in your community.

What Else?

Ask whether trash collection is included in the taxes or is a private matter. Find out if there are separate charges for water and sewer service. Inquire of owners about their heating and cooling costs. Ask to see their past utility bills.

A Word about Improvements

If you are considering buying a home that needs work, it's helpful to understand the difference between repairs and improvements.

Improvements are just that: permanent additions that increase the value of your house. The IRS considers them as part of your cost for the house. Every homeowner should keep a permanent record book detailing all expenses for improvements and should save checks and receipts. Some day, when the house is sold at a profit, these figures could reduce any income tax otherwise due.

Repairs don't count as improvements, and neither does redecorating. Typical improvements include adding a room, finishing a basement, fences, new furnace, new plumbing or wiring (as opposed to simple repairs), new roof and driveway paving.

Your own labor cannot count as part of the expense, by the way. And in some areas, capital improvements are exempt from local sales tax; inquire when you are having them done.

As you consider buying a home in need of improvements, remember that it is financially imprudent to make a house into the most expensive one on the street; you are not likely to recoup your investment when you eventually sell.

Open Houses

One good way to start your house-hunting is to visit open houses. Usually held on Saturday or Sunday afternoons, they are an invitation to the general public. You won't need any advance appointment or research; you can tour the neighborhoods that most interest you, stopping in at one house after another. It's a great way to get a feeling for prices.

Don't hesitate to visit even if you're not ready to buy. Brokers can be lonely, giving up a Sunday afternoon to sit in a house, and they will welcome you. Don't be worried if you're asked to sign in. If it were your house, wouldn't you want people to identify themselves before they came in? And of course you'll wipe your feet, restrain your children and put out your cigarette before entering.

Community practices differ in the matter of open-house etiquette among brokers. If you are working with one agent, discuss frankly the best way to visit open houses on your own when he or she isn't available. You don't want to find your dream house, only to discover that you've stepped into jurisdictional disputes. Most agents can offer suggestions on how to head off such problems.

Stay in Touch with Your Agent

Of course, you'll read the ads avidly while you are house-hunting. Particular real estate terms common to each area may puzzle you; don't hesitate to ask your agent to explain them.

If you want to work through a seller's agent who gives you good service, or if you have retained a buyer's broker, don't answer ads yourself. Phone the agent and mention the items that catch your eye. The broker can then do a little investigating, particularly where the multiple-listing service is involved. Then you'll receive a call back: "That ad on page five was the house I showed you last week; it sure looks different on paper, doesn't it? The one on the bottom of the page is about $60,000 over your price range. But the one on page six was just listed yesterday, and it sounds as if you might like it. I arranged with the listing agent for us to view it this afternoon."

CHAPTER NINE

Buying Investment Property

If you're looking for investment property, this chapter will give you some basic guidelines.

Investing in real estate usually means buying property and holding it for the production of income, not necessarily buying and selling for immediate profit.

Real estate has been called not only the best way to build an estate but even the only way. Real estate investment, though, takes constant effort on your part. You can buy shares of stock and then limit your effort to checking the quotations every week in the Sunday paper. Not so with a duplex three blocks from your home. You must be ready for a phone call at 6 AM that the water heater has burst, and ready to buy a replacement promptly and arrange for someone to meet the plumber that very day.

Despite the plumbing problems, real estate investment is not liquid. You can take your money out of the stock market with a simple phone call to your stockbroker. When your capital is in real estate, you shouldn't count on taking it out under, say, six months' notice. When things (such as low employment levels) get bad in your community, it's possible that you can't get your money out until the economic cycle changes.

Getting Started

As an investor, you face three challenges—finding the right property, buying it right and then managing it. You will need

- A lawyer who specializes in real estate,
- An accountant and
- A good real estate broker who is interested in helping you reach your goals.

Line up all three *before* you make your first purchase. You'll need them to locate and then analyze the proposed investment. To prepare, talk with brokers, read the papers, visit open houses and develop some expertise so you'll recognize a bargain when you see it.

Read everything you can find—but don't send hundreds of dollars for home study courses advertised on cable TV. The same material is available in local bookstores and for free in the public library. Take basic real estate courses at community colleges—the sort offered to beginning real estate salespersons. That'll give you the vocabulary and some basic information, and your fellow students may eventually prove helpful.

Start Small

It's wise to start small for your first few transactions so that you're not risking too much capital or taking on too much liability while you learn. A one-to-six-unit building, in a familiar neighborhood near your own home, is best. If the place needs fixing up, pay for a building engineer's inspection so that you'll know what you're getting into before your purchase offer becomes firm (the lawyer can help arrange that part). Try for property that will appeal to the largest number of responsible prospective tenants.

Avoid Land

Forget about vacant land or building lots in resort areas. Land has to appreciate markedly before it pays off because it produces no income, ties up your money and requires tax payments. Judging which areas will be in demand in years to come takes skill and expertise, and even long-time investors can get burned. Land is no investment for beginners.

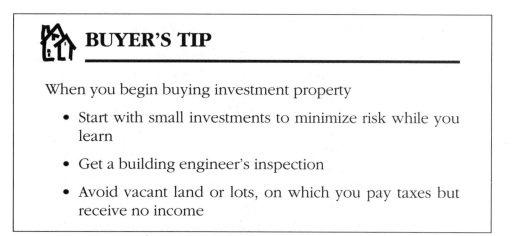

BUYER'S TIP

When you begin buying investment property

- Start with small investments to minimize risk while you learn

- Get a building engineer's inspection

- Avoid vacant land or lots, on which you pay taxes but receive no income

How Leverage Works

Traditionally, real estate investors have used *leverage* (other people's money) to pyramid a small amount of capital. If, for example, you had $100,000 and bought one piece that went up 5 percent in the next year, you'd make $5,000 in appreciation. To use leverage, you find ten such parcels, putting $10,000 down on each and taking out $90,000 mortgages. If they went up 5 percent, you'd have appreciation totaling $50,000 in the same one year—and you'd control a million dollars' worth of real estate.

This traditional technique runs into problems, however, where local conditions change, employment drops and it becomes difficult to find tenants who will pay enough to cover those ten mortgage payments. You may end up supporting the real estate by taking money out of your pocket each month—if you have enough money in your pocket.

Those cheery investors who give testimonials on cable TV may say, "Within a week I owned a million dollars' worth of real estate," but a more accurate statement would be, "Within a week I *owed on* a million dollars' worth."

Analyzing Your First Investment

An accountant can help analyze any purchase before you make it. You use annual figures, calculating first the *gross rental income*. If present rentals are below market average, it's permissible to estimate using the rentals you'd charge (just find out whether present figures are locked in with leases).

From the gross rental you subtract

- An estimated allowance for vacancies and uncollected rents (in normal times, typically 5 percent of gross rental income)
- Utilities paid by the landlord
- Heat (if furnished)
- Property taxes
- Insurance
- Water charges (if paid by the landlord)
- Trash removal
- Estimate for repairs
- Janitor service, snow removal, lawn care and the like
- A reserve for future large improvements (new roof, furnace)

An accountant can help estimate the proper amount for reserve, which might run, for example, 2 percent of the value of the property.

With projected expenses subtracted from gross rental, you have the *annual net operating income*. From that, you then subtract *debt service* (mortgage payments). The resulting figure is your *cash flow*—actual dollars you can expect to take out of the property each year. If you have a minus figure, you have negative cash flow and had better think hard and long before taking on the investment. The beginner needs positive cash flow. It might be small, but the good news is that it does not represent your total return.

To calculate your actual return, first figure your taxable income on the property. It should be less than cash flow, because of an artificial bookkeeping concept known as *depreciation* (cost recovery). You can charge as a so-called expense a portion of what you paid for the building (the lot is not depreciated). On residential property, divide the cost of the building by 27.5 to learn the amount you may charge each year for depreciation. (Commercial property is depreciated over 31.5 years.)

Subtract this depreciation amount from your net operating income to determine how much profit or loss you will declare on your federal income tax return. If it's a loss, discuss with an accountant whether you can take the loss against other sources of income. The rules are complex. If your total income is less than $100,000 and you actively manage the property, you may be able to claim up to $25,000 in losses against other types of income (salary, dividends, etc.).

With total income up to $150,000, part of a loss may be deducted. Otherwise, your paper loss can be taken only against other *passive income* (the category into which all rental income now falls for tax purposes).

If you can take any loss on your income tax return, the next step is to figure the income tax savings that result, depending on your tax bracket. This figure is one component in calculating the true return from the proposed investment, which consists of cash flow plus

- Principal paid down the first year on mortgage (amortization)
- Estimated annual appreciation
- Income tax saving (if any)

The *total annual return* is then analyzed as a percentage of the cash you will invest. In order for the investment to fly, this should be considerably higher than the return available on, for example, certificates of deposit. Otherwise, there's no point in risking your capital and making an additional investment of your time and effort.

The one-to-six-family residential buildings suitable for beginning investors will usually not support professional management and still show positive cash flow. In most cases, you'll have to manage the property yourself. It won't work if you have to pay someone else to change every faucet washer either, so now that you've found your first purchase, the next thing to analyze is:

Are you temperamentally suited to be a landlord?

But that's a question for another book. For now, let's stick to making the purchase.

CHAPTER TEN

Arriving at a Contract

When you've found your dream house—or your compromise house—or your investment property—what then? How do you reach a binding agreement with the seller?

The process resembles a tennis game. The homeowner makes the first serve, a public offer to sell the property at a given price. Now the ball is in your court.

Local customs differ, particularly in the area around New York and other large cities, which use a system of offers and bids, with the final contract written by attorneys.

In most localities, however, you start things off with an offer to buy, which includes not only price but many other provisions. The document you present to the seller is a written *purchase offer;* when the seller accepts it exactly as you presented it, it becomes a *binding contract,* which may be known in your community as a deposit receipt, contract of sale, or agreement to buy and sell.

All real estate contracts must be in writing in order to be enforceable. (Translation: "Oral agreements aren't worth the paper they're written on.") If, in front of 20 witnesses, a homeowner said he was willing to sell you the property for $150,000 cash and took your deposit check—you still could not legally hold him to it.

The written contract supersedes any oral agreements; if the sellers promise to leave the refrigerator, make sure that the contract mentions it, or you could be out of luck.

The Written Offer

Depending on local custom, a broker or attorney will usually help draw up a written purchase offer detailing the terms under which you propose to buy. In some areas this is a full-fledged contract, needing only the seller's acceptance to be complete. Elsewhere, local custom may employ a preliminary memorandum, articles of agreement, binder or deposit receipt.

Can you draw up the offer for yourself? Yes, and you could perform your own surgery, too. In either case, it'd be fine unless you happened to make an amateurish mistake. There's no use copying someone else's contract or a model; yours will differ in many respects according to the needs of the parties involved, local custom and state law. Brokers and lawyers must take courses, pass exams and gain related experience before they're allowed to fill out these forms. Don't try to do it yourself.

Ask the broker with whom you are working for a copy of a purchase offer that is common in your area, or obtain a copy of the contract generally used by your multiple-listing system or bar association. Study it at leisure in advance, for when it comes time to fill one in and sign it, you'll be too nervous for quiet consideration.

First Decision: Purchase Price

Before you begin and before emotions take over, settle in your mind the top price you really would invest in the house—a figure you will not share with the agent, unless it is someone you specifically hired as your own broker.

Should you expect to pay full asking price, or is there a formula for the amount of bargaining built in by the sellers?

The answer is simple: It all depends . . .

Homeowners who hate haggling may have listed their house at a rock-bottom price with no room for flexibility. Others may add a five percent cushion to what they'd really take.

The sellers' circumstances affect price. They may be under some of the pressures mentioned in the last chapter. Elderly homeowners, on the other hand, are often in no hurry to move. They may have emotional ties that make it difficult for them to view their property impartially.

If a house has been on the market a long time (more than five months), the buying public has voted that it isn't worth what they're asking. In that case, don't offer full price.

On the other hand, don't fool around if you've stumbled on a hot listing, one that has just come on the market and is uniquely appealing or underpriced. If there is a possibility of several offers within the next day, consider coming in somewhere over asking price. This gives you an advantage against competition. It sounds suspicious when a broker recommends such action; this is where it helps if you already know and trust the agent.

Look for Comparables

When you house-hunt extensively in a given area, you quickly become an expert on homes that fall within your price range. You can recognize a bargain when it comes on the market. You can also spot overpriced property. For a short time, you may know more than anyone else in the world about the proper price for a three-bedroom ranch in Milkwood.

In an unfamiliar area, ask the agent for sale prices of *comparables*. These are similar homes in the neighborhood that have recently changed hands; they'll give you something to judge by. Comparables, in fact, are the principal tool brokers themselves use to appraise property for market value. Other considerations in making price comparisons include the condition of the house, time of year, special financing available and the general economic climate—whether it's a buyers' or sellers' market.

You may be curious about what the homeowners paid three years ago for the place you want to buy today, but that is not relevant. If they had received it as a gift, must they then give it away? On the other hand, if they've invested $25,000 in a gold-plated bathroom, are you then obliged to reimburse them? Of course not.

How much money the sellers have invested in the property, and how much they need to get out of it, are their concerns, not yours. In the end, says the professional appraiser's maxim, "buyers make value." Selling price is set by the operation of supply and demand, in competition on the open market.

Your offering price will be affected by the terms under which you expect to buy. If the sellers have to wait around while you market your present home, they'll be less inclined to drop their price. The same applies if they must come up with a cash payment of points to your lender. By the same token, a clean offer with no contingencies is worth a price concession.

After price, the next big item in the contract is how you will finance your purchase. If you are going to assume a present loan or place your mortgage with the sellers themselves, these terms are detailed. You'll stipulate that the mortgage you are taking over must be current (paid up to date) at the time of transfer.

Allow for Contingencies

If you must obtain outside financing, the details of your proposed mortgage are spelled out, along with a statement that the contract is "contingent upon" or "subject to" your obtaining the loan. If you cannot find financing at the specific interest rate you have stipulated in the offer, you couldn't be required to go through with the purchase. The contract should state that in such a case your deposit would be returned.

There may be other *contingencies* (happenings) that must be satisfied before you will buy. You may need to sell your present home, or obtain the job you came to town to interview for or receive a satisfactory (to you) engineer's report. These conditions are inserted into the contract.

The sellers will be nervous about contingent offers. They will be taking their house off the market on your behalf, without any guarantee that the sale will go through. So it's customary to set a time limit on contingencies. The contract might state that it is "contingent upon buyer's receiving a satisfactory engineer's report on the property within three days of acceptance of this offer" or "contingent upon approval by the buyer's husband when he arrives in town before next Saturday, September 11, at 6 P.M."

For longer contingencies, particularly those involving the sale of your present house, the sellers may envision waiting around forever.

Instead of worrying about the sale of their home, they must now worry about yours, over which they have even less control.

So it's only fair to insert an *escape clause,* or *kick-out.* The wording may differ according to local practice, but the escape clause usually gives the seller the right to continue to show the house. If another good offer comes in, you may be required to remove the contingency and make your offer firm or else drop out.

If your contingency is called, you don't have to meet anyone else's offering price; your deal has been nailed down. But you would have to agree, for example, to buy the property whether or not you sell your present home. Otherwise, you could drop out and receive your deposit back.

Personal Property versus Real Estate

It is essential to spell out all the gray-area items (carpeting, fireplace equipment, chandeliers, drapes) about which there may be disputes as to whether they stay with the property or not.

In general, *personal property* that can be picked up and moved without leaving any nail or screw holes may be taken by the seller. By contrast, *real estate* is the land and anything permanently attached to it. The rules are complicated, though, and it's best to stipulate in the contract that "Stove and refrigerator are to remain" or "Seller may remove dining room chandelier."

Items like wall-to-wall carpeting, wood stoves, swing sets and satellite dishes are subject to occasional differences of opinion; head off trouble by detailing them in the written offer. If the listing agent did a proper job, the sellers will already have indicated which items they are taking or leaving. Ask the broker to do some delicate investigating about the sellers' plans for the above-ground pool or the tool shed.

Don't get bogged down over small items. Just make sure that your offer specifies what you expect to remain. Don't discuss furniture or rugs that you might like to buy at this point; wait until you have a firm purchase contract.

What Else in Your Offer?

It's a good idea to stipulate that you have the right to inspect the premises within 24 hours before closing. You will want to make sure that the sellers left the fireplace tools or removed the piles of magazines in the attic.

Also necessary in the contract are a target date and place for transfer of title. Choose a date that allows for processing of your mortgage application; the agent will have suggestions.

What if that date comes and goes? You still have a binding contract. If a certain deadline is absolutely essential, you can use the powerful legal phrase "time is of the essence," but this is strong medicine; don't do it without consulting your lawyer.

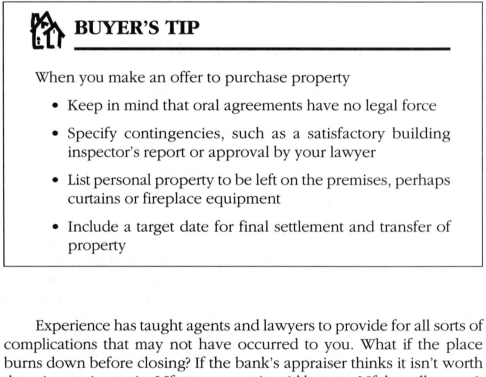

BUYER'S TIP

When you make an offer to purchase property

- Keep in mind that oral agreements have no legal force

- Specify contingencies, such as a satisfactory building inspector's report or approval by your lawyer

- List personal property to be left on the premises, perhaps curtains or fireplace equipment

- Include a target date for final settlement and transfer of property

Experience has taught agents and lawyers to provide for all sorts of complications that may not have occurred to you. What if the place burns down before closing? If the bank's appraiser thinks it isn't worth the price you're paying? If taxes weren't paid last year? If the sellers can't prove they have clear title (ownership)? If there's a full tank of oil left in the basement? Will you receive occupancy on the day you settle? Will you receive a full warranty deed, or does local custom use a lesser deed?

Your offer should have a time limit, and it should be a short one. A day or two is enough time for the sellers to consider your proposal. If you give them more time, they may be tempted to stall until after they see what next Sunday's open house might bring. They might also use your offer as an auction goad to bid up another prospective buyer. If the sellers are out of town, they should be available by phone and could answer your offer by fax with a confirming letter to follow.

Earnest Money

An offer to buy is usually accompanied by a substantial deposit, variously known as *binder* or *earnest money*. This sum serves several purposes. It proves to the sellers that you mean business. They are, after all, going to take the place off the market on your behalf. The deposit also serves as a source of damages if you back out for no good reason a month down the line. The deposit is usually placed with a broker or attorney, who puts it into a separate *escrow,* or trust, account. Avoid giving the deposit directly to the seller.

You may be told that 6 percent or 10 percent of the purchase price is necessary. If this is inconvenient, insist that you can come up with only a smaller amount. Remember, though, that the sellers are weighing your offer to see if it will result in a successful sale. Without much earnest money, it may not look convincing.

This earnest money, of course, counts toward the sum you'll need at closing. Your full deposit is credited toward the down payment or other settlement costs. The contract should clearly state under what circumstances it may be returned.

Legal Provisions

The contract provides that you will receive clear title, full unchallenged control and ownership, except for certain liens and easements that are spelled out. These are claims that third parties may have against the property. You agree to take it even though the telephone company has the right to run wires through the backyard, or the neighbor has the right to share the driveway; these are known as *easements of record*. You don't agree to be responsible for unknown *liens* (financial claims) that turn up later, like an unpaid roofing bill or an outstanding home-improvement loan.

Final Jitters

If this is your first homebuying experience, you will feel shaky when the time comes to sign the offer. You should receive an immediate duplicate of everything you sign; if it isn't offered, ask for it. You need not walk out wondering what you've just committed yourself to.

It's reassuring to take the contract to your lawyer before you sign it. Many sales, though, are made after office hours and on weekends, and you may risk losing the right house by delay. You can write above your signature "subject to the approval in form of my attorney." This means that you can go ahead and make your offer, while reserving for your lawyer the right to object later to any wording or provisions that don't protect your interests. The lawyer can even disapprove the whole contract.

Most lawyers refuse to give advice on price, feeling that this is out of their field of expertise. The attorney's job is to see that the contract protects you and accomplishes your objectives. You can safely follow local custom about who writes an uncomplicated contract.

Negotiation—The Tennis Game

Although local customs vary, in most areas the broker will present your offer to the seller, with you not present. You'll be advised to go home and wait by the phone. The agent, meanwhile, may contact the listing broker and the seller, to arrange for presentation of the offer as soon as possible; prompt forwarding of all offers is one of the broker's primary legal responsibilities. No broker has the right to refuse to convey a written offer, no matter how small.

The broker almost never reveals terms or price over the phone. The seller cannot accept over the phone and deserves the right to look over all the details of your proposal at leisure.

The tennis game is on, and the next move is the seller's. The response can be yes (acceptance), no (rejection) or maybe (counteroffer).

If it's yes, the seller accepts all your terms, and you have a binding contract. You can skip the rest of this chapter!

If it's no, the homeowners cannot later change their minds and get your offer back (unless you agree).

Then there's maybe. Rather than a rejection, a good negotiator will bring you a counteroffer: "We accept all terms and conditions except that purchase price shall be $183,000, and we'll throw in the stove and refrigerator."

The seller is now bound by the counteroffer, which probably contains a time limit, while you are free to consider its terms. You may want to counter the counteroffer, perhaps split the difference.

Too many volleys, though, result in hard feelings and often kill the deal. People begin to say, "It's not the money, it's the principle of the thing." Instead of working together toward what is legally known as a *meeting of the minds,* buyer and seller start to see the negotiation as a war. They concentrate on winning and lose sight of their original goals.

Before you start, make up your mind that you will not lose the house you really want over the last thousand dollars. When you cannot make any further concessions on price, try to include some face-saving gesture toward the seller: "We can't go any higher, but we'll move the closing date for their convenience."

Make your first offer, certainly your second one, close to the top price you'd really pay. The idea is to tempt the sellers to wrap up the deal, even if it isn't quite what they had in mind.

At each stage, the person who made the last proposal is bound by it until it's withdrawn or answered. The game ends when one side accepts unconditionally the other's last offer.

Remember that if your proposal is accepted, you will have a *binding legal contract* (see Figure 10.1). Don't fool around with a purchase offer unless you really want to buy the property. It should be a thrill when you finally receive the notification of acceptance that is the final legal requirement to make a contract binding:

"Congratulations! They said yes. You've just bought a house!"

FIGURE 10.1 Real Estate Sales Contract

PURCHASE AND SALE CONTRACT
FOR RESIDENTIAL PROPERTY

Plain English Form published by and only for use of members of the Greater Rochester Association of Realtors, Inc. and the Monroe County Bar Association.

COMMISSIONS OR FEES FOR THE REAL ESTATE SERVICES TO BE PROVIDED ARE NEGOTIABLE BETWEEN REALTOR AND CLIENT.

When Signed, This Document Becomes A Binding Contract. Buyer or Seller May Wish To Consult Their Own Attorney.

TO: _____ (Seller) FROM: _____ (Buyer)

OFFER TO PURCHASE

Buyer offers to purchase the property described below from Seller on the following terms:

1. PROPERTY DESCRIPTION.

Property known as No. _____ in the (Town) (City) (Village) of_____, State of New York, also

known as Tax No. _____ including all buildings and any other improvements and all rights which the Seller has in or with the property.

Approximate Lot Size: _____. **(Check if applicable)** [ ] As described in more detail in the attached description.

Description of Buildings on Property: _____

2. OTHER ITEMS INCLUDED IN PURCHASE. The following items, if any, now in or on the property are included in this purchase and sale. All heating, plumbing, septic and private water systems, lighting fixtures, flowers, shrubs, trees, window shades and blinds, curtain and traverse rods, storm windows, storm doors, screens, awnings, TV antennae, water softeners, sump pumps, window boxes, mail box, tool shed, fences, underground pet containment fencing with control devices, wall-to-wall carpeting and runners, exhaust fans, hoods, garbage disposal, electric garage door opener and remote control devices, intercom equipment, humidifier, security systems, smoke detectors, all fireplace screens and enclosures, swimming pool and all related equipment and accessories, and the following, if built-in: cabinets, mirrors, stoves, ovens, dishwashers, trash compactors, shelving and air conditioning (except window units). Buyer agrees to accept these items in their present conditions. Other items to be included in the purchase and sale are: _____

[ ] Seller represents to the best of Seller's knowledge that any heating, plumbing, air conditioning, electrical systems and included appliances are presently in good working order, except for

_____

Items not included are:_____

Seller represents that he has good title to all of the above items to be transferred to Buyer, and will deliver a Bill of Sale for the same at closing.

3. PRICE: AMOUNT AND HOW IT WILL BE PAID: The purchase price is _____ Dollars

$ _____, Buyer shall receive credit at closing for any deposit made hereunder. The balance of the purchase price shall be paid as follows: (Check and complete applicable provisions.)

[ ] (a) Seller agrees to pay a loan fee of _____% of the mortgage amount.

[ ] (b) All in cash, or certified check at closing.

[ ] (c) By Buyer assuming and agreeing to pay according to its terms, the principal balance of the mortgage in the approximate amount of $ _____

held by_____, provided that the mortgage is assumable without the holder's approval. Buyer

understands that the mortgage bears interest at the rate of _____% per year and the monthly payments are $ _____ which includes principal,

interest, taxes and insurance (strike out any item not included in payment), with the last payment due on approximately _____ 19/20_____. Buyer agrees to pay the

balance of the purchase price over the amount of the assumed mortgage in cash or certified check at closing. Buyer understands that principal balance may be lower at time of closing because of monthly payments made after this contract is signed. If the mortgage to be assumed provides for graduated or balloon payments, then a copy of the original bond and mortgage shall be furnished to Buyer's attorney for approval within ten days after acceptance of this offer.

[ ] (d) By Buyer delivering a purchase money bond and mortgage to Seller at closing. This purchase money bond and mortgage shall be in the amount of $_____

shall be amortized over a term of _____ years and all due and payable in _____ years from the date of closing, shall bear interest at the rate of _____% per year, and shall

be paid in monthly installments of $_____, including principal and interest. The mortgage shall contain the statutory clauses as to payment, insurance,

acceleration on default of thirty days, taxes, assessments, and water rates and also shall provide for late charges of 2% of any monthly payment which is not paid within 15 days after it is due and for recovery of reasonable attorney's fees if the mortgage is foreclosed.

The mortgage shall allow Buyer to prepay all or part of the mortgage without penalty at any time but shall also provide that the mortgage be paid in full if Buyer sells the property, unless Seller consents in writing to assumption of the mortgage debt. The balance of the purchase price will be paid at closing in cash, or certified check.

Source: Reprinted by permission of the Greater Rochester Association of REALTORS®

FIGURE 10.1 *(continued)*

4. CONTINGENCIES. Buyer makes this offer subject to the following contingencies. If any of these contingencies is not satisfied by the dates specified, then either Buyer or Seller may cancel this contract by written notice to the other. (Check and complete applicable provisions.)

[ ] (a) **Mortgage Contingency.** This offer subject to Buyer obtaining and accepting a _____ mortgage loan commitment in an amount not to exceed _____ at an interest rate not to exceed _____%, for a term of _____ years. Buyer shall immediately apply for this loan and shall have until _____ to obtain and accept a written mortgage commitment. The conditions of any such mortgage commitment shall not be deemed contingencies of this contract but shall be the sole responsibility of Buyer. If the loan commitment requires repairs, replacements, or improvements to be made or painting to be done, before closing, then Seller shall do the work and install the materials and improvements needed or have the same done, at Seller's expense. However, if the cost of doing so exceeds $_____ , Seller shall not be obligated to have such work done, and Buyer will be allowed either to receive credit at closing for the amount recited above and incur any necessary expenses to comply with the loan commitment requirements, or to cancel this contract by written notice to Seller, and any deposit shall be returned to Buyer. Issuance and acceptance by the Buyer of a written mortgage commitment shall be deemed a waiver and satisfaction of this contingency.

[ ] (b) **Mortgage Assumption Contingency.** This offer is subject to Buyer obtaining permission to assume the existing mortgage loan balance referred to above in (3c) by _____ 19_____ . If the mortgage holder requires that the interest rate be increased for such approval to be given, Buyer agrees to assume the mortgage at such rate as long as it does not exceed _____% at the time of the commitment. [ ]Buyer agrees to obtain a release of Seller's liability and to pay any assumption or release of liability fees.

[ ] (c) **Sale Contract Contingency.** This offer is subject to Buyer obtaining a contract for the sale of Buyer's property located at no later than _____ , 199____ . Unless and until Buyer has removed this sale contingency in writing, if Seller receives another acceptable purchase offer, Seller may notify Buyer in writing that Seller wants to accept the other offer and Buyer will then have _____ days to remove this sale contingency by written notice to the Seller. If Buyer does not remove this sale contingency after receiving notice from Seller, Buyer's rights under this contract shall end, and Seller shall be free to accept the other purchase offer and Buyer's deposit shall be returned. Buyer may not remove this sale contingency if Buyer's mortgage loan commitment requires the sale and/or transfer of this property as a condition of the mortgage loan funding, unless Buyer has a contract for the sale of this property which is not then subject to any unsatisfied contingencies.

[ ] (d) **Transfer of Title Contingency.** This offer is contingent upon the transfer of title to Buyer's property located at _____ no later than _____ , 199____ . [ ] Buyer represents that Buyer has entered into a contract for sale of Buyer's property which is now subject to the following contingencies: [ ] None; [ ] Mortgage; [ ] Assumption of Mortgage; [ ] Sale of Property; [ ] Transfer of Title; [ ] Attorney Approval; and/or [ ] Other_____. Unless and until Buyer has obtained a contract for sale of Buyer's property which is not subject to any unsatisfied contingencies, and has so notified the Seller in writing, if Seller receives another acceptable purchase offer, Seller may notify Buyer in writing that Seller wants to accept the other offer and Buyer will then have _____ days to remove this transfer of title contingency by written notice to the Seller. If Buyer does not remove this transfer of title contingency after receiving notice from Seller, Buyer's rights under this contract shall end, and Seller shall be free to accept the other purchase offer and Buyer's deposit shall be returned. Buyer may not remove this transfer of title contingency if Buyer's mortgage loan commitment requires the sale and transfer of this property as a condition of the mortgage loan funding, unless Buyer has a contract for sale of this property which is not then subject to any unsatisfied contingencies.

[ ] (e) **Attorney Approval.** This contract is subject to the written approval of attorneys for Buyer and Seller within _____ days from date of acceptance (the "Approval Period"). If either attorney makes written objection to the contract within the Approval Period, and such objection is not cured by written approval by both attorneys and all of the parties within the Approval Period, then either Buyer or Seller may cancel this contract by written notice to the other and any deposit shall be returned to the Buyer.

[ ] (f) **Waiver of Attorney Approval.** This offer is not subject to the Buyer's attorney approval.

[ ] (g) **Other Contingencies.** _____
_____

5. Closing Date and Place. Transfer of title shall take place at the _____County Clerk's Office or at the offices of Buyer's lender on or before _____ ,19_____ .

6. Buyer's Possession of Property.

[ ] Buyer shall have possession of the property on the day of closing, in broom clean condition, with all keys to the property delivered to Buyer at closing.

[ ] Seller shall have the right to retain possession for_____ days after closing at the cost of $_____ per day, plus utilities. At possession, the property shall be broom clean and all keys delivered to Buyer.

7. Title Documents. Seller shall provide the following documents in connection with the sale:

A. Deed. Seller will deliver to Buyer at closing a properly signed and notarized Warranty Deed with lien covenant (or Executor's Deed, Administrator's Deed or Trustee's Deed, if Seller holds title as such).

GRAR
3/94

B. Abstract, Bankruptcy and Tax Searches, and Instrument Survey Map. Seller will furnish and pay for and deliver to Buyer or Buyer's attorney at least 15 days prior to the date of closing, fully guaranteed tax, title and United States Court Searches dated or redated after the date of this contract with a local tax certificate for Village, or City taxes, if any, and an instrument survey map dated or redated after the date of this contract. Seller will pay for the map or redated map and for continuing such searches to and including the day of closing. Any survey map shall be prepared or redated and certified to meet the standards and requirements of Buyer's mortgage lender and of the Monroe County Bar Association.

8. Marketability of Title. The deed and other documents delivered by Seller shall be sufficient to convey good marketable title in fee simple, to the property free and clear of all liens and encumbrances. However, Buyer agrees to accept title to the property subject to restrictive covenants of record common to the tract or subdivision of which the property is a part, provided these restrictions have not been violated, or if they have been violated, that the time for anyone to complain of the violations has expired. Buyer also agrees to accept title to the property subject to public utility easements along lot lines as long as those easements do not interfere with any buildings now on the property or with any improvements Buyer may construct in compliance with all present restrictive covenants of record and zoning and building codes applicable to the Property. Seller agrees to furnish a smoke alarm affidavit at closing and to cooperate in executing any documents required by federal or state laws for transfer of title to residential property.

9. Objections to Title. If Buyer raises a valid written objection to Seller's title which means that the title to the property is unmarketable, Seller may cancel this contract by giving prompt written notice of cancellation to Buyer. Buyer's deposit shall be returned immediately, and if Buyer makes a written request for it, Seller shall reimburse Buyer for the reasonable cost of having the title examined. However, if Seller gives notice within 5 days that Seller will cure the problem prior to the closing date, or if the title objection is insurable and Buyer is willing to accept insurable title, then this contract shall continue in force until the closing date, subject to the Seller performing as promised and/or providing insurable title at Seller's expense. If Seller fails to cure the problem within such time, Buyer will not be obligated to purchase the property and Buyer's deposit shall be returned together with reimbursement for the reasonable cost of having the title examined.

10. Recording Costs, Mortgage Tax, Transfer Tax and Closing Adjustments. Seller will pay the real property transfer tax and special additional mortgage recording tax, if applicable. Buyer will pay mortgage assumption charges, if any, and will pay for recording the deed and the mortgage, and for mortgage tax. The following, as applicable, will be prorated and adjusted between Seller and Buyer as of the date of closing: current taxes computed on a fiscal year basis, excluding any delinquent items, interest and penalties; rent payments; fuel oil on the premises; water charges; pure water charges; sewer charges; mortgage interest; current common charges or assessments; prepaid F.H.A. Mortgage Insurance Premium (M.I.P.) of approximately $_____ , with the exact amount to be calculated at closing in accordance with F.H.A. formulae. Any F.H.A. insurance premium which is not prepaid, but rather paid monthly, shall be adjusted at closing. If there is a water meter at the property, Seller shall furnish an actual reading to a date not more than thirty (30) days before the closing date set forth in this contract. At closing the water charges and any sewer rent shall be apportioned on the basis of such actual reading.

FIGURE 10.1 *(continued)*

11. Zoning. Seller represents that the property is in full compliance with all zoning or building ordinances for use as a _____ .
If applicable laws require it, the Seller will furnish at or before closing, a Certificate of Occupancy for the property, dated within ninety (90) days of the closing, with Seller completing the work and installing the materials and improvements needed to obtain Certificate of Occupancy. However, if the cost of obtaining a Certificate of Occupancy exceeds $ _____ , Seller shall not be obligated to have such work done, and Buyer will be allowed either to receive credit at closing for the amount recited above, and incur the necessary expenses to obtain the Certificate of Occupancy, or to cancel this contract by written notice to Seller, and any deposit shall be returned to Buyer.

12. Risk of Loss. Risk of loss or damage to the property by fire or other casualty until transfer of title shall be assumed by the Seller. If damage to the property by fire or such other casualty occurs prior to transfer, Buyer may cancel this contract without any further liability to Seller and Buyer's deposit is to be returned. If Buyer does not cancel but elects to close, then Seller shall transfer to Buyer any insurance proceeds, or Seller's claim to insurance proceeds payable for such damage.

13. Condition of Property. Buyer agrees to purchase the property "as is" except as provided in paragraph 2, subject to reasonable use, wear, tear, and natural deterioration between now and the time of closing. However, this paragraph shall not relieve Seller from furnishing a Certificate of Occupancy as called for in paragraph 11, if applicable. Buyer shall have the right, after reasonable notice to Seller, to inspect the property within 48 hours before the time of closing.

14. Services. Seller represents that property is serviced by: _____ Public Water, _____ Public Sewers, _____ Septic System, _____ Private Well.

15. Deposit to Listing Broker. Buyer (has deposited) (will deposit upon acceptance) $ _____ in the form of a _____
with _____ (Escrow Agent) at _____ (bank), which deposit is to become part of the purchase price or returned if not accepted or if Buyer's contract thereafter fails to close for any reason not the fault of the Buyer. If Buyer fails to complete Buyer's part of this contract, Seller is allowed to retain the deposit to be applied to Seller's damages, and may also pursue other legal rights Seller has against the Buyer, including a lawsuit for any real estate brokerage commission paid by the Seller.

16. Real Estate Broker.
[ ] The parties agree that _____ brought about this purchase and sale.

[ ] It is understood and agreed by both Buyer and Seller that no broker secured this contract.

17. Life of Offer. This offer shall expire on _____ , 19_____ , at _____ .m.

18. Responsibility of Persons Under This Contract; Assignability. If more than one person signs this contract as Buyer, each person and any party who takes over that person's legal position will be responsible for keeping the promises made by Buyer in this contract. If more than one person signs this contract as Seller, each person or any party who takes over that person's legal position, will be fully responsible for keeping the promises made by Seller. However, this contract is personal to the parties and may not be assigned by either without the other's consent.

19. Entire Contract. This contract when signed by both Buyer and Seller will be the record of the complete agreement between the Buyer and Seller concerning the purchase and sale of the property. No verbal agreements or promises will be binding.

20. Notices. All notices under this contract shall be deemed delivered upon receipt. Any notices relating to this contract may be given by the attorneys for the parties.

21. Addenda. The following Addenda are incorporated into this contract:
[ ] All Parties Agreement [ ] Services [ ] Engineer's Inspection [ ] Mediation [ ] Electric Availability [ ] Utility Surcharge [ ] Lead Warning [ ] Other: _____

Dated: _____   BUYER _____

Witness: _____   BUYER _____

[ ] ACCEPTANCE OF OFFER BY SELLER   [ ] COUNTER OFFER BY SELLER
Seller certifies that Seller owns the property and has the power to sell the property. Seller accepts the offer and agrees to sell on the terms and conditions above set forth.

[ ] Waiver of Seller's attorney approval. This offer is not subject to Seller's attorney approval.

Dated: _____   SELLER _____

Witness: _____   SELLER _____

CHAPTER ELEVEN

Your Mortgage Application

Buyer's Remorse

As you approach the next phase of your adventure, watch out for a malady known by the scientific name of *Buyer's Remorse.* Onset may be from 24 hours to two weeks after your purchase offer was accepted. Symptoms usually develop rapidly around 2 AM, as you lie awake wondering why you ever got into this, if you can really afford the house, how you will get along without your present neighbors and whether the whole thing isn't a Big Mistake.

Buyer's Remorse is akin to the last-minute jitters that afflict brides and grooms before the wedding. One consolation: if it's all a big mistake, selling a house is simpler than getting a divorce.

Rather than lose any more sleep, call the real estate broker the next day asking if you can visit the house again, preferably when the sellers are absent. "Measuring for curtains" is a logical request; no need to alarm anyone at this point.

In nearly every case, the buyer is pleasantly surprised during the return visit. All that hard work, the research, the exhausting house-hunting really did pay off; this is clearly the best house in town for you.

If, as happens rarely, you are more depressed than ever after your return visit, it's time for a conference with your attorney to determine your legal position if you back out and how much money you stand to forfeit.

Mortgage Application

If you require a new mortgage to finance your purchase, the sale contract probably contains your promise to apply promptly at a lending institution. The real estate broker can often suggest the lender most favorable to your situation and the seller's. Perhaps the one that asks the fewest points this week, processes applications promptly or looks with favor on unusual older houses. Or you may be relying on a mortgage broker.

In some areas, the agent makes the appointment for you and even accompanies you to the application session. If you are on your own, sit down with the yellow pages open to "Mortgages" and ask to speak with a mortgage counselor or mortgage loan officer. Do your own research, using the charts in Chapter 7.

Come to the application session armed with as many facts as possible (see Figure 11.1). The lender will want to know a great deal about your financial situation, all aimed at not letting you get in over your head in debt.

Factors the underwriters will consider in deciding whether or not to make the loan: employment stability and other dependable income, your present assets, credit history, past mortgage experience and present debts.

The lender judges two things: your ability to meet your obligations in the future and your willingness to do so, as evidenced in the past.

Assets

You may not borrow elsewhere for the down payment (*secondary financing*) on most loans. You will be asked to prove that you already

FIGURE 11.1

☑ Checklist: Take to Your Mortgage Application

Some of these items, if not available, can be obtained later during the application process—VA eligibility certificate, for example, or legal description of property. To expedite your application, though, take as much as possible to your initial interview.

❑ Original purchase contract signed by all parties. It will be copied and returned to you.

❑ Cash or check for application fee, to cover appraisal of the property and credit report. Additional points or origination fee if required.

❑ Social Security numbers.

❑ List of all income.

❑ List of debts, credit cards, account numbers, payments, balances. Addresses of out-of-town creditors.

❑ List of two years' past employment and two years' past addresses.

❑ Seller's agreement to pay points (if not in contract).

❑ If self-employed, two years' signed income-tax returns. If on job less than two years, copies of previous W-2s.

❑ Expense and income statements on property presently rented out. Leases signed by tenants.

❑ Account numbers and balances on checking and saving accounts, branch addresses.

❑ Donor's name and address for gift letter.

❑ Explanation of any credit problems. Copies of bankruptcy papers.

❑ Certificate of Eligibility, if applying for VA loan.

❑ Legal description of property, survey (not required for all loans).

❑ List of stocks and bonds, current market value.

❑ List of other assets.

❑ True property tax figure on the projected purchase.

❑ Name and phone number of person who will give access to the lending institution's appraiser.

❑ Copy of divorce decree or separation agreement if paying child support or alimony; same documents if claiming them for income, along with proof that payments are being received.

have enough on hand for down payment and closing costs. Many institutions are skeptical about claims that your money is under the mattress, and will credit you with only a limited amount in cash—as little as $200, perhaps. They will also want an explanation for large sums of money that have suddenly turned up in your savings accounts within the past few months. (Maybe, they figure, you borrowed it somewhere, thus taking on too much debt.)

Bring in all details on your assets: numbers and balances on savings accounts (the lender will check with the bank to verify), list of stocks and bonds owned, income tax return if you anticipate a refund. Your earnest money deposit counts as an asset; the lender will verify it with the person holding it. You may have assets you've forgotten about: cash surrender value on your life insurance policy, valuable collections, jewelry, boats and RVs, IRA accounts, other real estate owned. List your furniture, appliances and automobiles; they might not bring much if you sold them, but they show that you won't need to go on a buying spree right after you close on the house.

A gift letter from a relative, promising to furnish some of the funds you need for closing with no repayment required or anticipated, can sometimes be used at mortgage application. Many lenders require the letter on their own form, and most want to verify that the relative does indeed have the funds in question.

Income To Qualify

The lending institution will analyze your income and will accept only figures that can be verified. More than one borrower (husband and wife or unrelated buyers) may pool their incomes to qualify for the loan.

The usual rule of thumb is that two years' continuous employment in the same field indicates employment stability. Exceptions are made for recent graduates or those who have just left the service. Lenders are nervous about those who jump often from one sort of job to another; employment changes that show upward movement within the same field are more acceptable.

Bonuses and overtime count toward qualification if your employer will verify them as dependable. Part-time and commission income count if they have been steady for the past year or two. Alimony and child support can be considered as income if you want to claim them, but you must be able to show that they are being paid dependably and are likely to continue for the next five years or so.

Older applicants will not be asked their ages, but they will be asked to prove dependable Social Security and pension income if they anticipate retirement within the next few years. Disability income counts if it is permanent.

Seasonal income may count if applicants can prove at least a two-year history of such a cycle, and they may even be able to count unemployment insurance in qualifying.

The self-employed will be asked to furnish income-tax returns for two years past and, where appropriate, audited profit-and-loss statements.

Other sources of income might include dividends and interest, and net rental from other properties (leases signed by your tenants may be required). If you will have rental income from the house you are buying (a duplex, for example, with the other side to be rented out), half or even all of the anticipated rent may be counted as further income.

Debts

Lenders give careful consideration to your present debts, your *liabilities*. Depending on the type of loan for which you are applying, they will count any debt on which you must pay for more than six, ten or twelve months. Car loans are among the most common liabilities in this category.

Before you arrive for mortgage application, list your debts, including loan numbers, monthly payments, balances and time left to run. Student loans are considered obligations if payments are presently due. Child support or alimony is considered an obligation; so is child care if you are applying for VA or FHA loans.

Credit History

It is essential to divulge information about past credit problems frankly during your interview. You should already have discussed judgments or bankruptcies with the real estate agent during your first meeting. Such problems won't necessarily prevent you from obtaining a mortgage, but if the lender's checking turns up any lies, you're in trouble.

To find out about your credit history, simply go to your local credit bureau and draw an inexpensive report on yourself. Do it early on. If any inaccuracies show up, the bureau will help you clear them up. TRW, one of the largest credit bureaus, will furnish you with a free report on yourself as often as once a year. If they have no local bureau, you can call them free of charge at 1-800-392-1122.

If you haven't borrowed money before, don't worry. An old wives' tale says that you must take out a loan and repay it to establish credit. Lenders know, though, that you've been around long enough to get into trouble if you were going to. No credit history is considered good credit.

Less-than-perfect credit may qualify you for one sort of loan and not another. VA and FHA guidelines are generally more lenient, though banks making their own portfolio loans can be flexible within certain limits.

The lender may ask you for written explanations of slow payment history or any derogatory report. You will have to pay off any open judgments, even if they flow from an "I won't pay as a matter of principle" dispute.

Bankruptcy guidelines vary, depending on the type of bankruptcy and type of loan. In general, one to two years must have elapsed since the discharge of your bankruptcy, though each case is considered separately. If your problem was due to something beyond your control, and your previous credit history was exemplary, exceptions can be made. Most important is your record of payments on any previous mortgage loan.

You'll be asked to sign a number of papers when you apply for the loan, many of them authorizing the release of verifying information from your employer, savings institution or credit bureau.

After the Application

While the lending institution completes all the paperwork (*assembling the exhibits*), the real estate agent should keep in touch in case any hitches develop. You might check yourself from time to time to see if things are going smoothly. Lenders have even been known to lose a whole file, so everything has to be done over again!

Within three days of your application, the lending institution must send you a good faith estimate of your closing costs, and notification of your APR, the *adjusted percentage rate.* If you paid for the appraisal, you are entitled to receive a copy; if it isn't offered, request it in writing.

BUYER'S TIP

After you have applied for a mortgage loan

- Check periodically on its progress
- Obtain an estimate of closing costs
- Don't incur any new debts

Keep the broker, or your lawyer, informed of any communication you receive from the lending institution, local government or FHA. Above all, don't go out and buy a car. This is not the time to incur additional debt or deplete your cash.

If you have questions for the seller, it's usually best to ask them through the broker, who can arrange for you to measure for curtains or show the place to your parents. Experience has proven that the transaction proceeds most efficiently when the broker and lawyers handle communication between buyer and seller. There are exceptions, of course; sellers have been known to host a barbecue to introduce the buyers to the neighbors.

After all the exhibits have been assembled, the lender's mortgage committee reviews the underwriting decision. It may then issue either a commitment letter or a conditional commitment dependent, for example, on certain repairs to the property before closing or on your clearing up an outstanding judgment. In any event, be sure to contact the broker and your lawyer or closing agent as soon as you hear from the lender.

Once you have the commitment safely in hand, nothing remains but to find a time (within the number of days stipulated in the commitment letter) that suits everyone for transferring the property. You are ready for closing.

CHAPTER
TWELVE

Buying Your Home at Last

In Maine they "pass papers"; in California they "go to escrow." It's closing, settlement, transfer of title—the moment when the seller gets the money and you get legal ownership and the front-door keys. In few real estate matters does local custom vary so widely.

In your area, closing may be conducted by attorneys, title companies, an escrow service, the lending institution, even by real estate brokers. It may take place at the county courthouse, a bank, attorney's office or other location. Sometimes everyone sits around a big table; sometimes buyer and seller never even meet.

Your purchase contract provides a blueprint for the final transfer. The seller's main responsibility is to prove title, to show that you are receiving clear and trouble-free ownership. Depending on the mortgagee's requirements and local custom, the seller may prove title by furnishing an abstract and lawyer's opinion, title insurance or, in some states, Torrens certificate.

Two types of *title insurance* are available. A fee policy, which may be required by your lender, protects the mortgagee—the lender—against loss if other parties challenge your ownership. If you need the policy for your mortgage loan, you may be asked to pay for it. The premium is a single payment, good for the whole time you own the property. For a relatively small additional fee, you can purchase at the same time an owner's policy, which protects *you* from loss if anyone challenges your ownership.

An *abstract* is a history of all transactions affecting the property, researched from the public records (see Figure 12.1). Typically, the seller must furnish an up-to-date abstract and forward it to you (better yet, to your attorney) for inspection before the closing, to make sure no problems exist. Where escrow or title companies handle closings, many of the same procedures are followed within the company.

The third method of proving title, the *Torrens system,* is used in some states and provides a central, permanent registration of title to the property.

Forms of Joint Ownership

If two persons are buying together, the wording of the deed determines their respective shares of ownership, their legal rights and the disposition of the property upon the death of one of them. Depending on state law, types of joint ownership include:

- **Tenancy in common.** Each owner has the right to leave his or her share to his estate.
- **Joint tenancy with right of survivorship.** The survivor automatically becomes complete owner.
- **Tenancy by the entirety.** This is a special form of joint tenancy for married couples.

If the owners have unequal shares, tenancy in common is the usual form. Except with tenancy by the entirety, any owner would have the right to force a division or sale of the property (partition).

When there is more than one owner, it is important to check with an attorney and to make sure that the deed clearly states the desired form of ownership.

FIGURE 12.1   Portion of an Abstract

A B S T R A C T   O F   T I T L E

- T O -

#47 W e s t   s i d e   R o w l e y   S t r e e t,   b e i n g

P a r t   o f   L o t s   #27   a n d   28   o f   t h e

B r o o k s   T r a c t   (N. P a r t)   i n   t h e

C i t y   o f   R o c h e s t e r

Maps: Liber 2 of Maps, page 120 and 138
Liber 3 of Maps, page 45
1935 Hopkins Atlas, Vol. 1, Plate 4

1   Ida May Hughey   Mortgage to secure $5000.00
Dated   June 3, 1947
same day
Rochester Savings   same day at 12:30 P. M.
47 Main Street
Rochester, New York   Liber 1800 of Mortgages, page 344

Conveys land in the City of Rochester, being on the

west side of Rowley Street in said City and being part of lots

Nos. 27 and 28 in the Brooks Tract as shown on a map of said

Tract made by M. D. Rowley, surveyor, May 15, 1869, and filed

in Monroe County Clerk's Office and counded and described as

follows:

Beginning at a point in the west line of Rowely

Street 15 feet northerly from the southeast corner of said

lot #27; thence northerly on the west line of Rowley Street,

forth (40) feet; thence westerly on a line parallel with the

south line of said lot #27, 121 feet; thence southerly on a

line parallel with the west line of Rowley Street, 40 feet;

thence easterly 121 feet to the place of beginning.

FIGURE 12.1   (*continued*)

       Being the same premises conveyed to the mortgagor by Liber 2258 of Deeds, page 178.

       Subject to any restrictions and public utility easements of record.

- -

2   Ida May Hughey, Landlord   Lease

            -To-   Dated May 23, 1952
                              Ack.   same day
Michael Franco   Rec.   August 4, 1952
Mildred Franco, his wife,
Tenants, 17 Glendale Park,   Liber 2769 of Deeds, page 290
Rochester, N.Y., (Second
parties not certified)

       First party leases to second parties premises described as #47 Rowley Street, Rochester, New York, being a 12 room house for a term of 5 years commencing July 16, 1952 and ending July 15, 1957 on certain terms and conditions set forth herein.

       Second parties shall have the right of renewal on the same terms and conditions as herein for an additional period of 5 years provided that written notice of intention to renew is served upon Landlord or her assigns at least 30 days prior to end of initial term hereof.

- -

3   Ida May Hughey,   Warranty Deed

        -To-   Dated Oct. 30, 1953
                              Ack. Same day
Michele Franco, Mildred   Rec. Same day at 10:50 A.M.
Franco, his wife, as
tenants by the entirety,   Liber 2861 of Deeds, page 411
#47 Rowley St., Rochester,
N.Y. (Second parties not
certified).

       Conveys same as #1.

       Subject to all covenants, easements and restrictions

That Clod of Earth—The Deed

The *deed,* the bill of sale for real estate, is drawn up ahead of time so that it can be examined and approved. A full *warranty deed* contains legal guarantees: that the seller really owns the property, for example, and that no one will ever challenge your right to it. In some areas, the standard is a *bargain and sale deed with covenant,* or *special warranty deed,* which contains some guarantees but not as many. If you buy from an estate, you receive an executor's deed. A *quitclaim deed* completely transfers whatever ownership the grantor (person signing the deed) may have had, but makes no claim of ownership in the first place.

In feudal times, when few could read or write, transfer of ownership was effected by buyer and seller first walking the boundaries of the land in question together. Often they would take along young boys, who would be there to serve as witnesses after buyer and seller were long gone. (One account says the boys were urged along with switches, on the theory that one doesn't forget painful experiences—beating the bounds.)

With the boundaries agreed upon, the seller would then dig up a clod of earth from the land being transferred and hand it to the buyer, who seized it and at that moment was the new owner, "seized of the land." The legal term *seizin* still refers to the claim of ownership.

Today, in a literate society, that clod of earth is replaced by a document, the deed, whose sole purpose is to transfer ownership. The beating of the bounds is replaced by the legal description in the deed. And you become owner at the exact moment when the deed is handed to you and accepted by you—physical transfer, just as it was with that clod of earth.

What To Do before Closing

You'll be alerted a few days before closing as to the exact amount of money needed. Cash or a certified check is usually required; no one wants to turn over so valuable an asset on a personal check. Except where you won't be in attendance (escrow closing), it's simplest to have a certified check or money order made out to your attorney or yourself; you can always endorse it, and matters are simpler if anything goes wrong. Bring a supply of your personal checks as well.

FIGURE 12.2

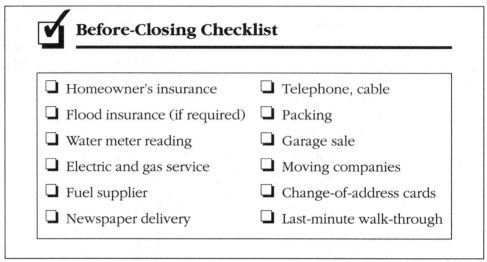

✓ **Before-Closing Checklist**	
❏ Homeowner's insurance	❏ Telephone, cable
❏ Flood insurance (if required)	❏ Packing
❏ Water meter reading	❏ Garage sale
❏ Electric and gas service	❏ Moving companies
❏ Fuel supplier	❏ Change-of-address cards
❏ Newspaper delivery	❏ Last-minute walk-through

You may be asked to bring proof that you are placing insurance on the property (see Figure 12.2). Real estate in a flood-prone area may be required to carry flood insurance. A survey proving that the building is located above the 100-year flood mark may allow you to drop a flood insurance requirement.

As closing approaches, request a last-minute walk-through of the property. If you see a window that was broken since you first inspected the house or a junked car in the backyard, don't talk directly with the seller. Instead, contact the agent and your lawyer immediately.

What Happens at Closing?

At closing, the seller gives you a deed to the property in return for the purchase money. But you can't give the seller the cash until the lender gives you the loan. You can't get the check for the loan until you sign the mortgage (or trust deed). And you can't sign a mortgage until you own the property.

You can see why it must all take place at once and in the right order. In some areas, buyer and seller sign all the documents ahead of time, and when everything is in order, an escrow agent, who holds all the papers, declares that the transfer has taken place.

If you are assuming a mortgage, you will receive a *reduction certificate,* the lender's statement that the principal has been paid down to a certain amount. You should receive proof that the payments are current and that property taxes are paid up to date. A last-minute title search will reassure you that the seller did not borrow money against the property earlier that morning.

Holding Proceeds in Escrow

It's extremely important to have problems cleared up *before* you hand over your check or the lenders'. Once transfer of title has taken place, many matters are merged into the closing—you have bought the problems along with the property. Don't rely, then, on promises that something will be taken care of "in the next few days." If it is impractical to solve the problem immediately, ask that part of the purchase price be held in escrow, to be turned over to the seller only after the matter is attended to.

If the seller is to remain in occupancy after closing, be sure that there is plenty of financial motivation to move out as promised; otherwise, you could find yourself stuck with a lengthy and expensive eviction. Per diem rental should be set at a high figure, with the provision that it will be deducted from that part of the purchase price held in escrow pending the seller's vacating as agreed.

Adjustments and Prorations

Many small items must be adjusted fairly between you and the seller. Your state will assume that the owner on the day of closing is either seller or buyer. Items adjusted as of the date of closing might include property taxes, interest in a mortgage being assumed or unpaid water bills.

If the tenants in the attic apartment have paid rent for the present month, part of that rent may belong to you. You should receive the security deposit they paid, because some day they will ask you to return it.

When all items are listed on a balance sheet, you'll receive full credit for the earnest money deposit you placed with the real estate agent. If the lender requires a trust account, you'll be asked to place in escrow several months' property taxes and insurance costs, mortgage insurance or other items.

Various sums charged to either buyer or seller may include recording fees (for the new deed and mortgage), attorney's fees, transfer tax (revenue stamps), notary fees, charges for document preparation, mortgage tax and closing agent's fee.

The Real Estate Settlement Procedures Act (RESPA) requires a uniform statement to be furnished to you (see Figure 12.3). In addition, your attorney or the person handling the closing should furnish you with a simpler account of your expenses and credits (see Figure 12.4).

Passing Papers

You'll find yourself signing two papers for the mortgage. One is the *bond,* or *note,* the personal promise to repay the loan. The other is the *mortgage* itself, the financial lien (claim) against the property, which gives the lender the right to foreclose if you default. Then the mortgagee gives you a check, probably the largest you'll ever see. You get to hold it just long enough to endorse it and turn it over to the seller.

The deed, which is signed only by the grantor (the seller), will be placed in your hands, then taken away to be recorded. It will probably be sent to you later. If no one is available to record the deed, go to the county recorder (usually the county clerk) and do it yourself immediately; this is of utmost importance.

You will also receive those keys, the garage door opener and security system codes. You'll walk out with a mass of papers and head for the nearest glass of champagne.

Congratulations! You've been on a long, complicated journey, but look at how much you've learned along the way. You and your new home are going to be very happy together.

FIGURE 12.3   RESPA Uniform Settlement Statement*

A. Settlement Statement

U.S. Department of Housing
and Urban Development

OMB Approval No. 2502-0265

B. Type of Loan

1. ☐ FHA 2. ☐ FmHA 3. ☐ Conv. Unins.	6. File Number
4. ☐ VA 5. ☐ Conv. Ins.	

7. Loan Number	8. Mortgage Insurance Case Number

C. Note: This form is furnished to give you a statement of actual settlement costs. Amounts paid to and by the settlement agent are shown. Items marked "(p.o.c.)" were paid outside the closing; they are shown here for informational purposes and are not included in the totals.

D. Name and Address of Borrower	E. Name and Address of Seller	F. Name and Address of Lender

G. Property Location	H. Settlement Agent
	Place of Settlement

I. Settlement Date

J. Summary of Borrower's Transaction		**K. Summary of Seller's Transaction**	
100. Gross Amount Due From Borrower		**400. Gross Amount Due To Seller**	
101. Contract sales price		401. Contract sales price	
102. Personal property		402. Personal property	
103. Settlement charges to borrower (line 1400)		403.	
104.		404.	
105.		405.	
Adjustments for items paid by seller in advance		**Adjustments for items paid by seller in advance**	
106. City/town taxes to		406. City/town taxes to	
107. County taxes to		407. County taxes to	
108. Assessments to		408. Assessments to	
109.		409.	
110.		410.	
111.		411.	
112.		412.	
120. Gross Amount Due From Borrower		**420. Gross Amount Due To Seller**	

FIGURE 12.3   (*continued*)

200. Amounts Paid By Or In Behalf Of Borrower		500. Reductions In Amount Due To Seller	
201. Deposit or earnest money		501. Excess deposit (see instructions)	
202. Principal amount of new loan(s)		502. Settlement charges to seller (line 1400)	
203. Existing loan(s) taken subject to		503. Existing loan(s) taken subject to	
204.		504. Payoff of first mortgage loan	
205.		505. Payoff of second mortgage loan	
206.		506.	
207.		507.	
208.		508.	
209.		509.	
Adjustments for items unpaid by seller		**Adjustments for items unpaid by seller**	
210. City/town taxes to		510. City/town taxes to	
211. County taxes to		511. County taxes to	
212. Assessments to		512. Assessments to	
213.		513.	
214.		514.	
215.		515.	
216.		516.	
217.		517.	
218.		518.	
219.		519.	
220. Total Paid By/For Borrower		**520. Total Reduction Amount Due Seller**	
300. Cash At Settlement From/To Borrower		**600. Cash At Settlement To/From Seller**	
301. Gross Amount due from borrower (line 120)		601. Gross amount due to seller (line 420)	
302. Less amounts paid by/for borrower (line 220) ( )		602. Less reductions in amt. due seller (line 520) ( )	
303. Cash ☐ From ☐ To Borrower		603. Cash ☐ To ☐ From Seller	

L. Settlement Charges

700. Total Sales/Broker's Commission based on price $ @ % =		Paid From Borrowers Funds at Settlement	Paid From Seller's Funds at Settlement
Division of Commission (line 700) as follows:			
701. $ to			
702. $ to			
703. Commission paid at Settlement			
704.			
800. Items Payable In Connection With Loan			
801. Loan Origination Fee %			
802. Loan Discount %			
803. Appraisal Fee to			
804. Credit Report to			
805. Lender's Inspection Fee			
806. Mortgage Insurance Application Fee to			
807. Assumption Fee			
808.			
809.			
810.			
811.			

FIGURE 12.3   *(continued)*

900. Items Required By Lender To Be Paid In Advance				
901. Interest from to @$ /day				
902. Mortgage Insurance Premium for months to				
903. Hazard Insurance Premium for years to				
904. years to				
905.				
1000. Reserves Deposited With Lender				
1001. Hazard insurance	months@$	per month		
1002. Mortgage insurance	months@$	per month		
1003. City property taxes	months@$	per month		
1004. County property taxes	months@$	per month		
1005. Annual assessments	months@$	per month		
1006.	months@$	per month		
1007.	months@$	per month		
1008.	months@$	per month		
1100. Title Charges				
1101. Settlement or closing fee	to			
1102. Abstract or title search	to			
1103. Title examination	to			
1104. Title insurance binder	to			
1105. Document preparation	to			
1106. Notary fees	to			
1107. Attorney's fees	to			
(includes above items numbers:		)		
1108. Title insurance	to			
(includes above items numbers:		)		
1109. Lender's coverage	$			
1110. Owner's coverage	$			
1111.				
1112.				
1113.				
1200. Government Recording and Transfer Charges				
1201. Recording fees: Deed $; Mortgage $; Releases $				
1202. City/county tax/stamps: Deed $; Mortgage $				
1203. State tax/stamps: Deed $; Mortgage $				
1204.				
1205.				
1300. Additional Settlement Charges				
1301. Survey to				
1302. Pest inspection to				
1303.				
1304.				
1305.				
1400. Total Settlement Charges (enter on lines 103, Section J and 502, Section K)				

Public Reporting Burden for this collection of information is estimated to average 0.25 hours per response, including the time for reviewing instructions, searching existing data sources, gathering and maintaining the data needed, and completing and reviewing the collection of information. Send comments regarding this burden estimate or any other aspect of this collection of information, including suggestions for reducing this burden, to the Reports Management Officer, Office of Information Policies and Systems, U.S. Department of Housing and Urban Development, Washington, D.C. 20410-3600; and to the Office of Management and Budget, Paperwork Reduction Project (2502-0265), Washington, D.C. 20503

FIGURE 12.4   Buyer's Closing Statement*

SELLER'S CREDITS

Sale Price _____ $ 89,500.00

ADJUSTMENT OF TAXES

School Tax 7/1/ to 6/30/   Amount $ 1176.35   Adj. 10 mos. 18 days $ 1,039.16

City/School Tax 7/1/ to 6/30/   Amount $_____ Adj._____ mos._____ days $_____

County Tax 19____   Amount $ 309.06   Adj. 4 mos. 18 days $ 118.52

Village Tax 6/1/ to 5/31/   Amount $_____ Adj._____ mos._____ days $_____

City Tax Embellishments   Amount $_____ Adj._____ mos._____ days $_____

Total Seller's Credits $ 90,657.68

PURCHASER'S CREDITS

Deposit with __Nothnagle__ $ 500.00

(Assumed) (New) Mortgage with Seller $480.07 p/m $ 40,000.00

beg. 9-12   12% int., 15 yrs. $_____

$_____

$_____

$_____

$_____

$_____

$_____

Total Purchaser's Credits $ 40,500.00

Cash (Rectd) (Paid) at Closing $ 50,157.68

<table>
<tr><td colspan="2">EXPENSES OF PURCHASER</td><td colspan="2">EXPENSES OF SELLER</td></tr>
<tr><td>Mortgage Tax</td><td>$ 275.00</td><td>Title Search Fee</td><td>$_____</td></tr>
<tr><td>Recording Mortgage</td><td>$ 11.00</td><td>Transfer Tax on Deed</td><td>$_____</td></tr>
<tr><td>Recording Deed</td><td>$ 12.00</td><td>Filing of Gains Tax Affidavit</td><td>$_____</td></tr>
<tr><td></td><td></td><td>Discharge Recording Fee</td><td>$_____</td></tr>
<tr><td>ESCROWS:</td><td></td><td>Mortgage Tax</td><td>$_____</td></tr>
<tr><td>____ mos. insurance</td><td>$_____</td><td>Surveyor's Fees</td><td>$_____</td></tr>
<tr><td>____ mos. school tax</td><td>$_____</td><td>Points</td><td>$_____</td></tr>
<tr><td>____ mos. county tax</td><td>$_____</td><td>Mortgage Payoff</td><td>$_____</td></tr>
<tr><td>____ mos. village tax</td><td>$_____</td><td>Real Estate Commission</td><td>$_____</td></tr>
<tr><td>PMI FHA Insurance</td><td>$_____</td><td>Water Escrow</td><td>$_____</td></tr>
<tr><td>Total:</td><td>$_____</td><td></td><td>$_____</td></tr>
<tr><td>Bank Attorney Fee</td><td>$_____</td><td></td><td>$_____</td></tr>
<tr><td>Points</td><td>$_____</td><td></td><td>$_____</td></tr>
<tr><td>Title Insurance</td><td>$_____</td><td></td><td>$_____</td></tr>
<tr><td>Interest</td><td>$_____</td><td>Legal Fee</td><td>$_____</td></tr>
<tr><td></td><td>$_____</td><td>Total</td><td>$_____</td></tr>
<tr><td></td><td>$_____</td><td></td><td></td></tr>
<tr><td></td><td>$_____</td><td></td><td></td></tr>
<tr><td>Legal Fee</td><td>$ 500.00</td><td>Cash Received:</td><td>$</td></tr>
<tr><td>Total</td><td>$ 798.00</td><td>Less Seller's Expenses:</td><td>$</td></tr>
<tr><td></td><td></td><td>Net Proceeds:</td><td>$</td></tr>
</table>

Cash paid to Seller: $ 50,157.68

Plus Purchaser's Expenses: $ 798.00

Total Disbursed: $ 50,955.68

*This statement, from the lawyer to the buyer, is relatively simple because no lending institution is involved. In this state, taxes are paid in advance.

Appendix A
Monthly Payment Tables

Your monthly mortgage payment will include interest on the amount borrowed, plus a bit more intended to whittle down the principal still owed. As the loan is gradually paid, less interest is owed, and a larger portion of each payment can go toward principal.

The following tables cover loan terms of 1 to 40 years, with interest rates between 2 percent and 19 percent.

To find your mortgage payment:

1. Search the left-hand column until you find the interest rate on your loan.
2. Search the top line for the number of years you will be making payments.
3. Follow the percentage line across and the "number of years" column down until the two intersect. The figure indicated is the monthly dollar amount necessary to amortize (pay off) a loan of $1,000 in the given time, at the given rate of interest.

   Example: If a 10 percent loan has a term of 25 years, the two lines intersect at 9.0870. This means that $9.087 a month, for 25 years, would pay off a loan of $1,000 at 10 percent interest.
4. Multiply the figure indicated by the number of thousands being borrowed. This gives you the monthly payment necessary to amortize the entire loan.

   Example: If, in the example given with step 3, the loan amount is $74,500, this represents 74.5 thousands. Multiplying $9.087 by 74.5 gives you $676.9816, which would be rounded off to a monthly payment of $676.98.

The figure you have found represents principal and interest only; if a lending institution requires escrow for taxes and insurance, one-twelfth of those costs must be added to arrive at PITI payment.

MONTHLY PAYMENT TO AMORTIZE A LOAN OF $1,000

Term of Loan

Interest Rate	1 Year	2 Years	3 Years	4 Years	5 Years	6 Years	7 Years	8 Years
2.000%	84.2389	42.5403	28.6426	21.6951	17.5278	14.7504	12.7674	11.2809
2.125%	84.2956	42.5952	28.6972	21.7497	17.5825	14.8054	12.8226	11.3364
2.250%	84.3524	42.6502	28.7518	21.8044	17.6373	14.8605	12.8780	11.3920
2.375%	84.4093	42.7053	28.8066	21.8592	17.6923	14.9157	12.9335	11.4478
2.500%	84.4661	42.7604	28.8614	21.9140	17.7474	14.9710	12.9892	11.5038
2.625%	84.5230	42.8155	28.9162	21.9690	17.8025	15.0265	13.0450	11.5600
2.750%	84.5799	42.8707	28.9712	22.0240	17.8578	15.0821	13.1009	11.6164
2.875%	84.6368	42.9259	29.0262	22.0791	17.9132	15.1378	13.1570	11.6729
3.000%	84.6937	42.9812	29.0812	22.1343	17.9687	15.1937	13.2133	11.7296
3.125%	84.7506	43.0365	29.1363	22.1896	18.0243	15.2497	13.2697	11.7864
3.250%	84.8076	43.0919	29.1915	22.2450	18.0800	15.3058	13.3263	11.8435
3.375%	84.8646	43.1473	29.2468	22.3005	18.1358	15.3620	13.3830	11.9007
3.500%	84.9216	43.2027	29.3021	22.3560	18.1917	15.4184	13.4399	11.9581
3.625%	84.9787	43.2582	29.3575	22.4116	18.2478	15.4749	13.4969	12.0156
3.750%	85.0357	43.3137	29.4129	22.4674	18.3039	15.5315	13.5540	12.0733
3.875%	85.0928	43.3693	29.4684	22.5232	18.3602	15.5883	13.6113	12.1312
4.000%	85.1499	43.4249	29.5240	22.5791	18.4165	15.6452	13.6688	12.1893
4.125%	85.2070	43.4806	29.5796	22.6350	18.4730	15.7022	13.7264	12.2475
4.250%	85.2642	43.5363	29.6353	22.6911	18.5296	15.7593	13.7842	12.3059
4.375%	85.3213	43.5920	29.6911	22.7472	18.5862	15.8166	13.8421	12.3645
4.500%	85.3785	43.6478	29.7469	22.8035	18.6430	15.8740	13.9002	12.4232
4.625%	85.4357	43.7036	29.8028	22.8598	18.6999	15.9316	13.9584	12.4822
4.750%	85.4930	43.7595	29.8588	22.9162	18.7569	15.9892	14.0167	12.5412
4.875%	85.5502	43.8154	29.9148	22.9727	18.8140	16.0470	14.0752	12.6005
5.000%	85.6075	43.8714	29.9709	23.0293	18.8712	16.1049	14.1339	12.6599
5.125%	85.6648	43.9274	30.0271	23.0860	18.9286	16.1630	14.1927	12.7195
5.250%	85.7221	43.9834	30.0833	23.1427	18.9860	16.2212	14.2517	12.7793
5.375%	85.7794	44.0395	30.1396	23.1996	19.0435	16.2795	14.3108	12.8392
5.500%	85.8368	44.0957	30.1959	23.2565	19.1012	16.3379	14.3700	12.8993
5.625%	85.8942	44.1518	30.2523	23.3135	19.1589	16.3964	14.4294	12.9596
5.750%	85.9516	44.2080	30.3088	23.3706	19.2168	16.4551	14.4890	13.0200
5.875%	86.0090	44.2643	30.3653	23.4278	19.2747	16.5139	14.5487	13.0807
6.000%	86.0664	44.3206	30.4219	23.4850	19.3328	16.5729	14.6086	13.1414
6.125%	86.1239	44.3770	30.4786	23.5424	19.3910	16.6320	14.6686	13.2024
6.250%	86.1814	44.4333	30.5353	23.5998	19.4493	16.6912	14.7287	13.2635
6.375%	86.2389	44.4898	30.5921	23.6573	19.5077	16.7505	14.7890	13.3248
6.500%	86.2964	44.5463	30.6490	23.7150	19.5661	16.8099	14.8494	13.3862
6.625%	86.3540	44.6028	30.7059	23.7726	19.6248	16.8695	14.9100	13.4479
6.750%	86.4115	44.6593	30.7629	23.8304	19.6835	16.9292	14.9708	13.5096
6.875%	86.4691	44.7159	30.8200	23.8883	19.7423	16.9890	15.0316	13.5716

MONTHLY PAYMENT TO AMORTIZE A LOAN OF $1,000

Term of Loan

Interest Rate	9 Years	10 Years	11 Years	12 Years	13 Years	14 Years	15 Years	16 Years
2.000%	10.1253	9.2013	8.4459	7.8168	7.2850	6.8295	6.4351	6.0903
2.125%	10.1811	9.2574	8.5023	7.8736	7.3420	6.8869	6.4928	6.1484
2.250%	10.2370	9.3137	8.5590	7.9305	7.3994	6.9446	6.5508	6.2068
2.375%	10.2932	9.3703	8.6158	7.9878	7.4570	7.0025	6.6092	6.2655
2.500%	10.3496	9.4270	8.6729	8.0453	7.5149	7.0608	6.6679	6.3246
2.625%	10.4061	9.4839	8.7303	8.1031	7.5730	7.1194	6.7269	6.3840
2.750%	10.4629	9.5411	8.7879	8.1611	7.6315	7.1783	6.7862	6.4438
2.875%	10.5198	9.5985	8.8457	8.2193	7.6902	7.2375	6.8459	6.5039
3.000%	10.5769	9.6561	8.9038	8.2779	7.7492	7.2970	6.9058	6.5643
3.125%	10.6343	9.7139	8.9621	8.3367	7.8085	7.3567	6.9661	6.6251
3.250%	10.6918	9.7719	9.0206	8.3957	7.8680	7.4168	7.0267	6.6862
3.375%	10.7495	9.8301	9.0793	8.4550	7.9279	7.4772	7.0876	6.7477
3.500%	10.8074	9.8886	9.1383	8.5145	7.9880	7.5378	7.1488	6.8095
3.625%	10.8655	9.9472	9.1976	8.5743	8.0484	7.5988	7.2104	6.8716
3.750%	10.9238	10.0061	9.2570	8.6344	8.1090	7.6601	7.2722	6.9340
3.875%	10.9823	10.0652	9.3167	8.6947	8.1700	7.7216	7.3344	6.9968
4.000%	11.0410	10.1245	9.3767	8.7553	8.2312	7.7835	7.3969	7.0600
4.125%	11.0998	10.1840	9.4368	8.8161	8.2926	7.8456	7.4597	7.1234
4.250%	11.1589	10.2438	9.4972	8.8772	8.3544	7.9080	7.5228	7.1872
4.375%	11.2181	10.3037	9.5579	8.9385	8.4164	7.9707	7.5862	7.2513
4.500%	11.2776	10.3638	9.6187	9.0001	8.4787	8.0338	7.6499	7.3158
4.625%	11.3372	10.4242	9.6798	9.0619	8.5413	8.0971	7.7140	7.3805
4.750%	11.3971	10.4848	9.7411	9.1240	8.6041	8.1607	7.7783	7.4456
4.875%	11.4571	10.5456	9.8027	9.1863	8.6672	8.2245	7.8430	7.5111
5.000%	11.5173	10.6066	9.8645	9.2489	8.7306	8.2887	7.9079	7.5768
5.125%	11.5777	10.6678	9.9265	9.3117	8.7942	8.3532	7.9732	7.6429
5.250%	11.6383	10.7292	9.9888	9.3748	8.8582	8.4179	8.0388	7.7093
5.375%	11.6990	10.7908	10.0512	9.4381	8.9223	8.4829	8.1047	7.7760
5.500%	11.7600	10.8526	10.1139	9.5017	8.9868	8.5483	8.1708	7.8430
5.625%	11.8212	10.9147	10.1769	9.5655	9.0515	8.6139	8.2373	7.9104
5.750%	11.8825	10.9769	10.2400	9.6296	9.1165	8.6797	8.3041	7.9781
5.875%	11.9440	11.0394	10.3034	9.6939	9.1817	8.7459	8.3712	8.0461
6.000%	12.0057	11.1021	10.3670	9.7585	9.2472	8.8124	8.4386	8.1144
6.125%	12.0677	11.1649	10.4309	9.8233	9.3130	8.8791	8.5062	8.1830
6.250%	12.1298	11.2280	10.4949	9.8884	9.3790	8.9461	8.5742	8.2519
6.375%	12.1920	11.2913	10.5592	9.9537	9.4453	9.0134	8.6425	8.3212
6.500%	12.2545	11.3548	10.6238	10.0192	9.5119	9.0810	8.7111	8.3908
6.625%	12.3172	11.4185	10.6885	10.0850	9.5787	9.1488	8.7799	8.4606
6.750%	12.3800	11.4824	10.7535	10.1510	9.6458	9.2169	8.8491	8.5308
6.875%	12.4431	11.5465	10.8187	10.2173	9.7131	9.2853	8.9185	8.6013

MONTHLY PAYMENT TO AMORTIZE A LOAN OF $1,000

Term of Loan

Interest Rate	17 Years	18 Years	19 Years	20 Years	21 Years	22 Years	23 Years	24 Years
2.000%	5.7865	5.5167	5.2756	5.0588	4.8630	4.6852	4.5232	4.3748
2.125%	5.8449	5.5754	5.3346	5.1182	4.9228	4.7453	4.5836	4.4356
2.250%	5.9036	5.6345	5.3941	5.1781	4.9830	4.8059	4.6445	4.4969
2.375%	5.9627	5.6940	5.4540	5.2383	5.0436	4.8669	4.7059	4.5587
2.500%	6.0222	5.7539	5.5143	5.2990	5.1047	4.9284	4.7678	4.6209
2.625%	6.0821	5.8142	5.5750	5.3601	5.1662	4.9904	4.8302	4.6837
2.750%	6.1423	5.8748	5.6360	5.4217	5.2282	5.0528	4.8930	4.7470
2.875%	6.2028	5.9358	5.6975	5.4836	5.2906	5.1156	4.9564	4.8108
3.000%	6.2637	5.9972	5.7594	5.5460	5.3534	5.1790	5.0202	4.8751
3.125%	6.3250	6.0590	5.8217	5.6088	5.4167	5.2427	5.0844	4.9399
3.250%	6.3867	6.1212	5.8844	5.6720	5.4804	5.3070	5.1492	5.0051
3.375%	6.4487	6.1837	5.9474	5.7356	5.5446	5.3717	5.2144	5.0709
3.500%	6.5110	6.2466	6.0109	5.7996	5.6092	5.4368	5.2801	5.1371
3.625%	6.5737	6.3099	6.0748	5.8640	5.6742	5.5024	5.3463	5.2039
3.750%	6.6368	6.3736	6.1390	5.9289	5.7396	5.5684	5.4129	5.2711
3.875%	6.7002	6.4376	6.2037	5.9941	5.8055	5.6349	5.4800	5.3387
4.000%	6.7639	6.5020	6.2687	6.0598	5.8718	5.7018	5.5475	5.4069
4.125%	6.8280	6.5667	6.3341	6.1259	5.9385	5.7692	5.6155	5.4755
4.250%	6.8925	6.6319	6.3999	6.1923	6.0056	5.8370	5.6840	5.5446
4.375%	6.9573	6.6974	6.4661	6.2592	6.0732	5.9052	5.7529	5.6142
4.500%	7.0225	6.7632	6.5327	6.3265	6.1412	5.9739	5.8222	5.6842
4.625%	7.0880	6.8295	6.5996	6.3942	6.2096	6.0430	5.8920	5.7547
4.750%	7.1538	6.8961	6.6670	6.4622	6.2784	6.1125	5.9623	5.8257
4.875%	7.2200	6.9630	6.7347	6.5307	6.3476	6.1824	6.0329	5.8971
5.000%	7.2866	7.0303	6.8028	6.5996	6.4172	6.2528	6.1041	5.9690
5.125%	7.3534	7.0980	6.8712	6.6688	6.4872	6.3236	6.1756	6.0413
5.250%	7.4206	7.1660	6.9401	6.7384	6.5576	6.3948	6.2476	6.1140
5.375%	7.4882	7.2344	7.0093	6.8085	6.6285	6.4664	6.3200	6.1872
5.500%	7.5561	7.3032	7.0789	6.8789	6.6997	6.5385	6.3929	6.2609
5.625%	7.6243	7.3723	7.1488	6.9497	6.7713	6.6109	6.4661	6.3350
5.750%	7.6929	7.4417	7.2191	7.0208	6.8434	6.6838	6.5398	6.4095
5.875%	7.7618	7.5115	7.2898	7.0924	6.9158	6.7571	6.6139	6.4844
6.000%	7.8310	7.5816	7.3608	7.1643	6.9886	6.8307	6.6885	6.5598
6.125%	7.9006	7.6521	7.4322	7.2366	7.0618	6.9048	6.7634	6.6356
6.250%	7.9705	7.7229	7.5040	7.3093	7.1353	6.9793	6.8387	6.7118
6.375%	8.0407	7.7941	7.5761	7.3823	7.2093	7.0541	6.9145	6.7884
6.500%	8.1112	7.8656	7.6486	7.4557	7.2836	7.1294	6.9906	6.8654
6.625%	8.1821	7.9375	7.7214	7.5295	7.3583	7.2050	7.0672	6.9429
6.750%	8.2533	8.0096	7.7945	7.6036	7.4334	7.2811	7.1441	7.0207
6.875%	8.3248	8.0822	7.8681	7.6781	7.5089	7.3575	7.2215	7.0990

MONTHLY PAYMENT TO AMORTIZE A LOAN OF $1,000

Term of Loan

Interest Rate	25 Years	26 Years	27 Years	28 Years	29 Years	30 Years	35 Years	40 Years
2.000%	4.2385	4.1130	3.9969	3.8893	3.7893	3.6962	3.3126	3.0283
2.125%	4.2997	4.1744	4.0587	3.9515	3.8518	3.7590	3.3771	3.0944
2.250%	4.3613	4.2364	4.1211	4.0142	3.9149	3.8225	3.4424	3.1614
2.375%	4.4235	4.2990	4.1840	4.0775	3.9786	3.8865	3.5083	3.2292
2.500%	4.4862	4.3621	4.2475	4.1414	4.0429	3.9512	3.5750	3.2978
2.625%	4.5494	4.4257	4.3115	4.2058	4.1078	4.0165	3.6423	3.3671
2.750%	4.6131	4.4899	4.3761	4.2709	4.1732	4.0824	3.7103	3.4373
2.875%	4.6774	4.5546	4.4413	4.3365	4.2393	4.1489	3.7791	3.5082
3.000%	4.7421	4.6198	4.5070	4.4027	4.3059	4.2160	3.8485	3.5798
3.125%	4.8074	4.6856	4.5733	4.4694	4.3732	4.2838	3.9186	3.6523
3.250%	4.8732	4.7519	4.6401	4.5367	4.4410	4.3521	3.9894	3.7254
3.375%	4.9394	4.8187	4.7074	4.6046	4.5094	4.4210	4.0608	3.7993
3.500%	5.0062	4.8860	4.7753	4.6730	4.5783	4.4904	4.1329	3.8739
3.625%	5.0735	4.9539	4.8437	4.7420	4.6478	4.5605	4.2057	3.9492
3.750%	5.1413	5.0222	4.9126	4.8115	4.7179	4.6312	4.2791	4.0253
3.875%	5.2096	5.0911	4.9821	4.8815	4.7885	4.7024	4.3531	4.1020
4.000%	5.2784	5.1605	5.0521	4.9521	4.8597	4.7742	4.4277	4.1794
4.125%	5.3476	5.2304	5.1226	5.0233	4.9315	4.8465	4.5030	4.2575
4.250%	5.4174	5.3008	5.1936	5.0949	5.0038	4.9194	4.5789	4.3362
4.375%	5.4876	5.3717	5.2652	5.1671	5.0766	4.9929	4.6555	4.4156
4.500%	5.5583	5.4430	5.3372	5.2398	5.1499	5.0669	4.7326	4.4956
4.625%	5.6295	5.5149	5.4098	5.3130	5.2238	5.1414	4.8103	4.5763
4.750%	5.7012	5.5873	5.4828	5.3868	5.2982	5.2165	4.8886	4.6576
4.875%	5.7733	5.6601	5.5564	5.4610	5.3732	5.2921	4.9674	4.7395
5.000%	5.8459	5.7334	5.6304	5.5357	5.4486	5.3682	5.0469	4.8220
5.125%	5.9190	5.8072	5.7049	5.6110	5.5246	5.4449	5.1269	4.9050
5.250%	5.9925	5.8815	5.7799	5.6867	5.6010	5.5220	5.2074	4.9887
5.375%	6.0665	5.9562	5.8554	5.7629	5.6780	5.5997	5.2885	5.0729
5.500%	6.1409	6.0314	5.9314	5.8397	5.7554	5.6779	5.3702	5.1577
5.625%	6.2157	6.1071	6.0078	5.9168	5.8334	5.7566	5.4523	5.2430
5.750%	6.2911	6.1832	6.0847	5.9945	5.9118	5.8357	5.5350	5.3289
5.875%	6.3668	6.2598	6.1620	6.0726	5.9907	5.9154	5.6182	5.4153
6.000%	6.4430	6.3368	6.2399	6.1512	6.0700	5.9955	5.7019	5.5021
6.125%	6.5196	6.4142	6.3181	6.2303	6.1499	6.0761	5.7861	5.5895
6.250%	6.5967	6.4921	6.3968	6.3098	6.2302	6.1572	5.8708	5.6774
6.375%	6.6742	6.5704	6.4760	6.3898	6.3109	6.2387	5.9559	5.7657
6.500%	6.7521	6.6492	6.5555	6.4702	6.3921	6.3207	6.0415	5.8546
6.625%	6.8304	6.7284	6.6356	6.5510	6.4738	6.4031	6.1276	5.9438
6.750%	6.9091	6.8079	6.7160	6.6323	6.5558	6.4860	6.2142	6.0336
6.875%	6.9883	6.8880	6.7969	6.7140	6.6384	6.5693	6.3011	6.1237

MONTHLY PAYMENT TO AMORTIZE A LOAN OF $1,000

Term of Loan

Interest Rate	1 Year	2 Years	3 Years	4 Years	5 Years	6 Years	7 Years	8 Years
7.000%	86.5267	44.7726	30.8771	23.9462	19.8012	17.0490	15.0927	13.6337
7.125%	86.5844	44.8293	30.9343	24.0043	19.8602	17.1091	15.1539	13.6960
7.250%	86.6420	44.8860	30.9915	24.0624	19.9194	17.1693	15.2152	13.7585
7.375%	86.6997	44.9428	31.0488	24.1206	19.9786	17.2296	15.2767	13.8211
7.500%	86.7574	44.9996	31.1062	24.1789	20.0379	17.2901	15.3383	13.8839
7.625%	86.8151	45.0565	31.1637	24.2373	20.0974	17.3507	15.4000	13.9468
7.750%	86.8729	45.1134	31.2212	24.2957	20.1570	17.4114	15.4620	14.0099
7.875%	86.9306	45.1703	31.2787	24.3543	20.2166	17.4723	15.5240	14.0732
8.000%	86.9884	45.2273	31.3364	24.4129	20.2764	17.5332	15.5862	14.1367
8.125%	87.0462	45.2843	31.3941	24.4716	20.3363	17.5943	15.6486	14.2003
8.250%	87.1041	45.3414	31.4518	24.5304	20.3963	17.6556	15.7111	14.2641
8.375%	87.1619	45.3985	31.5096	24.5893	20.4563	17.7169	15.7737	14.3280
8.500%	87.2198	45.4557	31.5675	24.6483	20.5165	17.7784	15.8365	14.3921
8.625%	87.2777	45.5129	31.6255	24.7074	20.5768	17.8400	15.8994	14.4564
8.750%	87.3356	45.5701	31.6835	24.7665	20.6372	17.9017	15.9625	14.5208
8.875%	87.3935	45.6274	31.7416	24.8257	20.6977	17.9636	16.0257	14.5854
9.000%	87.4515	45.6847	31.7997	24.8850	20.7584	18.0255	16.0891	14.6502
9.125%	87.5095	45.7421	31.8579	24.9444	20.8191	18.0876	16.1526	14.7151
9.250%	87.5675	45.7995	31.9162	25.0039	20.8799	18.1499	16.2162	14.7802
9.375%	87.6255	45.8570	31.9745	25.0635	20.9408	18.2122	16.2800	14.8455
9.500%	87.6835	45.9145	32.0329	25.1231	21.0019	18.2747	16.3440	14.9109
9.625%	87.7416	45.9720	32.0914	25.1829	21.0630	18.3373	16.4081	14.9765
9.750%	87.7997	46.0296	32.1499	25.2427	21.1242	18.4000	16.4723	15.0422
9.875%	87.8578	46.0873	32.2085	25.3026	21.1856	18.4629	16.5367	15.1081
10.000%	87.9159	46.1449	32.2672	25.3626	21.2470	18.5258	16.6012	15.1742
10.125%	87.9740	46.2026	32.3259	25.4227	21.3086	18.5889	16.6658	15.2404
10.250%	88.0322	46.2604	32.3847	25.4828	21.3703	18.6522	16.7306	15.3068
10.375%	88.0904	46.3182	32.4435	25.5431	21.4320	18.7155	16.7956	15.3733
10.500%	88.1486	46.3760	32.5024	25.6034	21.4939	18.7790	16.8607	15.4400
10.625%	88.2068	46.4339	32.5614	25.6638	21.5559	18.8426	16.9259	15.5069
10.750%	88.2651	46.4919	32.6205	25.7243	21.6180	18.9063	16.9913	15.5739
10.875%	88.3234	46.5498	32.6796	25.7849	21.6801	18.9701	17.0568	15.6411
11.000%	88.3817	46.6078	32.7387	25.8455	21.7424	19.0341	17.1224	15.7084
11.125%	88.4400	46.6659	32.7979	25.9063	21.8048	19.0982	17.1882	15.7759
11.250%	88.4983	46.7240	32.8572	25.9671	21.8673	19.1624	17.2542	15.8436
11.375%	88.5567	46.7821	32.9166	26.0280	21.9299	19.2267	17.3202	15.9114
11.500%	88.6151	46.8403	32.9760	26.0890	21.9926	19.2912	17.3865	15.9794
11.625%	88.6735	46.8985	33.0355	26.1501	22.0554	19.3557	17.4528	16.0475
11.750%	88.7319	46.9568	33.0950	26.2113	22.1183	19.4204	17.5193	16.1158
11.875%	88.7903	47.0151	33.1546	26.2725	22.1813	19.4853	17.5860	16.1842

MONTHLY PAYMENT TO AMORTIZE A LOAN OF $1,000

Term of Loan

Interest Rate	9 Years	10 Years	11 Years	12 Years	13 Years	14 Years	15 Years	16 Years
7.000%	12.5063	11.6108	10.8841	10.2838	9.7807	9.3540	8.9883	8.6721
7.125%	12.5697	11.6754	10.9497	10.3506	9.8486	9.4230	9.0583	8.7432
7.250%	12.6333	11.7401	11.0156	10.4176	9.9167	9.4922	9.1286	8.8146
7.375%	12.6971	11.8050	11.0817	10.4848	9.9851	9.5617	9.1992	8.8863
7.500%	12.7610	11.8702	11.1480	10.5523	10.0537	9.6314	9.2701	8.9583
7.625%	12.8252	11.9355	11.2145	10.6200	10.1226	9.7015	9.3413	9.0306
7.750%	12.8895	12.0011	11.2813	10.6879	10.1917	9.7718	9.4128	9.1032
7.875%	12.9540	12.0668	11.3483	10.7561	10.2611	9.8423	9.4845	9.1761
8.000%	13.0187	12.1328	11.4154	10.8245	10.3307	9.9132	9.5565	9.2493
8.125%	13.0836	12.1989	11.4829	10.8932	10.4006	9.9843	9.6288	9.3227
8.250%	13.1487	12.2653	11.5505	10.9621	10.4708	10.0557	9.7014	9.3965
8.375%	13.2139	12.3318	11.6183	11.0312	10.5412	10.1273	9.7743	9.4706
8.500%	13.2794	12.3986	11.6864	11.1006	10.6118	10.1992	9.8474	9.5449
8.625%	13.3450	12.4655	11.7547	11.1701	10.6827	10.2713	9.9208	9.6195
8.750%	13.4108	12.5327	11.8232	11.2400	10.7538	10.3438	9.9945	9.6945
8.875%	13.4767	12.6000	11.8919	11.3100	10.8252	10.4164	10.0684	9.7697
9.000%	13.5429	12.6676	11.9608	11.3803	10.8968	10.4894	10.1427	9.8452
9.125%	13.6093	12.7353	12.0299	11.4508	10.9687	10.5626	10.2172	9.9209
9.250%	13.6758	12.8033	12.0993	11.5216	11.0408	10.6360	10.2919	9.9970
9.375%	13.7425	12.8714	12.1689	11.5925	11.1131	10.7097	10.3670	10.0733
9.500%	13.8094	12.9398	12.2386	11.6637	11.1857	10.7837	10.4422	10.1499
9.625%	13.8764	13.0083	12.3086	11.7352	11.2586	10.8579	10.5178	10.2268
9.750%	13.9437	13.0770	12.3788	11.8068	11.3316	10.9324	10.5936	10.3039
9.875%	14.0111	13.1460	12.4493	11.8787	11.4049	11.0071	10.6697	10.3813
10.000%	14.0787	13.2151	12.5199	11.9508	11.4785	11.0820	10.7461	10.4590
10.125%	14.1465	13.2844	12.5907	12.0231	11.5523	11.1572	10.8227	10.5370
10.250%	14.2144	13.3539	12.6618	12.0957	11.6263	11.2327	10.8995	10.6152
10.375%	14.2826	13.4236	12.7330	12.1684	11.7005	11.3084	10.9766	10.6937
10.500%	14.3509	13.4935	12.8045	12.2414	11.7750	11.3843	11.0540	10.7724
10.625%	14.4193	13.5636	12.8761	12.3146	11.8497	11.4605	11.1316	10.8514
10.750%	14.4880	13.6339	12.9480	12.3880	11.9247	11.5370	11.2095	10.9307
10.875%	14.5568	13.7043	13.0201	12.4617	11.9999	11.6136	11.2876	11.0102
11.000%	14.6259	13.7750	13.0923	12.5356	12.0753	11.6905	11.3660	11.0900
11.125%	14.6950	13.8459	13.1648	12.6096	12.1509	11.7677	11.4446	11.1700
11.250%	14.7644	13.9169	13.2375	12.6839	12.2268	11.8451	11.5234	11.2503
11.375%	14.8339	13.9881	13.3104	12.7584	12.3029	11.9227	11.6026	11.3309
11.500%	14.9037	14.0595	13.3835	12.8332	12.3792	12.0006	11.6819	11.4116
11.625%	14.9735	14.1312	13.4568	12.9081	12.4557	12.0786	11.7615	11.4927
11.750%	15.0436	14.2029	13.5303	12.9833	12.5325	12.1570	11.8413	11.5740
11.875%	15.1138	14.2749	13.6040	13.0586	12.6095	12.2355	11.9214	11.6555

MONTHLY PAYMENT TO AMORTIZE A LOAN OF $1,000

Term of Loan

Interest Rate	17 Years	18 Years	19 Years	20 Years	21 Years	22 Years	23 Years	24 Years
7.000%	8.3966	8.1550	7.9419	7.7530	7.5847	7.4342	7.2992	7.1776
7.125%	8.4688	8.2282	8.0161	7.8282	7.6609	7.5114	7.3773	7.2566
7.250%	8.5412	8.3017	8.0907	7.9038	7.7375	7.5889	7.4558	7.3361
7.375%	8.6140	8.3756	8.1656	7.9797	7.8144	7.6668	7.5347	7.4159
7.500%	8.6871	8.4497	8.2408	8.0559	7.8917	7.7451	7.6139	7.4960
7.625%	8.7605	8.5242	8.3163	8.1325	7.9693	7.8237	7.6935	7.5766
7.750%	8.8342	8.5990	8.3922	8.2095	8.0473	7.9027	7.7735	7.6576
7.875%	8.9082	8.6742	8.4685	8.2868	8.1256	7.9821	7.8538	7.7389
8.000%	8.9826	8.7496	8.5450	8.3644	8.2043	8.0618	7.9345	7.8205
8.125%	9.0572	8.8254	8.6219	8.4424	8.2833	8.1418	8.0156	7.9026
8.250%	9.1321	8.9015	8.6991	8.5207	8.3627	8.2222	8.0970	7.9850
8.375%	9.2074	8.9779	8.7766	8.5993	8.4424	8.3030	8.1788	8.0677
8.500%	9.2829	9.0546	8.8545	8.6782	8.5224	8.3841	8.2609	8.1508
8.625%	9.3588	9.1316	8.9326	8.7575	8.6028	8.4655	8.3433	8.2343
8.750%	9.4349	9.2089	9.0111	8.8371	8.6834	8.5472	8.4261	8.3181
8.875%	9.5113	9.2865	9.0899	8.9170	8.7645	8.6293	8.5092	8.4022
9.000%	9.5880	9.3644	9.1690	8.9973	8.8458	8.7117	8.5927	8.4866
9.125%	9.6650	9.4427	9.2484	9.0778	8.9275	8.7945	8.6765	8.5714
9.250%	9.7423	9.5212	9.3281	9.1587	9.0094	8.8775	8.7606	8.6566
9.375%	9.8199	9.6000	9.4081	9.2398	9.0917	8.9609	8.8450	8.7420
9.500%	9.8978	9.6791	9.4884	9.3213	9.1743	9.0446	8.9297	8.8277
9.625%	9.9760	9.7585	9.5690	9.4031	9.2573	9.1286	9.0148	8.9138
9.750%	10.0544	9.8382	9.6499	9.4852	9.3405	9.2129	9.1002	9.0002
9.875%	10.1331	9.9182	9.7311	9.5675	9.4240	9.2975	9.1858	9.0869
10.000%	10.2121	9.9984	9.8126	9.6502	9.5078	9.3825	9.2718	9.1739
10.125%	10.2914	10.0790	9.8944	9.7332	9.5919	9.4677	9.3581	9.2612
10.250%	10.3709	10.1598	9.9764	9.8164	9.6763	9.5532	9.4447	9.3488
10.375%	10.4507	10.2409	10.0588	9.9000	9.7610	9.6390	9.5315	9.4366
10.500%	10.5308	10.3223	10.1414	9.9838	9.8460	9.7251	9.6187	9.5248
10.625%	10.6112	10.4039	10.2243	10.0679	9.9312	9.8114	9.7061	9.6133
10.750%	10.6918	10.4858	10.3075	10.1523	10.0168	9.8981	9.7938	9.7020
10.875%	10.7727	10.5680	10.3909	10.2370	10.1026	9.9850	9.8818	9.7910
11.000%	10.8538	10.6505	10.4746	10.3219	10.1887	10.0722	9.9701	9.8803
11.125%	10.9352	10.7332	10.5586	10.4071	10.2751	10.1597	10.0586	9.9698
11.250%	11.0169	10.8162	10.6429	10.4926	10.3617	10.2475	10.1474	10.0596
11.375%	11.0988	10.8994	10.7274	10.5783	10.4486	10.3355	10.2365	10.1497
11.500%	11.1810	10.9830	10.8122	10.6643	10.5358	10.4237	10.3258	10.2400
11.625%	11.2634	11.0667	10.8972	10.7506	10.6232	10.5123	10.4154	10.3306
11.750%	11.3461	11.1507	10.9825	10.8371	10.7109	10.6011	10.5052	10.4214
11.875%	11.4290	11.2350	11.0681	10.9238	10.7988	10.6901	10.5953	10.5125

MONTHLY PAYMENT TO AMORTIZE A LOAN OF $1,000

Term of Loan

Interest Rate	25 Years	26 Years	27 Years	28 Years	29 Years	30 Years	35 Years	40 Years
7.000%	7.0678	6.9684	6.8781	6.7961	6.7213	6.6530	6.3886	6.2143
7.125%	7.1477	7.0492	6.9598	6.8786	6.8047	6.7372	6.4764	6.3053
7.250%	7.2281	7.1304	7.0419	6.9616	6.8884	6.8218	6.5647	6.3967
7.375%	7.3088	7.2121	7.1244	7.0449	6.9726	6.9068	6.6533	6.4885
7.500%	7.3899	7.2941	7.2073	7.1287	7.0572	6.9921	6.7424	6.5807
7.625%	7.4714	7.3765	7.2906	7.2128	7.1422	7.0779	6.8319	6.6733
7.750%	7.5533	7.4593	7.3743	7.2974	7.2276	7.1641	6.9218	6.7662
7.875%	7.6355	7.5424	7.4584	7.3823	7.3133	7.2507	7.0120	6.8595
8.000%	7.7182	7.6260	7.5428	7.4676	7.3995	7.3376	7.1026	6.9531
8.125%	7.8012	7.7099	7.6276	7.5533	7.4860	7.4250	7.1936	7.0471
8.250%	7.8845	7.7942	7.7128	7.6393	7.5729	7.5127	7.2849	7.1414
8.375%	7.9682	7.8788	7.7983	7.7257	7.6601	7.6007	7.3766	7.2360
8.500%	8.0523	7.9638	7.8842	7.8125	7.7477	7.6891	7.4686	7.3309
8.625%	8.1367	8.0491	7.9705	7.8996	7.8357	7.7779	7.5610	7.4262
8.750%	8.2214	8.1348	8.0570	7.9871	7.9240	7.8670	7.6536	7.5217
8.875%	8.3065	8.2209	8.1440	8.0749	8.0126	7.9564	7.7466	7.6175
9.000%	8.3920	8.3072	8.2313	8.1630	8.1016	8.0462	7.8399	7.7136
9.125%	8.4777	8.3939	8.3189	8.2515	8.1909	8.1363	7.9335	7.8100
9.250%	8.5638	8.4810	8.4068	8.3403	8.2805	8.2268	8.0274	7.9066
9.375%	8.6502	8.5683	8.4950	8.4294	8.3705	8.3175	8.1216	8.0035
9.500%	8.7370	8.6560	8.5836	8.5188	8.4607	8.4085	8.2161	8.1006
9.625%	8.8240	8.7440	8.6725	8.6086	8.5513	8.4999	8.3109	8.1980
9.750%	8.9114	8.8323	8.7617	8.6986	8.6421	8.5915	8.4059	8.2956
9.875%	8.9990	8.9209	8.8512	8.7890	8.7333	8.6835	8.5012	8.3934
10.000%	9.0870	9.0098	8.9410	8.8796	8.8248	8.7757	8.5967	8.4915
10.125%	9.1753	9.0990	9.0311	8.9705	8.9165	8.8682	8.6925	8.5897
10.250%	9.2638	9.1885	9.1214	9.0618	9.0085	8.9610	8.7886	8.6882
10.375%	9.3527	9.2782	9.2121	9.1533	9.1008	9.0541	8.8848	8.7868
10.500%	9.4418	9.3683	9.3030	9.2450	9.1934	9.1474	8.9813	8.8857
10.625%	9.5312	9.4586	9.3943	9.3371	9.2862	9.2410	9.0781	8.9847
10.750%	9.6209	9.5492	9.4857	9.4294	9.3793	9.3348	9.1750	9.0840
10.875%	9.7109	9.6401	9.5775	9.5220	9.4727	9.4289	9.2722	9.1834
11.000%	9.8011	9.7313	9.6695	9.6148	9.5663	9.5232	9.3696	9.2829
11.125%	9.8916	9.8227	9.7618	9.7079	9.6601	9.6178	9.4672	9.3827
11.250%	9.9824	9.9143	9.8543	9.8012	9.7542	9.7126	9.5649	9.4826
11.375%	10.0734	10.0063	9.9471	9.8948	9.8486	9.8077	9.6629	9.5826
11.500%	10.1647	10.0984	10.0401	9.9886	9.9431	9.9029	9.7611	9.6828
11.625%	10.2562	10.1909	10.1333	10.0826	10.0379	9.9984	9.8594	9.7832
11.750%	10.3480	10.2835	10.2268	10.1769	10.1329	10.0941	9.9579	9.8836
11.875%	10.4400	10.3764	10.3205	10.2714	10.2281	10.1900	10.0566	9.9843

MONTHLY PAYMENT TO AMORTIZE A LOAN OF $1,000

Term of Loan

Interest Rate	1 Year	2 Years	3 Years	4 Years	5 Years	6 Years	7 Years	8 Years
12.000%	88.8488	47.0735	33.2143	26.3338	22.2444	19.5502	17.6527	16.2528
12.125%	88.9073	47.1319	33.2740	26.3953	22.3077	19.6153	17.7197	16.3216
12.250%	88.9658	47.1903	33.3338	26.4568	22.3710	19.6804	17.7867	16.3905
12.375%	89.0243	47.2488	33.3937	26.5183	22.4344	19.7457	17.8539	16.4596
12.500%	89.0829	47.3073	33.4536	26.5800	22.4979	19.8112	17.9212	16.5288
12.625%	89.1414	47.3659	33.5136	26.6417	22.5616	19.8767	17.9887	16.5982
12.750%	89.2000	47.4245	33.5737	26.7036	22.6253	19.9424	18.0563	16.6677
12.875%	89.2586	47.4831	33.6338	26.7655	22.6891	20.0082	18.1241	16.7374
13.000%	89.3173	47.5418	33.6940	26.8275	22.7531	20.0741	18.1920	16.8073
13.125%	89.3759	47.6006	33.7542	26.8896	22.8171	20.1401	18.2600	16.8773
13.250%	89.4346	47.6593	33.8145	26.9517	22.8813	20.2063	18.3282	16.9474
13.375%	89.4933	47.7182	33.8749	27.0140	22.9455	20.2726	18.3965	17.0177
13.500%	89.5520	47.7770	33.9353	27.0763	23.0098	20.3390	18.4649	17.0882
13.625%	89.6108	47.8359	33.9958	27.1387	23.0743	20.4055	18.5335	17.1588
13.750%	89.6695	47.8949	34.0563	27.2012	23.1388	20.4721	18.6022	17.2295
13.875%	89.7283	47.9539	34.1169	27.2638	23.2035	20.5389	18.6710	17.3004
14.000%	89.7871	48.0129	34.1776	27.3265	23.2683	20.6057	18.7400	17.3715
14.125%	89.8459	48.0720	34.2384	27.3892	23.3331	20.6727	18.8091	17.4427
14.250%	89.9048	48.1311	34.2992	27.4520	23.3981	20.7398	18.8784	17.5141
14.375%	89.9637	48.1902	34.3600	27.5150	23.4631	20.8071	18.9478	17.5856
14.500%	90.0225	48.2494	34.4210	27.5780	23.5283	20.8744	19.0173	17.6573
14.625%	90.0815	48.3087	34.4820	27.6410	23.5935	20.9419	19.0870	17.7291
14.750%	90.1404	48.3680	34.5430	27.7042	23.6589	21.0095	19.1568	17.8010
14.875%	90.1993	48.4273	34.6041	27.7674	23.7244	21.0772	19.2267	17.8731
15.000%	90.2583	48.4866	34.6653	27.8307	23.7899	21.1450	19.2968	17.9454
15.125%	90.3173	48.5461	34.7266	27.8942	23.8556	21.2130	19.3670	18.0178
15.250%	90.3763	48.6055	34.7879	27.9576	23.9214	21.2810	19.4373	18.0904
15.375%	90.4354	48.6650	34.8492	28.0212	23.9872	21.3492	19.5077	18.1631
15.500%	90.4944	48.7245	34.9107	28.0849	24.0532	21.4175	19.5783	18.2359
15.625%	90.5535	48.7841	34.9722	28.1486	24.1193	21.4859	19.6491	18.3089
15.750%	90.6126	48.8437	35.0337	28.2124	24.1854	21.5544	19.7199	18.3821
15.875%	90.6717	48.9034	35.0954	28.2763	24.2517	21.6231	19.7909	18.4554
16.000%	90.7309	48.9631	35.1570	28.3403	24.3181	21.6918	19.8621	18.5288
16.125%	90.7900	49.0229	35.2188	28.4043	24.3845	21.7607	19.9333	18.6024
16.250%	90.8492	49.0826	35.2806	28.4685	24.4511	21.8297	20.0047	18.6761
16.375%	90.9084	49.1425	35.3425	28.5327	24.5178	21.8988	20.0762	18.7500
16.500%	90.9676	49.2024	35.4044	28.5970	24.5845	21.9681	20.1479	18.8240
16.625%	91.0269	49.2623	35.4664	28.6614	24.6514	22.0374	20.2197	18.8981
16.750%	91.0862	49.3222	35.5284	28.7259	24.7184	22.1069	20.2916	18.9724
16.875%	91.1454	49.3822	35.5905	28.7904	24.7854	22.1764	20.3636	19.0469

MONTHLY PAYMENT TO AMORTIZE A LOAN OF $1,000

Term of Loan

Interest Rate	9 Years	10 Years	11 Years	12 Years	13 Years	14 Years	15 Years	16 Years
12.000%	15.1842	14.3471	13.6779	13.1342	12.6867	12.3143	12.0017	11.7373
12.125%	15.2548	14.4194	13.7520	13.2100	12.7641	12.3933	12.0822	11.8193
12.250%	15.3256	14.4920	13.8263	13.2860	12.8417	12.4725	12.1630	11.9015
12.375%	15.3965	14.5647	13.9007	13.3622	12.9196	12.5520	12.2440	11.9840
12.500%	15.4676	14.6376	13.9754	13.4386	12.9977	12.6317	12.3252	12.0667
12.625%	15.5388	14.7107	14.0503	13.5152	13.0760	12.7116	12.4067	12.1496
12.750%	15.6102	14.7840	14.1254	13.5920	13.1545	12.7917	12.4884	12.2328
12.875%	15.6818	14.8574	14.2006	13.6690	13.2332	12.8721	12.5703	12.3162
13.000%	15.7536	14.9311	14.2761	13.7463	13.3121	12.9526	12.6524	12.3999
13.125%	15.8255	15.0049	14.3518	13.8237	13.3912	13.0334	12.7348	12.4837
13.250%	15.8976	15.0789	14.4276	13.9013	13.4706	13.1144	12.8174	12.5678
13.375%	15.9699	15.1531	14.5036	13.9791	13.5502	13.1956	12.9002	12.6521
13.500%	16.0423	15.2274	14.5799	14.0572	13.6299	13.2771	12.9832	12.7367
13.625%	16.1149	15.3020	14.6563	14.1354	13.7099	13.3587	13.0664	12.8214
13.750%	16.1877	15.3767	14.7329	14.2138	13.7901	13.4406	13.1499	12.9064
13.875%	16.2606	15.4516	14.8097	14.2925	13.8704	13.5226	13.2335	12.9916
14.000%	16.3337	15.5266	14.8867	14.3713	13.9510	13.6049	13.3174	13.0770
14.125%	16.4070	15.6019	14.9638	14.4503	14.0318	13.6874	13.4015	13.1626
14.250%	16.4804	15.6773	15.0412	14.5295	14.1128	13.7701	13.4858	13.2484
14.375%	16.5540	15.7529	15.1187	14.6089	14.1940	13.8529	13.5703	13.3345
14.500%	16.6277	15.8287	15.1964	14.6885	14.2754	13.9360	13.6550	13.4207
14.625%	16.7016	15.9046	15.2743	14.7683	14.3570	14.0193	13.7399	13.5071
14.750%	16.7757	15.9807	15.3524	14.8483	14.4387	14.1028	13.8250	13.5938
14.875%	16.8499	16.0570	15.4307	14.9284	14.5207	14.1865	13.9104	13.6806
15.000%	16.9243	16.1335	15.5091	15.0088	14.6029	14.2704	13.9959	13.7677
15.125%	16.9989	16.2101	15.5878	15.0893	14.6852	14.3545	14.0816	13.8549
15.250%	17.0736	16.2869	15.6666	15.1700	14.7678	14.4388	14.1675	13.9424
15.375%	17.1485	16.3639	15.7456	15.2509	14.8505	14.5232	14.2536	14.0300
15.500%	17.2235	16.4411	15.8247	15.3320	14.9335	14.6079	14.3399	14.1179
15.625%	17.2987	16.5184	15.9041	15.4133	15.0166	14.6928	14.4264	14.2059
15.750%	17.3741	16.5958	15.9836	15.4948	15.0999	14.7778	14.5131	14.2941
15.875%	17.4496	16.6735	16.0633	15.5764	15.1834	14.8630	14.5999	14.3825
16.000%	17.5253	16.7513	16.1432	15.6583	15.2670	14.9485	14.6870	14.4711
16.125%	17.6011	16.8293	16.2232	15.7403	15.3509	15.0341	14.7743	14.5599
16.250%	17.6771	16.9074	16.3034	15.8224	15.4349	15.1199	14.8617	14.6488
16.375%	17.7532	16.9858	16.3838	15.9048	15.5192	15.2058	14.9493	14.7380
16.500%	17.8295	17.0642	16.4644	15.9873	15.6036	15.2920	15.0371	14.8273
16.625%	17.9059	17.1429	16.5451	16.0700	15.6881	15.3783	15.1251	14.9168
16.750%	17.9825	17.2217	16.6260	16.1529	15.7729	15.4648	15.2132	15.0065
16.875%	18.0593	17.3006	16.7071	16.2360	15.8578	15.5515	15.3015	15.0963

MONTHLY PAYMENT TO AMORTIZE A LOAN OF $1,000

Term of Loan

Interest Rate	17 Years	18 Years	19 Years	20 Years	21 Years	22 Years	23 Years	24 Years
12.000%	11.5122	11.3195	11.1539	11.0109	10.8870	10.7794	10.6856	10.6038
12.125%	11.5956	11.4043	11.2399	11.0981	10.9754	10.8689	10.7762	10.6954
12.250%	11.6792	11.4893	11.3262	11.1856	11.0641	10.9587	10.8670	10.7872
12.375%	11.7631	11.5745	11.4127	11.2734	11.1530	11.0487	10.9581	10.8792
12.500%	11.8473	11.6600	11.4995	11.3614	11.2422	11.1390	11.0494	10.9714
12.625%	11.9316	11.7457	11.5865	11.4496	11.3316	11.2294	11.1409	11.0639
12.750%	12.0162	11.8317	11.6738	11.5381	11.4212	11.3202	11.2326	11.1566
12.875%	12.1011	11.9179	11.7613	11.6268	11.5111	11.4111	11.3246	11.2495
13.000%	12.1861	12.0043	11.8490	11.7158	11.6011	11.5023	11.4168	11.3427
13.125%	12.2714	12.0910	11.9369	11.8049	11.6915	11.5937	11.5092	11.4360
13.250%	12.3570	12.1779	12.0251	11.8943	11.7820	11.6853	11.6018	11.5296
13.375%	12.4427	12.2650	12.1135	11.9839	11.8727	11.7771	11.6946	11.6233
13.500%	12.5287	12.3523	12.2021	12.0737	11.9637	11.8691	11.7876	11.7173
13.625%	12.6149	12.4399	12.2910	12.1638	12.0549	11.9613	11.8808	11.8114
13.750%	12.7013	12.5276	12.3800	12.2541	12.1463	12.0538	11.9743	11.9058
13.875%	12.7879	12.6156	12.4693	12.3445	12.2379	12.1464	12.0679	12.0003
14.000%	12.8748	12.7038	12.5588	12.4352	12.3297	12.2393	12.1617	12.0950
14.125%	12.9618	12.7922	12.6485	12.5261	12.4217	12.3323	12.2557	12.1900
14.250%	13.0491	12.8809	12.7384	12.6172	12.5139	12.4256	12.3500	12.2851
14.375%	13.1366	12.9697	12.8285	12.7085	12.6063	12.5190	12.4443	12.3803
14.500%	13.2242	13.0587	12.9188	12.8000	12.6989	12.6126	12.5389	12.4758
14.625%	13.3121	13.1480	13.0093	12.8917	12.7917	12.7065	12.6337	12.5714
14.750%	13.4002	13.2374	13.1000	12.9836	12.8847	12.8004	12.7286	12.6672
14.875%	13.4885	13.3271	13.1909	13.0756	12.9778	12.8946	12.8237	12.7632
15.000%	13.5770	13.4169	13.2820	13.1679	13.0712	12.9890	12.9190	12.8593
15.125%	13.6657	13.5069	13.3733	13.2603	13.1647	13.0835	13.0144	12.9556
15.250%	13.7546	13.5972	13.4647	13.3530	13.2584	13.1782	13.1100	13.0520
15.375%	13.8437	13.6876	13.5564	13.4458	13.3523	13.2731	13.2058	13.1486
15.500%	13.9329	13.7782	13.6483	13.5388	13.4464	13.3681	13.3018	13.2454
15.625%	14.0224	13.8690	13.7403	13.6320	13.5406	13.4633	13.3979	13.3423
15.750%	14.1120	13.9600	13.8325	13.7253	13.6350	13.5587	13.4941	13.4394
15.875%	14.2019	14.0511	13.9249	13.8189	13.7296	13.6542	13.5905	13.5366
16.000%	14.2919	14.1425	14.0175	13.9126	13.8243	13.7499	13.6871	13.6339
16.125%	14.3821	14.2340	14.1102	14.0064	13.9192	13.8457	13.7838	13.7314
16.250%	14.4725	14.3257	14.2031	14.1005	14.0143	13.9417	13.8806	13.8290
16.375%	14.5630	14.4176	14.2962	14.1946	14.1095	14.0379	13.9776	13.9268
16.500%	14.6538	14.5096	14.3894	14.2890	14.2048	14.1342	14.0747	14.0247
16.625%	14.7447	14.6018	14.4829	14.3835	14.3004	14.2306	14.1720	14.1227
16.750%	14.8358	14.6942	14.5764	14.4782	14.3960	14.3272	14.2694	14.2208
16.875%	14.9270	14.7868	14.6702	14.5730	14.4919	14.4239	14.3669	14.3191

MONTHLY PAYMENT TO AMORTIZE A LOAN OF $1,000

Term of Loan

Interest Rate	25 Years	26 Years	27 Years	28 Years	29 Years	30 Years	35 Years	40 Years
12.000%	10.5322	10.4695	10.4145	10.3661	10.3236	10.2861	10.1555	10.0850
12.125%	10.6247	10.5629	10.5087	10.4611	10.4192	10.3824	10.2545	10.1859
12.250%	10.7174	10.6565	10.6030	10.5562	10.5151	10.4790	10.3537	10.2869
12.375%	10.8104	10.7503	10.6977	10.6516	10.6112	10.5757	10.4531	10.3880
12.500%	10.9035	10.8443	10.7925	10.7471	10.7074	10.6726	10.5525	10.4892
12.625%	10.9969	10.9385	10.8875	10.8429	10.8039	10.7697	10.6522	10.5905
12.750%	11.0905	11.0329	10.9827	10.9388	10.9005	10.8669	10.7520	10.6920
12.875%	11.1843	11.1276	11.0781	11.0350	10.9973	10.9644	10.8519	10.7935
13.000%	11.2784	11.2224	11.1738	11.1313	11.0943	11.0620	10.9519	10.8951
13.125%	11.3726	11.3175	11.2696	11.2279	11.1915	11.1598	11.0521	10.9969
13.250%	11.4670	11.4127	11.3656	11.3246	11.2888	11.2577	11.1524	11.0987
13.375%	11.5616	11.5082	11.4618	11.4214	11.3864	11.3558	11.2529	11.2006
13.500%	11.6564	11.6038	11.5581	11.5185	11.4841	11.4541	11.3534	11.3026
13.625%	11.7515	11.6996	11.6547	11.6157	11.5819	11.5525	11.4541	11.4047
13.750%	11.8467	11.7956	11.7514	11.7131	11.6799	11.6511	11.5549	11.5069
13.875%	11.9420	11.8917	11.8483	11.8107	11.7781	11.7498	11.6557	11.6091
14.000%	12.0376	11.9881	11.9453	11.9084	11.8764	11.8487	11.7567	11.7114
14.125%	12.1334	12.0846	12.0425	12.0062	11.9749	11.9477	11.8578	11.8138
14.250%	12.2293	12.1813	12.1399	12.1043	12.0735	12.0469	11.9590	11.9162
14.375%	12.3254	12.2781	12.2375	12.2024	12.1722	12.1461	12.0603	12.0187
14.500%	12.4216	12.3751	12.3351	12.3007	12.2711	12.2456	12.1617	12.1213
14.625%	12.5181	12.4723	12.4330	12.3992	12.3701	12.3451	12.2632	12.2240
14.750%	12.6146	12.5696	12.5310	12.4978	12.4693	12.4448	12.3647	12.3267
14.875%	12.7114	12.6671	12.6291	12.5965	12.5686	12.5445	12.4664	12.4294
15.000%	12.8083	12.7647	12.7274	12.6954	12.6680	12.6444	12.5681	12.5322
15.125%	12.9054	12.8625	12.8258	12.7944	12.7675	12.7445	12.6699	12.6351
15.250%	13.0026	12.9604	12.9243	12.8935	12.8672	12.8446	12.7718	12.7380
15.375%	13.0999	13.0584	13.0230	12.9928	12.9669	12.9448	12.8738	12.8410
15.500%	13.1975	13.1566	13.1218	13.0922	13.0668	13.0452	12.9758	12.9440
15.625%	13.2951	13.2550	13.2208	13.1916	13.1668	13.1456	13.0780	13.0471
15.750%	13.3929	13.3534	13.3198	13.2913	13.2669	13.2462	13.1801	13.1502
15.875%	13.4908	13.4520	13.4190	13.3910	13.3671	13.3468	13.2824	13.2533
16.000%	13.5889	13.5507	13.5183	13.4908	13.4674	13.4476	13.3847	13.3565
16.125%	13.6871	13.6496	13.6178	13.5908	13.5679	13.5484	13.4871	13.4597
16.250%	13.7854	13.7485	13.7173	13.6908	13.6684	13.6493	13.5895	13.5630
16.375%	13.8839	13.8476	13.8169	13.7910	13.7690	13.7504	13.6920	13.6663
16.500%	13.9824	13.9468	13.9167	13.8912	13.8697	13.8515	13.7945	13.7696
16.625%	14.0811	14.0461	14.0166	13.9916	13.9705	13.9527	13.8971	13.8730
16.750%	14.1800	14.1456	14.1165	14.0921	14.0714	14.0540	13.9998	13.9764
16.875%	14.2789	14.2451	14.2166	14.1926	14.1724	14.1553	14.1025	14.0798

MONTHLY PAYMENT TO AMORTIZE A LOAN OF $1,000

Term of Loan

Interest Rate	1 Year	2 Years	3 Years	4 Years	5 Years	6 Years	7 Years	8 Years
17.000%	91.2048	49.4423	35.6527	28.8550	24.8526	22.2461	20.4358	19.1215
17.125%	91.2641	49.5023	35.7150	28.9198	24.9198	22.3159	20.5081	19.1962
17.250%	91.3234	49.5625	35.7773	28.9845	24.9872	22.3859	20.5805	19.2710
17.375%	91.3828	49.6226	35.8396	29.0494	25.0547	22.4559	20.6531	19.3461
17.500%	91.4422	49.6828	35.9021	29.1144	25.1222	22.5260	20.7258	19.4212
17.625%	91.5016	49.7431	35.9646	29.1794	25.1899	22.5963	20.7986	19.4965
17.750%	91.5611	49.8034	36.0271	29.2445	25.2576	22.6667	20.8716	19.5719
17.875%	91.6205	49.8637	36.0897	29.3097	25.3255	22.7372	20.9446	19.6475
18.000%	91.6800	49.9241	36.1524	29.3750	25.3934	22.8078	21.0178	19.7232
18.125%	91.7395	49.9845	36.2151	29.4404	25.4615	22.8785	21.0912	19.7991
18.250%	91.7990	50.0450	36.2779	29.5058	25.5296	22.9493	21.1646	19.8751
18.375%	91.8586	50.1055	36.3408	29.5713	25.5979	23.0203	21.2382	19.9512
18.500%	91.9181	50.1660	36.4037	29.6369	25.6662	23.0914	21.3119	20.0274
18.625%	91.9777	50.2266	36.4667	29.7026	25.7346	23.1625	21.3858	20.1038
18.750%	92.0373	50.2872	36.5297	29.7684	25.8032	23.2338	21.4597	20.1804
18.875%	92.0969	50.3479	36.5929	29.8342	25.8718	23.3052	21.5338	20.2571
19.000%	92.1566	50.4086	36.6560	29.9001	25.9406	23.3767	21.6080	20.3339

MONTHLY PAYMENT TO AMORTIZE A LOAN OF $1,000

Term of Loan

Interest Rate	9 Years	10 Years	11 Years	12 Years	13 Years	14 Years	15 Years	16 Years
17.000%	18.1362	17.3798	16.7883	16.3192	15.9430	15.6384	15.3900	15.1863
17.125%	18.2132	17.4591	16.8697	16.4026	16.0282	15.7254	15.4787	15.2765
17.250%	18.2905	17.5385	16.9513	16.4862	16.1137	15.8126	15.5676	15.3669
17.375%	18.3678	17.6181	17.0330	16.5700	16.1993	15.9000	15.6566	15.4574
17.500%	18.4453	17.6979	17.1149	16.6539	16.2851	15.9876	15.7458	15.5481
17.625%	18.5230	17.7778	17.1970	16.7380	16.3711	16.0753	15.8351	15.6390
17.750%	18.6008	17.8579	17.2792	16.8222	16.4572	16.1632	15.9247	15.7300
17.875%	18.6788	17.9381	17.3616	16.9066	16.5435	16.2513	16.0144	15.8212
18.000%	18.7569	18.0185	17.4442	16.9912	16.6300	16.3395	16.1042	15.9126
18.125%	18.8351	18.0991	17.5269	17.0759	16.7166	16.4279	16.1942	16.0041
18.250%	18.9136	18.1798	17.6098	17.1608	16.8034	16.5165	16.2844	16.0957
18.375%	18.9921	18.2606	17.6928	17.2459	16.8904	16.6052	16.3747	16.1875
18.500%	19.0708	18.3417	17.7760	17.3311	16.9775	16.6941	16.4652	16.2795
18.625%	19.1497	18.4228	17.8593	17.4165	17.0648	16.7831	16.5559	16.3716
18.750%	19.2287	18.5041	17.9428	19.5021	17.1523	16.8723	16.6467	16.4639
18.875%	19.3078	18.5856	18.0265	17.5878	17.2399	16.9616	16.7376	16.5564
19.000%	19.3871	18.6672	18.1103	17.6736	17.3276	17.0511	16.8288	16.6489

MONTHLY PAYMENT TO AMORTIZE A LOAN OF $1,000

Term of Loan

Interest Rate	17 Years	18 Years	19 Years	20 Years	21 Years	22 Years	23 Years	24 Years
17.000%	15.0184	14.8795	14.7641	14.6680	14.5878	14.5208	14.4646	14.4175
17.125%	15.1100	14.9724	14.8581	14.7631	14.6839	14.6178	14.5624	14.5160
17.250%	15.2018	15.0654	14.9524	14.8584	14.7802	14.7149	14.6603	14.6147
17.375%	15.2937	15.1586	15.0467	14.9538	14.8766	14.8122	14.7584	14.7134
17.500%	15.3858	15.2519	15.1412	15.0494	14.9731	14.9095	14.8565	14.8123
17.625%	15.4780	15.3455	15.2359	15.1451	15.0698	15.0071	14.9548	14.9113
17.750%	15.5704	15.4391	15.3307	15.2410	15.1666	15.1047	15.0532	15.0104
17.875%	15.6630	15.5329	15.4257	15.3370	15.2635	15.2025	15.1518	15.1096
18.000%	15.7557	15.6269	15.5208	15.4331	15.3605	15.3004	15.2504	15.2089
18.125%	15.8486	15.7210	15.6160	15.5294	15.4577	15.3984	15.3492	15.3083
18.250%	15.9146	15.8153	15.7114	15.6258	15.5550	15.4965	15.4480	15.4078
18.375%	16.0348	15.9097	15.8069	15.7223	15.6525	15.5948	15.5470	15.5074
18.500%	16.1281	16.0042	15.9026	15.8190	15.7500	15.6931	15.6461	15.6071
18.625%	16.2216	16.0989	15.9984	15.9158	15.8477	15.7916	15.7452	15.7069
18.750%	16.3152	16.1938	16.0943	16.0127	15.9455	15.8902	15.8445	15.8068
18.875%	16.4090	16.2887	16.1904	16.1097	16.0434	15.9889	15.9429	15.9068
19.000%	16.5029	16.3838	16.2866	16.2068	16.1414	16.0876	16.0434	16.0069

MONTHLY PAYMENT TO AMORTIZE A LOAN OF $1,000

Term of Loan

Interest Rate	25 Years	26 Years	27 Years	28 Years	29 Years	30 Years	35 Years	40 Years
17.000%	14.3780	14.3447	14.3168	14.2933	14.2734	14.2568	14.2053	14.1832
17.125%	14.4771	14.4445	14.4171	14.3940	14.3746	14.3583	14.3081	14.2867
17.250%	14.5764	14.5443	14.5174	14.4948	14.4758	14.4599	14.4109	14.3902
17.375%	14.6758	14.6443	14.6179	14.5957	14.5771	14.5615	14.5138	14.4938
17.500%	14.7753	14.7443	14.7184	14.6967	14.6785	14.6633	14.6168	14.5973
17.625%	14.8749	14.8445	14.8191	14.7978	14.7800	14.7651	14.7197	14.7009
17.750%	14.9746	14.9447	14.9198	14.8989	14.8815	14.8669	14.8228	14.8045
17.875%	15.0744	15.0451	15.0206	15.0002	14.9831	14.9689	14.9258	14.9082
18.000%	15.1743	15.1455	15.1215	15.1015	15.0848	15.0709	15.0289	15.0118
18.125%	15.2743	15.2460	15.2225	15.2029	15.1865	15.1729	15.1321	15.1155
18.250%	15.3744	15.3466	15.3235	15.3043	15.2883	15.2750	15.2352	15.2192
18.375%	15.4746	15.4473	15.4247	15.4059	15.3902	15.3772	15.3384	15.3229
18.500%	15.5748	15.5481	15.5259	15.5075	15.4922	15.4794	15.4417	15.4266
18.625%	15.6752	15.6489	15.6272	15.6091	15.5942	15.5817	15.5449	15.5304
18.750%	15.7757	15.7499	15.7285	15.7109	15.6962	15.6841	15.6483	15.6342
18.875%	15.8762	15.8509	15.8300	15.8127	15.7983	15.7865	15.7516	15.7379
19.000%	15.9768	15.9520	15.9315	15.9145	15.9005	15.8889	15.8549	15.8417

Appendix B
Remaining Principal Balance

If you arrange a balloon mortgage, monthly payments will be set on a long-term schedule. At some point during the life of the loan, though, the entire remaining balance will suddenly become due and payable.

How much will that final (balloon) payment be? In the early years of a loan, interest charges absorb most of the monthly payment, and little is left to reduce the principal. It is not unusual for the final payment to be almost as much as the original debt.

To calculate the amount:

1. Find the table with the interest rate on your mortgage.
2. Follow across the top line until you find the original term of the loan (the number of years that were used to calculate the monthly payment).
3. Go down the left-hand column until you find the number of years the loan will actually last (the age of the loan when you will make that balloon payment).
4. Find the spot where the two lines intersect.
   Example: On the chart for 10 percent loans, with an original term of 25 years, a ten-year balloon has a factor of .846. Almost 85 percent of the original loan is still due.
5. Multiply the original loan amount by the factor.
   Example: A loan of $74,500 × .846 (84.6%) = $63,027. This represents the remaining balance after ten years' payments have been made, and it represents the final balloon payment.

Remaining Principal Balance Factors

For Mortgages with an Interest Rate of 2.00% and an Original Term of:

Age of Loan in Years	5 Years	6 Years	7 Years	8 Years	9 Years	10 Years	11 Years	12 Years	15 Years	20 Years	25 Years	30 Years	35 Years	40 Years
1	0.808	0.842	0.866	0.884	0.898	0.909	0.918	0.926	0.942	0.959	0.969	0.975	0.980	0.984
2	0.612	0.680	0.728	0.765	0.793	0.816	0.834	0.850	0.883	0.917	0.937	0.950	0.960	0.967
3	0.412	0.515	0.588	0.644	0.686	0.721	0.749	0.772	0.823	0.874	0.905	0.925	0.939	0.950
4	0.208	0.347	0.446	0.520	0.578	0.624	0.662	0.693	0.762	0.831	0.872	0.899	0.918	0.932
5	0.000	0.175	0.300	0.394	0.467	0.525	0.573	0.612	0.699	0.786	0.838	0.872	0.896	0.914
6		0.000	0.152	0.265	0.354	0.424	0.482	0.530	0.636	0.741	0.803	0.845	0.874	0.896
7			0.000	0.134	0.238	0.321	0.389	0.446	0.570	0.694	0.768	0.817	0.852	0.877
8				0.000	0.120	0.216	0.295	0.360	0.504	0.647	0.732	0.789	0.829	0.858
9					0.000	0.109	0.199	0.273	0.436	0.599	0.696	0.760	0.805	0.839
10						0.000	0.100	0.184	0.367	0.550	0.659	0.731	0.782	0.819
11							0.000	0.093	0.297	0.500	0.621	0.701	0.757	0.799
12								0.000	0.225	0.448	0.582	0.670	0.732	0.779
15									0.000	0.289	0.461	0.574	0.655	0.714
20										0.000	0.242	0.402	0.515	0.599
25											0.000	0.211	0.360	0.471
30												0.000	0.189	0.329
35													0.000	0.173
40														0.000

For Mortgages with an Interest Rate of 2.25% and an Original Term of:

Age of Loan in Years	5 Years	6 Years	7 Years	8 Years	9 Years	10 Years	11 Years	12 Years	15 Years	20 Years	25 Years	30 Years	35 Years	40 Years
1	0.809	0.843	0.867	0.885	0.899	0.910	0.919	0.927	0.943	0.960	0.970	0.976	0.981	0.984
2	0.613	0.682	0.730	0.767	0.795	0.818	0.836	0.851	0.885	0.919	0.939	0.952	0.962	0.968
3	0.414	0.517	0.591	0.646	0.689	0.723	0.751	0.775	0.826	0.877	0.907	0.928	0.942	0.952
4	0.209	0.348	0.448	0.522	0.580	0.627	0.665	0.696	0.765	0.834	0.875	0.902	0.921	0.935
5	0.000	0.176	0.302	0.396	0.469	0.528	0.576	0.616	0.703	0.790	0.842	0.876	0.901	0.918
6		0.000	0.153	0.267	0.356	0.427	0.485	0.534	0.640	0.746	0.809	0.850	0.879	0.901
7			0.000	0.135	0.240	0.324	0.393	0.450	0.575	0.700	0.774	0.823	0.858	0.883
8				0.000	0.121	0.218	0.298	0.364	0.509	0.653	0.739	0.795	0.835	0.865
9					0.000	0.110	0.201	0.276	0.441	0.605	0.703	0.767	0.813	0.846
10						0.000	0.101	0.186	0.371	0.556	0.666	0.738	0.789	0.827
11							0.000	0.094	0.300	0.506	0.628	0.709	0.766	0.808
12								0.000	0.228	0.455	0.589	0.678	0.741	0.788
15									0.000	0.294	0.468	0.584	0.665	0.725
20														
25											0.000	0.217	0.370	0.483
30												0.000	0.195	0.339
35													0.000	0.179
40														0.000

Remaining Principal Balance Factors

For Mortgages with an Interest Rate of 2.50% and an Original Term of:

Age of Loan in Years	5 Years	6 Years	7 Years	8 Years	9 Years	10 Years	11 Years	12 Years	15 Years	20 Years	25 Years	30 Years	35 Years	40 Years
1	0.810	0.844	0.868	0.886	0.900	0.911	0.920	0.928	0.944	0.961	0.971	0.977	0.982	0.985
2	0.615	0.683	0.732	0.768	0.797	0.819	0.838	0.853	0.887	0.921	0.941	0.954	0.963	0.970
3	0.415	0.519	0.593	0.648	0.691	0.726	0.754	0.777	0.829	0.880	0.910	0.930	0.944	0.955
4	0.210	0.350	0.450	0.525	0.583	0.630	0.668	0.699	0.769	0.838	0.879	0.906	0.925	0.939
5	0.000	0.177	0.304	0.399	0.472	0.531	0.579	0.619	0.707	0.795	0.847	0.881	0.905	0.922
6		0.000	0.154	0.269	0.359	0.430	0.489	0.537	0.644	0.750	0.814	0.855	0.884	0.906
7			0.000	0.136	0.242	0.327	0.396	0.453	0.580	0.705	0.780	0.829	0.863	0.889
8				0.000	0.123	0.220	0.301	0.367	0.513	0.659	0.745	0.802	0.842	0.871
9					0.000	0.112	0.203	0.279	0.445	0.611	0.709	0.774	0.820	0.853
10						0.000	0.103	0.188	0.376	0.562	0.673	0.746	0.797	0.835
11							0.000	0.095	0.304	0.512	0.635	0.717	0.774	0.816
12								0.000	0.231	0.461	0.597	0.687	0.750	0.796
15									0.000	0.299	0.476	0.593	0.675	0.735
20										0.000	0.253	0.419	0.536	0.622
25											0.000	0.223	0.379	0.495
30												0.000	0.201	0.350
35													0.000	0.186
40														0.000

For Mortgages with an Interest Rate of 2.75% and an Original Term of:

Age of Loan in Years	5 Years	6 Years	7 Years	8 Years	9 Years	10 Years	11 Years	12 Years	15 Years	20 Years	25 Years	30 Years	35 Years	40 Years
1	0.811	0.845	0.869	0.887	0.901	0.912	0.921	0.929	0.945	0.962	0.972	0.978	0.983	0.986
2	0.616	0.685	0.734	0.770	0.799	0.821	0.840	0.855	0.889	0.923	0.943	0.956	0.965	0.972
3	0.417	0.521	0.595	0.650	0.694	0.728	0.757	0.780	0.832	0.883	0.913	0.933	0.947	0.957
4	0.211	0.352	0.452	0.527	0.586	0.633	0.671	0.703	0.772	0.841	0.882	0.909	0.928	0.942
5	0.000	0.178	0.306	0.401	0.475	0.534	0.583	0.623	0.711	0.799	0.851	0.885	0.909	0.926
6		0.000	0.155	0.271	0.361	0.433	0.492	0.541	0.649	0.755	0.819	0.860	0.889	0.910
7			0.000	0.137	0.244	0.329	0.399	0.457	0.584	0.710	0.785	0.834	0.869	0.894
8				0.000	0.124	0.223	0.303	0.371	0.518	0.664	0.751	0.808	0.848	0.877
9					0.000	0.113	0.205	0.282	0.450	0.617	0.716	0.781	0.826	0.860
10						0.000	0.104	0.190	0.380	0.568	0.680	0.753	0.804	0.842
11							0.000	0.096	0.308	0.518	0.643	0.724	0.782	0.824
12								0.000	0.234	0.467	0.604	0.695	0.758	0.805
15									0.000	0.304	0.483	0.602	0.684	0.745
20										0.000	0.258	0.428	0.547	0.634
25											0.000	0.229	0.389	0.507
30												0.000	0.208	0.360
35													0.000	0.192
40														0.000

Remaining Principal Balance Factors

For Mortgages with an Interest Rate of 3.00% and an Original Term of:

Age of Loan in Years	5 Years	6 Years	7 Years	8 Years	9 Years	10 Years	11 Years	12 Years	15 Years	20 Years	25 Years	30 Years	35 Years	40 Years
1	0.812	0.846	0.870	0.888	0.902	0.913	0.922	0.930	0.946	0.963	0.973	0.979	0.984	0.987
2	0.618	0.686	0.735	0.772	0.800	0.823	0.842	0.857	0.891	0.925	0.945	0.958	0.967	0.973
3	0.418	0.522	0.597	0.653	0.696	0.731	0.759	0.783	0.834	0.885	0.916	0.935	0.949	0.959
4	0.212	0.353	0.454	0.530	0.589	0.636	0.674	0.706	0.776	0.845	0.886	0.913	0.931	0.945
5	0.000	0.179	0.307	0.403	0.478	0.537	0.586	0.626	0.715	0.803	0.855	0.889	0.913	0.930
6		0.000	0.156	0.273	0.364	0.436	0.496	0.545	0.653	0.760	0.823	0.865	0.894	0.915
7			0.000	0.138	0.246	0.332	0.402	0.461	0.589	0.716	0.791	0.840	0.874	0.899
8				0.000	0.125	0.225	0.306	0.374	0.523	0.670	0.757	0.814	0.854	0.883
9					0.000	0.114	0.207	0.285	0.455	0.623	0.722	0.788	0.833	0.866
10						0.000	0.105	0.193	0.384	0.574	0.687	0.760	0.812	0.849
11							0.000	0.098	0.312	0.524	0.650	0.732	0.789	0.831
12								0.000	0.237	0.473	0.612	0.703	0.767	0.813
15									0.000	0.309	0.491	0.611	0.694	0.755
20										0.000	0.264	0.437	0.557	0.645
25											0.000	0.235	0.399	0.518
30												0.000	0.214	0.371
35													0.000	0.199
40														0.000

For Mortgages with an Interest Rate of 3.25% and an Original Term of:

Age of Loan in Years	5 Years	6 Years	7 Years	8 Years	9 Years	10 Years	11 Years	12 Years	15 Years	20 Years	25 Years	30 Years	35 Years	40 Years
1	0.813	0.847	0.871	0.889	0.903	0.914	0.923	0.931	0.947	0.964	0.974	0.980	0.984	0.988
2	0.619	0.688	0.737	0.774	0.802	0.825	0.844	0.859	0.893	0.927	0.946	0.959	0.968	0.975
3	0.420	0.524	0.599	0.655	0.699	0.733	0.762	0.785	0.837	0.888	0.918	0.938	0.952	0.962
4	0.213	0.355	0.457	0.532	0.591	0.638	0.677	0.709	0.779	0.848	0.889	0.916	0.934	0.948
5	0.000	0.180	0.309	0.406	0.481	0.540	0.589	0.630	0.719	0.807	0.859	0.893	0.917	0.934
6		0.000	0.157	0.275	0.366	0.439	0.499	0.549	0.657	0.765	0.828	0.870	0.898	0.919
7			0.000	0.140	0.248	0.335	0.406	0.464	0.593	0.721	0.796	0.845	0.879	0.904
8				0.000	0.126	0.227	0.309	0.377	0.527	0.676	0.763	0.820	0.860	0.889
9					0.000	0.115	0.209	0.288	0.459	0.629	0.729	0.794	0.840	0.873
10						0.000	0.106	0.195	0.389	0.580	0.694	0.767	0.819	0.856
11							0.000	0.099	0.316	0.530	0.657	0.740	0.797	0.839
12								0.000	0.241	0.479	0.619	0.711	0.775	0.821
15									0.000	0.314	0.499	0.619	0.703	0.764
20										0.000	0.270	0.445	0.568	0.657
25											0.000	0.241	0.408	0.530
30												0.000	0.221	0.381
35													0.000	0.206
40														0.000

Remaining Principal Balance Factors

For Mortgages with an Interest Rate of 3.50% and an Original Term of:

Age of Loan in Years	5 Years	6 Years	7 Years	8 Years	9 Years	10 Years	11 Years	12 Years	15 Years	20 Years	25 Years	30 Years	35 Years	40 Years
1	0.814	0.848	0.872	0.890	0.904	0.915	0.924	0.932	0.948	0.965	0.975	0.981	0.985	0.988
2	0.621	0.690	0.739	0.776	0.804	0.827	0.846	0.861	0.895	0.928	0.948	0.961	0.970	0.976
3	0.421	0.526	0.601	0.657	0.701	0.736	0.764	0.788	0.840	0.891	0.921	0.940	0.954	0.964
4	0.214	0.357	0.459	0.535	0.594	0.641	0.680	0.712	0.782	0.852	0.893	0.919	0.937	0.951
5	0.000	0.182	0.311	0.408	0.483	0.544	0.593	0.634	0.723	0.811	0.863	0.897	0.920	0.937
6		0.000	0.158	0.277	0.369	0.442	0.502	0.552	0.661	0.769	0.833	0.874	0.903	0.923
7			0.000	0.141	0.250	0.337	0.409	0.468	0.598	0.726	0.801	0.850	0.884	0.909
8				0.000	0.127	0.229	0.312	0.381	0.532	0.681	0.769	0.826	0.865	0.894
9					0.000	0.116	0.212	0.291	0.464	0.635	0.735	0.801	0.846	0.879
10						0.000	0.108	0.197	0.393	0.586	0.700	0.774	0.826	0.863
11							0.000	0.100	0.320	0.537	0.664	0.747	0.805	0.846
12								0.000	0.244	0.485	0.627	0.719	0.783	0.829
15									0.000	0.319	0.506	0.628	0.713	0.774
20										0.000	0.275	0.454	0.578	0.668
25											0.000	0.247	0.418	0.542
30												0.000	0.227	0.392
35													0.000	0.213
40														0.000

For Mortgages with an Interest Rate of 3.75% and an Original Term of:

Age of Loan in Years	5 Years	6 Years	7 Years	8 Years	9 Years	10 Years	11 Years	12 Years	15 Years	20 Years	25 Years	30 Years	35 Years	40 Years
1	0.815	0.849	0.873	0.891	0.905	0.916	0.925	0.933	0.949	0.966	0.975	0.982	0.986	0.989
2	0.622	0.691	0.740	0.777	0.806	0.829	0.847	0.863	0.897	0.930	0.950	0.963	0.971	0.978
3	0.423	0.528	0.603	0.660	0.703	0.738	0.767	0.790	0.842	0.893	0.923	0.943	0.956	0.966
4	0.215	0.359	0.461	0.537	0.597	0.644	0.683	0.715	0.786	0.855	0.896	0.922	0.940	0.953
5	0.000	0.183	0.313	0.410	0.486	0.547	0.596	0.637	0.727	0.815	0.867	0.901	0.924	0.941
6		0.000	0.159	0.279	0.371	0.445	0.506	0.556	0.666	0.774	0.837	0.879	0.907	0.927
7			0.000	0.142	0.252	0.340	0.412	0.472	0.602	0.731	0.807	0.856	0.889	0.914
8				0.000	0.128	0.231	0.315	0.384	0.537	0.687	0.775	0.832	0.871	0.899
9					0.000	0.118	0.214	0.294	0.468	0.640	0.741	0.807	0.852	0.885
10						0.000	0.109	0.199	0.397	0.593	0.707	0.781	0.832	0.869
11							0.000	0.102	0.324	0.543	0.671	0.754	0.812	0.853
12								0.000	0.247	0.491	0.634	0.727	0.791	0.837
15									0.000	0.324	0.514	0.637	0.722	0.783
20										0.000	0.281	0.463	0.588	0.679
25											0.000	0.253	0.428	0.554
30												0.000	0.234	0.402
35													0.000	0.220
40														0.000

Remaining Principal Balance Factors

For Mortgages with an Interest Rate of 4.00% and an Original Term of:

Age of Loan in Years	5 Years	6 Years	7 Years	8 Years	9 Years	10 Years	11 Years	12 Years	15 Years	20 Years	25 Years	30 Years	35 Years	40 Years
1	0.816	0.850	0.874	0.892	0.906	0.917	0.926	0.934	0.950	0.967	0.976	0.982	0.987	0.990
2	0.624	0.693	0.742	0.779	0.808	0.831	0.849	0.865	0.899	0.932	0.951	0.964	0.973	0.979
3	0.424	0.530	0.605	0.662	0.706	0.741	0.769	0.793	0.845	0.896	0.926	0.945	0.958	0.968
4	0.216	0.360	0.463	0.540	0.600	0.647	0.686	0.718	0.789	0.858	0.899	0.925	0.943	0.956
5	0.000	0.184	0.315	0.413	0.489	0.550	0.599	0.641	0.731	0.819	0.871	0.904	0.927	0.944
6		0.000	0.161	0.281	0.374	0.448	0.509	0.560	0.670	0.779	0.842	0.883	0.911	0.931
7			0.000	0.143	0.254	0.343	0.415	0.475	0.607	0.736	0.812	0.861	0.894	0.918
8				0.000	0.130	0.233	0.318	0.388	0.541	0.692	0.780	0.837	0.876	0.904
9					0.000	0.119	0.216	0.297	0.473	0.646	0.748	0.813	0.858	0.890
10						0.000	0.110	0.202	0.402	0.599	0.714	0.788	0.839	0.875
11							0.000	0.103	0.328	0.549	0.678	0.762	0.819	0.860
12								0.000	0.251	0.497	0.641	0.734	0.798	0.844
15									0.000	0.329	0.521	0.645	0.731	0.792
20										0.000	0.287	0.472	0.599	0.690
25											0.000	0.259	0.437	0.565
30												0.000	0.240	0.413
35													0.000	0.227
40														0.000

For Mortgages with an Interest Rate of 4.25% and an Original Term of:

Age of Loan in Years	5 Years	6 Years	7 Years	8 Years	9 Years	10 Years	11 Years	12 Years	15 Years	20 Years	25 Years	30 Years	35 Years	40 Years
1	0.817	0.850	0.875	0.893	0.907	0.918	0.927	0.935	0.951	0.968	0.977	0.983	0.987	0.990
2	0.625	0.695	0.744	0.781	0.810	0.832	0.851	0.867	0.900	0.934	0.953	0.966	0.974	0.980
3	0.426	0.532	0.607	0.664	0.708	0.743	0.772	0.796	0.847	0.898	0.928	0.947	0.960	0.970
4	0.217	0.362	0.465	0.542	0.602	0.650	0.689	0.721	0.792	0.862	0.902	0.928	0.946	0.959
5	0.000	0.185	0.317	0.415	0.492	0.553	0.603	0.644	0.734	0.823	0.875	0.908	0.931	0.947
6		0.000	0.162	0.283	0.377	0.451	0.513	0.563	0.674	0.783	0.846	0.887	0.915	0.935
7			0.000	0.144	0.256	0.346	0.419	0.479	0.611	0.741	0.817	0.865	0.899	0.922
8				0.000	0.131	0.235	0.320	0.391	0.546	0.698	0.786	0.843	0.882	0.909
9					0.000	0.120	0.218	0.300	0.477	0.652	0.754	0.819	0.864	0.896
10						0.000	0.111	0.204	0.406	0.604	0.720	0.794	0.845	0.881
11							0.000	0.104	0.332	0.555	0.685	0.769	0.826	0.867
12								0.000	0.254	0.503	0.648	0.742	0.806	0.851
15									0.000	0.334	0.529	0.654	0.739	0.800
20										0.000	0.292	0.480	0.609	0.700
25											0.000	0.265	0.447	0.576
30												0.000	0.247	0.423
35													0.000	0.234
40														0.000

Remaining Principal Balance Factors

For Mortgages with an Interest Rate of 4.50% and an Original Term of:

Age of Loan in Years	5 Years	6 Years	7 Years	8 Years	9 Years	10 Years	11 Years	12 Years	15 Years	20 Years	25 Years	30 Years	35 Years	40 Years
1	0.818	0.851	0.876	0.894	0.908	0.919	0.928	0.936	0.952	0.968	0.978	0.984	0.988	0.991
2	0.627	0.696	0.746	0.783	0.811	0.834	0.853	0.868	0.902	0.935	0.955	0.967	0.975	0.981
3	0.427	0.534	0.610	0.666	0.710	0.746	0.774	0.798	0.850	0.901	0.930	0.949	0.962	0.971
4	0.218	0.364	0.467	0.545	0.605	0.653	0.692	0.724	0.795	0.865	0.905	0.931	0.948	0.961
5	0.000	0.186	0.318	0.418	0.495	0.556	0.606	0.647	0.738	0.827	0.879	0.912	0.934	0.950
6		0.000	0.163	0.285	0.379	0.454	0.516	0.567	0.678	0.787	0.851	0.891	0.919	0.938
7			0.000	0.146	0.258	0.348	0.422	0.483	0.616	0.746	0.822	0.870	0.903	0.927
8				0.000	0.132	0.237	0.323	0.395	0.550	0.703	0.792	0.848	0.887	0.914
9					0.000	0.121	0.220	0.303	0.482	0.658	0.760	0.825	0.869	0.901
10						0.000	0.113	0.206	0.410	0.610	0.727	0.801	0.851	0.887
11							0.000	0.105	0.335	0.561	0.692	0.776	0.833	0.873
12								0.000	0.257	0.509	0.656	0.749	0.813	0.858
15									0.000	0.339	0.536	0.662	0.748	0.809
20										0.000	0.298	0.489	0.619	0.711
25											0.000	0.272	0.457	0.588
30												0.000	0.254	0.434
35													0.000	0.241
40														0.000

For Mortgages with an Interest Rate of 4.75% and an Original Term of:

Age of Loan in Years	5 Years	6 Years	7 Years	8 Years	9 Years	10 Years	11 Years	12 Years	15 Years	20 Years	25 Years	30 Years	35 Years	40 Years
1	0.818	0.852	0.877	0.895	0.909	0.920	0.929	0.937	0.953	0.969	0.979	0.985	0.989	0.991
2	0.628	0.698	0.747	0.784	0.813	0.836	0.855	0.870	0.904	0.937	0.956	0.968	0.977	0.982
3	0.429	0.535	0.612	0.669	0.713	0.748	0.777	0.801	0.853	0.903	0.933	0.951	0.964	0.973
4	0.219	0.365	0.469	0.547	0.608	0.656	0.695	0.728	0.799	0.868	0.908	0.934	0.951	0.963
5	0.000	0.187	0.320	0.420	0.497	0.559	0.609	0.651	0.742	0.831	0.882	0.915	0.937	0.953
6		0.000	0.164	0.287	0.382	0.458	0.519	0.571	0.682	0.792	0.855	0.895	0.923	0.942
7			0.000	0.147	0.260	0.351	0.425	0.486	0.620	0.751	0.827	0.875	0.908	0.930
8				0.000	0.133	0.240	0.326	0.398	0.555	0.708	0.797	0.853	0.892	0.919
9					0.000	0.123	0.223	0.306	0.486	0.663	0.766	0.831	0.875	0.906
10						0.000	0.114	0.209	0.415	0.616	0.733	0.807	0.857	0.893
11							0.000	0.107	0.339	0.567	0.699	0.782	0.839	0.879
12								0.000	0.261	0.515	0.663	0.756	0.820	0.865
15									0.000	0.345	0.544	0.671	0.756	0.817
20										0.000	0.304	0.498	0.628	0.721
25											0.000	0.278	0.466	0.599
30												0.000	0.261	0.444
35													0.000	0.248
40														0.000

Remaining Principal Balance Factors

For Mortgages with an Interest Rate of 5.00% and an Original Term of:

Age of Loan in Years	5 Years	6 Years	7 Years	8 Years	9 Years	10 Years	11 Years	12 Years	15 Years	20 Years	25 Years	30 Years	35 Years	40 Years
1	0.819	0.853	0.878	0.896	0.910	0.921	0.930	0.938	0.954	0.970	0.979	0.985	0.989	0.992
2	0.630	0.699	0.749	0.786	0.815	0.838	0.856	0.872	0.906	0.939	0.958	0.970	0.978	0.983
3	0.430	0.537	0.614	0.671	0.715	0.750	0.779	0.803	0.855	0.906	0.935	0.953	0.966	0.975
4	0.220	0.367	0.472	0.550	0.610	0.659	0.698	0.731	0.802	0.871	0.911	0.936	0.953	0.965
5	0.000	0.188	0.322	0.422	0.500	0.562	0.613	0.654	0.746	0.835	0.886	0.918	0.940	0.955
6		0.000	0.165	0.289	0.384	0.461	0.523	0.574	0.687	0.796	0.859	0.899	0.926	0.945
7			0.000	0.148	0.263	0.354	0.428	0.490	0.625	0.756	0.832	0.879	0.912	0.934
8				0.000	0.135	0.242	0.329	0.402	0.560	0.714	0.802	0.859	0.896	0.923
9					0.000	0.124	0.225	0.309	0.491	0.669	0.772	0.837	0.880	0.911
10						0.000	0.115	0.211	0.419	0.622	0.739	0.813	0.863	0.898
11							0.000	0.108	0.343	0.573	0.705	0.789	0.846	0.885
12								0.000	0.264	0.521	0.670	0.764	0.827	0.871
15									0.000	0.350	0.551	0.679	0.765	0.825
20										0.000	0.310	0.506	0.638	0.731
25											0.000	0.284	0.476	0.610
30												0.000	0.267	0.455
35													0.000	0.256
40														0.000

For Mortgages with an Interest Rate of 5.25% and an Original Term of:

Age of Loan in Years	5 Years	6 Years	7 Years	8 Years	9 Years	10 Years	11 Years	12 Years	15 Years	20 Years	25 Years	30 Years	35 Years	40 Years
1	0.820	0.854	0.879	0.897	0.911	0.922	0.931	0.939	0.955	0.971	0.980	0.986	0.990	0.992
2	0.631	0.701	0.751	0.788	0.817	0.840	0.858	0.874	0.908	0.940	0.959	0.971	0.979	0.985
3	0.432	0.539	0.616	0.673	0.717	0.753	0.782	0.806	0.857	0.908	0.937	0.955	0.968	0.976
4	0.221	0.369	0.474	0.552	0.613	0.661	0.701	0.734	0.805	0.874	0.914	0.939	0.956	0.967
5	0.000	0.189	0.324	0.425	0.503	0.565	0.616	0.658	0.749	0.838	0.889	0.921	0.943	0.958
6		0.000	0.166	0.291	0.387	0.464	0.526	0.578	0.691	0.800	0.863	0.903	0.930	0.948
7			0.000	0.149	0.265	0.357	0.432	0.494	0.629	0.761	0.836	0.884	0.916	0.938
8				0.000	0.136	0.244	0.332	0.405	0.564	0.719	0.808	0.864	0.901	0.927
9					0.000	0.125	0.227	0.312	0.496	0.675	0.777	0.842	0.885	0.916
10						0.000	0.117	0.213	0.423	0.628	0.745	0.819	0.869	0.903
11							0.000	0.109	0.347	0.579	0.712	0.796	0.852	0.891
12								0.000	0.267	0.527	0.676	0.771	0.834	0.877
15									0.000	0.355	0.559	0.687	0.773	0.832
20										0.000	0.316	0.515	0.648	0.740
25											0.000	0.291	0.485	0.621
30												0.000	0.274	0.465
35													0.000	0.263
40														0.000

Remaining Principal Balance Factor

Factors For Mortgages with an Interest Rate of 5.50% and an Original Term of:

Age of Loan in Years	5 Years	6 Years	7 Years	8 Years	9 Years	10 Years	11 Years	12 Years	15 Years	20 Years	25 Years	30 Years	35 Years	40 Years
1	0.821	0.855	0.880	0.898	0.912	0.923	0.932	0.939	0.956	0.972	0.981	0.987	0.990	0.993
2	0.633	0.703	0.752	0.790	0.818	0.841	0.860	0.876	0.909	0.942	0.961	0.972	0.980	0.985
3	0.433	0.541	0.618	0.675	0.720	0.755	0.784	0.808	0.860	0.910	0.939	0.957	0.969	0.978
4	0.223	0.371	0.476	0.555	0.616	0.664	0.704	0.737	0.808	0.877	0.917	0.941	0.958	0.969
5	0.000	0.190	0.326	0.427	0.506	0.568	0.619	0.661	0.753	0.842	0.893	0.925	0.946	0.960
6		0.000	0.167	0.293	0.389	0.467	0.529	0.582	0.695	0.805	0.867	0.907	0.933	0.951
7			0.000	0.150	0.267	0.359	0.435	0.497	0.633	0.765	0.841	0.888	0.920	0.941
8				0.000	0.137	0.246	0.335	0.409	0.569	0.724	0.813	0.868	0.905	0.931
9					0.000	0.126	0.229	0.315	0.500	0.680	0.783	0.847	0.890	0.920
10						0.000	0.118	0.215	0.428	0.634	0.752	0.825	0.874	0.908
11							0.000	0.111	0.351	0.585	0.718	0.802	0.858	0.896
12								0.000	0.271	0.533	0.683	0.777	0.840	0.883
15									0.000	0.360	0.566	0.695	0.781	0.840
20										0.000	0.321	0.523	0.657	0.750
25											0.000	0.297	0.495	0.631
30												0.000	0.281	0.475
35													0.000	0.270
40														0.000

For Mortgages with an Interest Rate of 5.75% and an Original Term of:

Age of Loan in Years	5 Years	6 Years	7 Years	8 Years	9 Years	10 Years	11 Years	12 Years	15 Years	20 Years	25 Years	30 Years	35 Years	40 Years
1	0.822	0.856	0.881	0.899	0.913	0.924	0.933	0.940	0.957	0.973	0.982	0.987	0.991	0.993
2	0.634	0.704	0.754	0.791	0.820	0.843	0.862	0.877	0.911	0.943	0.962	0.974	0.981	0.986
3	0.435	0.543	0.620	0.678	0.722	0.758	0.786	0.810	0.862	0.913	0.941	0.959	0.971	0.979
4	0.224	0.372	0.478	0.557	0.618	0.667	0.707	0.740	0.811	0.880	0.919	0.944	0.960	0.971
5	0.000	0.191	0.328	0.430	0.508	0.571	0.622	0.665	0.757	0.845	0.896	0.928	0.948	0.963
6		0.000	0.169	0.295	0.392	0.470	0.533	0.585	0.699	0.809	0.871	0.910	0.936	0.954
7			0.000	0.151	0.269	0.362	0.438	0.501	0.638	0.770	0.845	0.892	0.923	0.945
8				0.000	0.138	0.248	0.338	0.412	0.573	0.729	0.818	0.873	0.910	0.935
9					0.000	0.128	0.232	0.318	0.505	0.686	0.789	0.853	0.895	0.924
10						0.000	0.119	0.218	0.432	0.640	0.758	0.831	0.880	0.913
11							0.000	0.112	0.355	0.591	0.725	0.808	0.864	0.901
12								0.000	0.274	0.539	0.690	0.784	0.846	0.889
15									0.000	0.365	0.573	0.703	0.788	0.847
20										0.000	0.327	0.532	0.667	0.759
25											0.000	0.304	0.504	0.642
30												0.000	0.288	0.485
35													0.000	0.277
40														0.000

Remaining Principal Balance Factors

For Mortgages with an Interest Rate of 6.00% and an Original Term of:

Age of Loan in Years	5 Years	6 Years	7 Years	8 Years	9 Years	10 Years	11 Years	12 Years	15 Years	20 Years	25 Years	30 Years	35 Years	40 Years
1	0.823	0.857	0.881	0.900	0.914	0.925	0.934	0.941	0.958	0.973	0.982	0.988	0.991	0.994
2	0.635	0.706	0.756	0.793	0.822	0.845	0.864	0.879	0.913	0.945	0.963	0.975	0.982	0.987
3	0.436	0.545	0.622	0.680	0.724	0.760	0.789	0.813	0.865	0.915	0.943	0.961	0.972	0.980
4	0.225	0.374	0.480	0.560	0.621	0.670	0.710	0.743	0.814	0.883	0.922	0.946	0.962	0.973
5	0.000	0.193	0.330	0.432	0.511	0.574	0.626	0.668	0.760	0.849	0.899	0.931	0.951	0.965
6		0.000	0.170	0.297	0.395	0.473	0.536	0.589	0.703	0.813	0.875	0.914	0.939	0.957
7			0.000	0.153	0.271	0.365	0.441	0.505	0.642	0.775	0.850	0.896	0.927	0.948
8				0.000	0.139	0.250	0.341	0.416	0.578	0.734	0.823	0.878	0.914	0.938
9					0.000	0.129	0.234	0.321	0.509	0.691	0.794	0.858	0.900	0.928
10						0.000	0.120	0.220	0.436	0.645	0.764	0.837	0.885	0.918
11							0.000	0.113	0.359	0.597	0.731	0.815	0.869	0.906
12								0.000	0.277	0.545	0.697	0.791	0.852	0.894
15									0.000	0.371	0.580	0.710	0.796	0.854
20										0.000	0.333	0.540	0.676	0.768
25											0.000	0.310	0.514	0.652
30												0.000	0.295	0.496
35													0.000	0.285
40												•		0.000

For Mortgages with an Interest Rate of 6.25% and an Original Term of:

Age of Loan in Years	5 Years	6 Years	7 Years	8 Years	9 Years	10 Years	11 Years	12 Years	15 Years	20 Years	25 Years	30 Years	35 Years	40 Years
1	0.824	0.858	0.882	0.901	0.915	0.926	0.935	0.942	0.958	0.974	0.983	0.988	0.992	0.994
2	0.637	0.707	0.757	0.795	0.824	0.847	0.865	0.881	0.914	0.946	0.965	0.976	0.983	0.988
3	0.438	0.547	0.624	0.682	0.727	0.762	0.791	0.815	0.867	0.917	0.945	0.963	0.974	0.981
4	0.226	0.376	0.482	0.562	0.624	0.673	0.713	0.746	0.817	0.886	0.925	0.948	0.964	0.974
5	0.000	0.194	0.331	0.434	0.514	0.577	0.629	0.671	0.764	0.852	0.903	0.933	0.953	0.967
6		0.000	0.171	0.299	0.397	0.476	0.540	0.592	0.707	0.817	0.879	0.917	0.942	0.959
7			0.000	0.154	0.273	0.368	0.445	0.508	0.646	0.779	0.854	0.900	0.930	0.951
8				0.000	0.141	0.253	0.344	0.419	0.582	0.739	0.828	0.882	0.918	0.942
9					0.000	0.130	0.236	0.324	0.514	0.696	0.799	0.863	0.904	0.932
10						0.000	0.122	0.223	0.441	0.651	0.769	0.842	0.890	0.922
11							0.000	0.115	0.363	0.603	0.737	0.821	0.875	0.911
12								0.000	0.281	0.551	0.703	0.797	0.858	0.900
15									0.000	0.376	0.588	0.718	0.803	0.861
20										0.000	0.339	0.548	0.685	0.777
25											0.000	0.317	0.523	0.662
30												0.000	0.302	0.506
35													0.000	0.292
40														0.000

Remaining Principal Balance Factors

For Mortgages with an Interest Rate of 6.50% and an Original Term of:

Age of Loan in Years	5 Years	6 Years	7 Years	8 Years	9 Years	10 Years	11 Years	12 Years	15 Years	20 Years	25 Years	30 Years	35 Years	40 Years
1	0.825	0.859	0.883	0.901	0.915	0.927	0.936	0.943	0.959	0.975	0.983	0.989	0.992	0.995
2	0.638	0.709	0.759	0.796	0.825	0.848	0.867	0.882	0.916	0.948	0.966	0.977	0.984	0.989
3	0.439	0.548	0.626	0.684	0.729	0.765	0.794	0.818	0.869	0.919	0.947	0.964	0.975	0.983
4	0.227	0.377	0.484	0.564	0.626	0.675	0.715	0.748	0.820	0.889	0.927	0.951	0.966	0.976
5	0.000	0.195	0.333	0.437	0.517	0.580	0.632	0.675	0.767	0.856	0.906	0.936	0.956	0.969
6		0.000	0.172	0.301	0.400	0.479	0.543	0.596	0.711	0.821	0.883	0.921	0.945	0.962
7			0.000	0.155	0.275	0.370	0.448	0.512	0.651	0.784	0.858	0.904	0.934	0.954
8				0.000	0.142	0.255	0.347	0.422	0.587	0.744	0.832	0.887	0.922	0.945
9					0.000	0.132	0.238	0.327	0.518	0.702	0.805	0.868	0.909	0.936
10						0.000	0.123	0.225	0.445	0.657	0.775	0.848	0.895	0.926
11							0.000	0.116	0.367	0.608	0.744	0.826	0.880	0.916
12								0.000	0.284	0.557	0.710	0.804	0.864	0.905
15									0.000	0.381	0.595	0.726	0.810	0.867
20										0.000	0.345	0.557	0.694	0.785
25											0.000	0.323	0.532	0.672
30												0.000	0.309	0.516
35													0.000	0.299
40														0.000

For Mortgages with an Interest Rate of 6.75% and an Original Term of:

Age of Loan in Years	5 Years	6 Years	7 Years	8 Years	9 Years	10 Years	11 Years	12 Years	15 Years	20 Years	25 Years	30 Years	35 Years	40 Years
1	0.826	0.860	0.884	0.902	0.916	0.927	0.937	0.944	0.960	0.976	0.984	0.989	0.993	0.995
2	0.640	0.710	0.761	0.798	0.827	0.850	0.869	0.884	0.917	0.949	0.967	0.978	0.985	0.990
3	0.441	0.550	0.628	0.686	0.731	0.767	0.796	0.820	0.872	0.921	0.949	0.966	0.977	0.984
4	0.228	0.379	0.487	0.567	0.629	0.678	0.718	0.751	0.823	0.891	0.929	0.953	0.968	0.978
5	0.000	0.196	0.335	0.439	0.520	0.583	0.635	0.678	0.771	0.859	0.909	0.939	0.958	0.971
6		0.000	0.173	0.303	0.402	0.482	0.546	0.600	0.715	0.825	0.886	0.924	0.948	0.964
7			0.000	0.156	0.277	0.373	0.451	0.516	0.655	0.788	0.863	0.908	0.937	0.956
8				0.000	0.143	0.257	0.350	0.426	0.591	0.749	0.837	0.891	0.925	0.948
9					0.000	0.133	0.241	0.330	0.523	0.707	0.810	0.873	0.913	0.940
10						0.000	0.124	0.227	0.450	0.662	0.781	0.853	0.899	0.930
11							0.000	0.117	0.371	0.614	0.750	0.832	0.885	0.920
12								0.000	0.288	0.563	0.716	0.810	0.870	0.910
15									0.000	0.386	0.602	0.733	0.817	0.873
20										0.000	0.351	0.565	0.702	0.794
25											0.000	0.330	0.541	0.682
30												0.000	0.316	0.525
35													0.000	0.307
40														0.000

Remaining Principal Balance Factors

For Mortgages with an Interest Rate of 7.00% and an Original Term of:

Age of Loan in Years	5 Years	6 Years	7 Years	8 Years	9 Years	10 Years	11 Years	12 Years	15 Years	20 Years	25 Years	30 Years	35 Years	40 Years
1	0.827	0.861	0.885	0.903	0.917	0.928	0.937	0.945	0.961	0.976	0.985	0.990	0.993	0.995
2	0.641	0.712	0.762	0.800	0.829	0.852	0.870	0.886	0.919	0.951	0.968	0.979	0.986	0.990
3	0.442	0.552	0.630	0.689	0.734	0.769	0.798	0.822	0.874	0.923	0.951	0.967	0.978	0.985
4	0.229	0.381	0.489	0.569	0.632	0.681	0.721	0.754	0.826	0.894	0.932	0.955	0.969	0.979
5	0.000	0.197	0.337	0.442	0.522	0.586	0.638	0.681	0.774	0.863	0.912	0.941	0.960	0.973
6		0.000	0.174	0.305	0.405	0.485	0.550	0.603	0.719	0.829	0.890	0.927	0.950	0.966
7			0.000	0.158	0.279	0.376	0.455	0.519	0.659	0.793	0.867	0.911	0.940	0.959
8				0.000	0.145	0.259	0.352	0.429	0.596	0.754	0.842	0.895	0.929	0.951
9					0.000	0.134	0.243	0.333	0.527	0.712	0.815	0.877	0.917	0.943
10						0.000	0.126	0.230	0.454	0.668	0.786	0.858	0.904	0.934
11							0.000	0.119	0.375	0.620	0.756	0.838	0.890	0.925
12								0.000	0.291	0.569	0.723	0.816	0.875	0.914
15									0.000	0.392	0.609	0.740	0.824	0.879
20										0.000	0.357	0.573	0.711	0.802
25											0.000	0.336	0.550	0.691
30												0.000	0.323	0.535
35													0.000	0.314
40														0.000

For Mortgages with an Interest Rate of 7.25% and an Original Term of:

Age of Loan in Years	5 Years	6 Years	7 Years	8 Years	9 Years	10 Years	11 Years	12 Years	15 Years	20 Years	25 Years	30 Years	35 Years	40 Years
1	0.828	0.862	0.886	0.904	0.918	0.929	0.938	0.946	0.962	0.977	0.985	0.990	0.994	0.996
2	0.643	0.714	0.764	0.801	0.830	0.853	0.872	0.887	0.921	0.952	0.969	0.980	0.987	0.991
3	0.444	0.554	0.632	0.691	0.736	0.772	0.801	0.825	0.876	0.925	0.952	0.969	0.979	0.986
4	0.230	0.383	0.491	0.572	0.634	0.684	0.724	0.757	0.829	0.897	0.934	0.957	0.971	0.980
5	0.000	0.198	0.339	0.444	0.525	0.589	0.642	0.685	0.778	0.866	0.915	0.944	0.962	0.974
6		0.000	0.176	0.307	0.408	0.488	0.553	0.607	0.723	0.833	0.893	0.930	0.953	0.968
7			0.000	0.159	0.281	0.379	0.458	0.523	0.663	0.797	0.871	0.915	0.943	0.961
8				0.000	0.146	0.262	0.355	0.433	0.600	0.759	0.846	0.899	0.932	0.954
9					0.000	0.136	0.245	0.336	0.532	0.718	0.820	0.882	0.921	0.946
10						0.000	0.127	0.232	0.458	0.673	0.792	0.863	0.908	0.938
11							0.000	0.120	0.379	0.626	0.761	0.843	0.895	0.929
12								0.000	0.295	0.574	0.729	0.822	0.880	0.919
15									0.000	0.397	0.616	0.747	0.831	0.885
20										0.000	0.363	0.581	0.719	0.809
25											0.000	0.342	0.559	0.701
30												0.000	0.330	0.545
35													0.000	0.321
40														0.000

Remaining Principal Balance Factors

For Mortgages with an Interest Rate of 7.50% and an Original Term of:

Age of Loan in Years	5 Years	6 Years	7 Years	8 Years	9 Years	10 Years	11 Years	12 Years	15 Years	20 Years	25 Years	30 Years	35 Years	40 Years
1	0.829	0.863	0.887	0.905	0.919	0.930	0.939	0.947	0.962	0.978	0.986	0.991	0.994	0.996
2	0.644	0.715	0.765	0.803	0.832	0.855	0.874	0.889	0.922	0.953	0.971	0.981	0.987	0.991
3	0.445	0.556	0.634	0.693	0.738	0.774	0.803	0.827	0.878	0.927	0.954	0.970	0.980	0.987
4	0.231	0.384	0.493	0.574	0.637	0.687	0.727	0.760	0.832	0.899	0.936	0.959	0.973	0.982
5	0.000	0.199	0.341	0.446	0.528	0.592	0.645	0.688	0.781	0.869	0.917	0.946	0.964	0.976
6		0.000	0.177	0.309	0.410	0.491	0.556	0.610	0.726	0.836	0.897	0.933	0.955	0.970
7			0.000	0.160	0.284	0.382	0.461	0.527	0.668	0.801	0.875	0.918	0.946	0.964
8				0.000	0.147	0.264	0.358	0.436	0.604	0.763	0.851	0.903	0.935	0.957
9					0.000	0.137	0.248	0.339	0.536	0.723	0.825	0.886	0.924	0.949
10						0.000	0.128	0.234	0.463	0.679	0.797	0.868	0.912	0.941
11							0.000	0.122	0.383	0.631	0.767	0.848	0.899	0.932
12								0.000	0.298	0.580	0.735	0.827	0.886	0.923
15									0.000	0.402	0.623	0.754	0.837	0.890
20										0.000	0.369	0.589	0.727	0.817
25											0.000	0.349	0.568	0.710
30												0.000	0.336	0.554
35													0.000	0.328
40														0.000

For Mortgages with an Interest Rate of 7.75% and an Original Term of:

Age of Loan in Years	5 Years	6 Years	7 Years	8 Years	9 Years	10 Years	11 Years	12 Years	15 Years	20 Years	25 Years	30 Years	35 Years	40 Years
1	0.830	0.864	0.888	0.906	0.920	0.931	0.940	0.947	0.963	0.978	0.986	0.991	0.994	0.996
2	0.646	0.717	0.767	0.805	0.834	0.857	0.875	0.891	0.924	0.955	0.972	0.982	0.988	0.992
3	0.447	0.558	0.636	0.695	0.740	0.776	0.805	0.829	0.881	0.929	0.956	0.971	0.981	0.988
4	0.232	0.386	0.495	0.577	0.639	0.689	0.730	0.763	0.834	0.902	0.939	0.960	0.974	0.983
5	0.000	0.200	0.343	0.449	0.531	0.595	0.648	0.691	0.784	0.872	0.920	0.948	0.966	0.978
6		0.000	0.178	0.311	0.413	0.494	0.560	0.614	0.730	0.840	0.900	0.936	0.958	0.972
7			0.000	0.161	0.286	0.384	0.464	0.530	0.672	0.806	0.878	0.922	0.949	0.966
8				0.000	0.148	0.266	0.361	0.440	0.609	0.768	0.855	0.907	0.939	0.959
9					0.000	0.138	0.250	0.342	0.541	0.728	0.830	0.890	0.928	0.952
10						0.000	0.130	0.237	0.467	0.684	0.802	0.873	0.916	0.944
11							0.000	0.123	0.387	0.637	0.773	0.854	0.904	0.936
12								0.000	0.301	0.586	0.741	0.833	0.890	0.927
15									0.000	0.407	0.629	0.761	0.843	0.896
20										0.000	0.375	0.597	0.735	0.824
25											0.000	0.355	0.577	0.719
30												0.000	0.343	0.564
35													0.000	0.336
40														0.000

Remaining Principal Balance Factors

For Mortgages with an Interest Rate of 8.00% and an Original Term of:

Age of Loan in Years	5 Years	6 Years	7 Years	8 Years	9 Years	10 Years	11 Years	12 Years	15 Years	20 Years	25 Years	30 Years	35 Years	40 Years
1	0.831	0.865	0.889	0.907	0.921	0.932	0.941	0.948	0.964	0.979	0.987	0.992	0.995	0.996
2	0.647	0.718	0.769	0.806	0.835	0.858	0.877	0.892	0.925	0.956	0.973	0.983	0.989	0.993
3	0.448	0.560	0.638	0.697	0.743	0.778	0.808	0.831	0.883	0.931	0.957	0.973	0.982	0.988
4	0.233	0.388	0.497	0.579	0.642	0.692	0.732	0.766	0.837	0.904	0.941	0.962	0.975	0.984
5	0.000	0.202	0.345	0.451	0.533	0.598	0.651	0.694	0.788	0.875	0.923	0.951	0.968	0.979
6		0.000	0.179	0.313	0.415	0.497	0.563	0.617	0.734	0.844	0.903	0.938	0.960	0.974
7			0.000	0.163	0.288	0.387	0.468	0.534	0.676	0.810	0.882	0.925	0.951	0.968
8				0.000	0.150	0.268	0.364	0.443	0.613	0.773	0.859	0.910	0.942	0.962
9					0.000	0.139	0.252	0.345	0.545	0.733	0.834	0.894	0.931	0.955
10						0.000	0.131	0.239	0.471	0.689	0.808	0.877	0.920	0.948
11							0.000	0.124	0.391	0.642	0.779	0.859	0.908	0.940
12								0.000	0.305	0.592	0.747	0.839	0.895	0.931
15									0.000	0.413	0.636	0.768	0.849	0.901
20										0.000	0.381	0.605	0.743	0.831
25											0.000	0.362	0.585	0.728
30												0.000	0.350	0.573
35													0.000	0.343
40														0.000

For Mortgages with an Interest Rate of 8.25% and an Original Term of:

Age of Loan in Years	5 Years	6 Years	7 Years	8 Years	9 Years	10 Years	11 Years	12 Years	15 Years	20 Years	25 Years	30 Years	35 Years	40 Years
1	0.831	0.866	0.890	0.908	0.922	0.933	0.942	0.949	0.965	0.979	0.987	0.992	0.995	0.997
2	0.648	0.720	0.770	0.808	0.837	0.860	0.878	0.894	0.927	0.957	0.974	0.983	0.989	0.993
3	0.450	0.561	0.640	0.699	0.745	0.781	0.810	0.834	0.885	0.933	0.959	0.974	0.983	0.989
4	0.234	0.389	0.500	0.581	0.645	0.695	0.735	0.769	0.840	0.907	0.943	0.964	0.977	0.985
5	0.000	0.203	0.347	0.454	0.536	0.601	0.654	0.698	0.791	0.878	0.925	0.953	0.970	0.980
6		0.000	0.180	0.315	0.418	0.500	0.566	0.621	0.738	0.847	0.906	0.941	0.962	0.975
7			0.000	0.164	0.290	0.390	0.471	0.537	0.680	0.814	0.886	0.928	0.954	0.970
8				0.000	0.151	0.271	0.367	0.447	0.617	0.777	0.863	0.914	0.945	0.964
9					0.000	0.141	0.255	0.349	0.549	0.738	0.839	0.898	0.935	0.958
10						0.000	0.133	0.242	0.476	0.695	0.813	0.882	0.924	0.951
11							0.000	0.126	0.395	0.648	0.784	0.864	0.912	0.943
12								0.000	0.308	0.597	0.753	0.844	0.900	0.935
15									0.000	0.418	0.643	0.774	0.855	0.906
20										0.000	0.387	0.613	0.751	0.838
25											0.000	0.368	0.594	0.736
30												0.000	0.357	0.582
35													0.000	0.250
40														0.000

Remaining Principal Balance Factors

For Mortgages with an Interest Rate of 8.50% and an Original Term of:

Age of Loan in Years	5 Years	6 Years	7 Years	8 Years	9 Years	10 Years	11 Years	12 Years	15 Years	20 Years	25 Years	30 Years	35 Years	40 Years
1	0.832	0.867	0.891	0.909	0.923	0.934	0.943	0.950	0.966	0.980	0.988	0.992	0.995	0.997
2	0.650	0.721	0.772	0.810	0.839	0.861	0.880	0.895	0.928	0.958	0.975	0.984	0.990	0.994
3	0.451	0.563	0.642	0.701	0.747	0.783	0.812	0.836	0.887	0.935	0.960	0.975	0.984	0.990
4	0.235	0.391	0.502	0.584	0.647	0.697	0.738	0.771	0.843	0.909	0.945	0.966	0.978	0.986
5	0.000	0.204	0.348	0.456	0.539	0.604	0.657	0.701	0.794	0.881	0.928	0.955	0.971	0.982
6		0.000	0.182	0.317	0.421	0.503	0.570	0.624	0.742	0.851	0.909	0.943	0.964	0.977
7			0.000	0.165	0.292	0.393	0.474	0.541	0.684	0.818	0.889	0.931	0.956	0.972
8				0.000	0.152	0.273	0.370	0.450	0.622	0.782	0.867	0.917	0.947	0.966
9					0.000	0.142	0.257	0.352	0.554	0.743	0.844	0.902	0.938	0.960
10						0.000	0.134	0.244	0.480	0.700	0.818	0.886	0.928	0.953
11							0.000	0.127	0.400	0.654	0.790	0.868	0.916	0.946
12								0.000	0.312	0.603	0.759	0.849	0.904	0.938
15									0.000	0.423	0.649	0.781	0.861	0.910
20										0.000	0.392	0.620	0.758	0.845
25											0.000	0.375	0.602	0.744
30												0.000	0.364	0.591
35													0.000	0.357
40														0.000

For Mortgages with an Interest Rate of 8.75% and an Original Term of:

Age of Loan in Years	5 Years	6 Years	7 Years	8 Years	9 Years	10 Years	11 Years	12 Years	15 Years	20 Years	25 Years	30 Years	35 Years	40 Years
1	0.833	0.867	0.892	0.910	0.924	0.935	0.943	0.951	0.966	0.981	0.988	0.993	0.995	0.997
2	0.651	0.723	0.773	0.811	0.840	0.863	0.882	0.897	0.929	0.960	0.976	0.985	0.991	0.994
3	0.453	0.565	0.645	0.704	0.749	0.785	0.814	0.838	0.889	0.937	0.962	0.976	0.985	0.991
4	0.236	0.393	0.504	0.586	0.650	0.700	0.741	0.774	0.845	0.912	0.947	0.967	0.979	0.987
5	0.000	0.205	0.350	0.458	0.541	0.607	0.660	0.704	0.797	0.884	0.930	0.957	0.973	0.983
6		0.000	0.183	0.319	0.423	0.506	0.573	0.628	0.745	0.854	0.912	0.946	0.966	0.978
7			0.000	0.166	0.294	0.396	0.477	0.545	0.688	0.822	0.893	0.934	0.958	0.973
8				0.000	0.154	0.275	0.373	0.454	0.626	0.786	0.871	0.920	0.950	0.968
9					0.000	0.144	0.259	0.355	0.558	0.747	0.848	0.906	0.941	0.962
10						0.000	0.135	0.247	0.484	0.705	0.823	0.890	0.931	0.956
11							0.000	0.129	0.404	0.659	0.795	0.873	0.920	0.949
12								0.000	0.315	0.609	0.765	0.854	0.908	0.942
15									0.000	0.428	0.656	0.787	0.866	0.915
20										0.000	0.398	0.628	0.766	0.851
25											0.000	0.381	0.611	0.753
30												0.000	0.371	0.600
35													0.000	0.364
40														0.000

Remaining Principal Balance Factors

For Mortgages with an Interest Rate of 9.00% and an Original Term of:

Age of Loan in Years	5 Years	6 Years	7 Years	8 Years	9 Years	10 Years	11 Years	12 Years	15 Years	20 Years	25 Years	30 Years	35 Years	40 Years
1	0.834	0.868	0.893	0.911	0.924	0.935	0.944	0.951	0.967	0.981	0.989	0.993	0.996	0.997
2	0.653	0.724	0.775	0.813	0.842	0.865	0.883	0.898	0.931	0.961	0.977	0.986	0.991	0.994
3	0.454	0.567	0.647	0.706	0.751	0.787	0.816	0.840	0.891	0.938	0.963	0.978	0.986	0.991
4	0.237	0.395	0.506	0.589	0.652	0.703	0.743	0.777	0.848	0.914	0.949	0.969	0.980	0.988
5	0.000	0.206	0.352	0.461	0.544	0.610	0.664	0.707	0.801	0.887	0.933	0.959	0.974	0.984
6		0.000	0.184	0.321	0.426	0.509	0.576	0.631	0.749	0.858	0.915	0.948	0.968	0.980
7			0.000	0.168	0.296	0.398	0.481	0.548	0.692	0.826	0.896	0.936	0.960	0.975
8				0.000	0.155	0.277	0.376	0.457	0.630	0.791	0.875	0.924	0.952	0.970
9					0.000	0.145	0.262	0.358	0.563	0.752	0.852	0.910	0.944	0.965
10						0.000	0.137	0.249	0.489	0.710	0.827	0.894	0.934	0.959
11							0.000	0.130	0.408	0.664	0.800	0.878	0.924	0.952
12								0.000	0.319	0.614	0.770	0.859	0.912	0.945
15									0.000	0.433	0.662	0.793	0.871	0.919
20										0.000	0.404	0.635	0.773	0.857
25											0.000	0.388	0.619	0.761
30												0.000	0.378	0.609
35													0.000	0.372
40														0.000

For Mortgages with an Interest Rate of 9.25% and an Original Term of:

Age of Loan in Years	5 Years	6 Years	7 Years	8 Years	9 Years	10 Years	11 Years	12 Years	15 Years	20 Years	25 Years	30 Years	35 Years	40 Years
1	0.835	0.869	0.893	0.911	0.925	0.936	0.945	0.952	0.968	0.982	0.989	0.994	0.996	0.998
2	0.654	0.726	0.777	0.814	0.843	0.866	0.885	0.900	0.932	0.962	0.978	0.986	0.992	0.995
3	0.456	0.569	0.649	0.708	0.753	0.790	0.819	0.842	0.893	0.940	0.965	0.979	0.987	0.992
4	0.238	0.396	0.508	0.591	0.655	0.705	0.746	0.780	0.851	0.916	0.951	0.970	0.982	0.989
5	0.000	0.207	0.354	0.463	0.547	0.613	0.667	0.710	0.804	0.890	0.935	0.961	0.976	0.985
6		0.000	0.185	0.323	0.428	0.512	0.579	0.635	0.753	0.861	0.918	0.950	0.969	0.981
7			0.000	0.169	0.299	0.401	0.484	0.552	0.696	0.830	0.899	0.939	0.962	0.977
8				0.000	0.156	0.280	0.379	0.461	0.635	0.795	0.879	0.927	0.955	0.972
9					0.000	0.146	0.264	0.361	0.567	0.757	0.857	0.913	0.947	0.967
10						0.000	0.138	0.252	0.493	0.715	0.832	0.898	0.937	0.961
11							0.000	0.132	0.412	0.670	0.805	0.882	0.927	0.955
12								0.000	0.322	0.620	0.776	0.864	0.916	0.948
15									0.000	0.439	0.669	0.799	0.876	0.923
20										0.000	0.410	0.643	0.780	0.863
25											0.000	0.394	0.627	0.768
30												0.000	0.384	0.618
35													0.000	0.379
40														0.000

Remaining Principal Balance Factors

For Mortgages with an Interest Rate of 9.50% and an Original Term of:

Age of Loan in Years	5 Years	6 Years	7 Years	8 Years	9 Years	10 Years	11 Years	12 Years	15 Years	20 Years	25 Years	30 Years	35 Years	40 Years
1	0.836	0.870	0.894	0.912	0.926	0.937	0.946	0.953	0.968	0.982	0.990	0.994	0.996	0.998
2	0.656	0.727	0.778	0.816	0.845	0.868	0.886	0.901	0.934	0.963	0.978	0.987	0.992	0.995
3	0.457	0.570	0.651	0.710	0.756	0.792	0.821	0.845	0.895	0.942	0.966	0.980	0.988	0.992
4	0.240	0.398	0.510	0.594	0.658	0.708	0.749	0.782	0.853	0.918	0.952	0.971	0.983	0.989
5	0.000	0.208	0.356	0.465	0.550	0.616	0.670	0.714	0.807	0.893	0.937	0.962	0.977	0.986
6		0.000	0.186	0.325	0.431	0.515	0.583	0.638	0.756	0.864	0.921	0.953	0.971	0.982
7			0.000	0.170	0.301	0.404	0.487	0.555	0.700	0.833	0.903	0.942	0.964	0.978
8				0.000	0.157	0.282	0.382	0.464	0.639	0.799	0.883	0.930	0.957	0.974
9					0.000	0.148	0.267	0.364	0.571	0.762	0.861	0.917	0.949	0.969
10						0.000	0.140	0.254	0.497	0.720	0.837	0.902	0.940	0.963
11							0.000	0.133	0.416	0.675	0.810	0.886	0.931	0.957
12								0.000	0.326	0.625	0.781	0.869	0.920	0.951
15									0.000	0.444	0.675	0.805	0.881	0.927
20										0.000	0.416	0.650	0.787	0.869
25											0.000	0.400	0.635	0.776
30												0.000	0.391	0.626
35													0.000	0.386
40														0.000

For Mortgages with an Interest Rate of 9.75% and an Original Term of:

Age of Loan in Years	5 Years	6 Years	7 Years	8 Years	9 Years	10 Years	11 Years	12 Years	15 Years	20 Years	25 Years	30 Years	35 Years	40 Years
1	0.837	0.871	0.895	0.913	0.927	0.938	0.947	0.954	0.969	0.983	0.990	0.994	0.996	0.998
2	0.657	0.729	0.780	0.818	0.846	0.869	0.888	0.903	0.935	0.964	0.979	0.988	0.993	0.995
3	0.459	0.572	0.653	0.712	0.758	0.794	0.823	0.847	0.897	0.943	0.967	0.981	0.988	0.993
4	0.241	0.400	0.512	0.596	0.660	0.711	0.751	0.785	0.856	0.921	0.954	0.973	0.984	0.990
5	0.000	0.210	0.358	0.468	0.552	0.619	0.673	0.717	0.810	0.895	0.940	0.964	0.978	0.987
6		0.000	0.188	0.327	0.434	0.518	0.586	0.642	0.760	0.868	0.923	0.955	0.973	0.983
7			0.000	0.171	0.303	0.407	0.490	0.559	0.704	0.837	0.906	0.944	0.966	0.980
8				0.000	0.159	0.284	0.385	0.468	0.643	0.803	0.886	0.933	0.959	0.975
9					0.000	0.149	0.269	0.367	0.576	0.766	0.865	0.920	0.952	0.971
10						0.000	0.141	0.257	0.501	0.725	0.841	0.906	0.943	0.966
11							0.000	0.134	0.420	0.680	0.815	0.890	0.934	0.960
12								0.000	0.330	0.631	0.786	0.873	0.924	0.954
15									0.000	0.449	0.681	0.811	0.886	0.931
20										0.000	0.422	0.657	0.793	0.875
25											0.000	0.407	0.643	0.783
30												0.000	0.398	0.634
35													0.000	0.393
40														0.000

Remaining Principal Balance Factors

For Mortgages with an Interest Rate of 10.00% and an Original Term of:

Age of Loan in Years	5 Years	6 Years	7 Years	8 Years	9 Years	10 Years	11 Years	12 Years	15 Years	20 Years	25 Years	30 Years	35 Years	40 Years
1	0.838	0.872	0.896	0.914	0.928	0.939	0.947	0.955	0.970	0.983	0.991	0.994	0.997	0.998
2	0.658	0.730	0.781	0.819	0.848	0.871	0.889	0.904	0.936	0.965	0.980	0.988	0.993	0.996
3	0.460	0.574	0.655	0.714	0.760	0.796	0.825	0.849	0.899	0.945	0.969	0.982	0.989	0.993
4	0.242	0.401	0.514	0.598	0.663	0.713	0.754	0.788	0.858	0.923	0.956	0.974	0.985	0.991
5	0.000	0.211	0.360	0.470	0.555	0.622	0.676	0.720	0.813	0.898	0.942	0.966	0.980	0.988
6		0.000	0.189	0.329	0.436	0.521	0.589	0.645	0.763	0.871	0.926	0.957	0.974	0.984
7			0.000	0.173	0.305	0.410	0.494	0.562	0.708	0.841	0.909	0.946	0.968	0.981
8				0.000	0.160	0.286	0.388	0.471	0.647	0.807	0.890	0.935	0.961	0.977
9					0.000	0.150	0.271	0.370	0.580	0.771	0.869	0.923	0.954	0.972
10						0.000	0.142	0.259	0.506	0.730	0.846	0.909	0.946	0.968
11							0.000	0.136	0.424	0.685	0.820	0.894	0.937	0.962
12								0.000	0.333	0.636	0.792	0.878	0.927	0.956
15									0.000	0.454	0.688	0.817	0.891	0.934
20										0.000	0.428	0.664	0.800	0.880
25											0.000	0.413	0.651	0.790
30												0.000	0.405	0.643
35													0.000	0.400
40														0.000

For Mortgages with an Interest Rate of 10.25% and an Original Term of:

Age of Loan in Years	5 Years	6 Years	7 Years	8 Years	9 Years	10 Years	11 Years	12 Years	15 Years	20 Years	25 Years	30 Years	35 Years	40 Years
1	0.839	0.873	0.897	0.915	0.929	0.939	0.948	0.955	0.970	0.984	0.991	0.995	0.997	0.998
2	0.660	0.732	0.783	0.821	0.850	0.872	0.891	0.906	0.937	0.966	0.981	0.989	0.993	0.996
3	0.462	0.576	0.657	0.716	0.762	0.798	0.827	0.851	0.901	0.947	0.970	0.982	0.990	0.994
4	0.243	0.403	0.517	0.601	0.665	0.716	0.757	0.790	0.861	0.925	0.957	0.975	0.985	0.991
5	0.000	0.212	0.362	0.473	0.558	0.625	0.679	0.723	0.816	0.901	0.944	0.967	0.981	0.989
6		0.000	0.190	0.331	0.439	0.524	0.592	0.648	0.767	0.874	0.929	0.959	0.976	0.986
7			0.000	0.174	0.307	0.412	0.497	0.566	0.712	0.844	0.912	0.949	0.970	0.982
8				0.000	0.161	0.289	0.391	0.475	0.651	0.812	0.893	0.938	0.964	0.978
9					0.000	0.152	0.274	0.373	0.584	0.775	0.873	0.926	0.956	0.974
10						0.000	0.144	0.261	0.510	0.735	0.850	0.913	0.949	0.970
11							0.000	0.137	0.428	0.691	0.825	0.898	0.940	0.964
12								0.000	0.337	0.641	0.797	0.882	0.931	0.959
15									0.000	0.459	0.694	0.822	0.895	0.938
20										0.000	0.433	0.671	0.806	0.885
25											0.000	0.419	0.658	0.797
30												0.000	0.411	0.651
35													0.000	0.407
40														0.000

Remaining Principal Balance Factors

For Mortgages with an Interest Rate of 10.50% and an Original Term of:

Age of Loan in Years	5 Years	6 Years	7 Years	8 Years	9 Years	10 Years	11 Years	12 Years	15 Years	20 Years	25 Years	30 Years	35 Years	40 Years
1	0.839	0.874	0.898	0.916	0.929	0.940	0.949	0.956	0.971	0.984	0.991	0.995	0.997	0.998
2	0.661	0.733	0.784	0.822	0.851	0.874	0.892	0.907	0.939	0.967	0.982	0.989	0.994	0.996
3	0.463	0.578	0.659	0.718	0.764	0.800	0.829	0.853	0.903	0.948	0.971	0.983	0.990	0.994
4	0.244	0.405	0.519	0.603	0.668	0.719	0.759	0.793	0.863	0.927	0.959	0.976	0.986	0.992
5	0.000	0.213	0.364	0.475	0.561	0.628	0.682	0.726	0.819	0.903	0.946	0.969	0.982	0.989
6		0.000	0.191	0.333	0.442	0.527	0.596	0.652	0.770	0.877	0.931	0.960	0.977	0.986
7			0.000	0.175	0.309	0.415	0.500	0.570	0.716	0.848	0.915	0.951	0.971	0.983
8				0.000	0.163	0.291	0.394	0.478	0.656	0.816	0.897	0.941	0.965	0.980
9					0.000	0.153	0.276	0.377	0.589	0.780	0.876	0.929	0.959	0.976
10						0.000	0.145	0.264	0.514	0.740	0.854	0.916	0.951	0.971
11							0.000	0.139	0.432	0.696	0.829	0.902	0.943	0.967
12								0.000	0.340	0.647	0.802	0.886	0.934	0.961
15									0.000	0.464	0.700	0.828	0.900	0.941
20										0.000	0.439	0.678	0.812	0.890
25											0.000	0.426	0.666	0.804
30												0.000	0.418	0.659
35													0.000	0.413
40														0.000

For Mortgages with an Interest Rate of 10.75% and an Original Term of:

Age of Loan in Years	5 Years	6 Years	7 Years	8 Years	9 Years	10 Years	11 Years	12 Years	15 Years	20 Years	25 Years	30 Years	35 Years	40 Years
1	0.840	0.875	0.899	0.917	0.930	0.941	0.950	0.957	0.972	0.985	0.992	0.995	0.997	0.998
2	0.663	0.735	0.786	0.824	0.853	0.875	0.894	0.909	0.940	0.968	0.982	0.990	0.994	0.997
3	0.465	0.580	0.661	0.720	0.766	0.802	0.831	0.855	0.905	0.950	0.972	0.984	0.991	0.995
4	0.245	0.407	0.521	0.605	0.670	0.721	0.762	0.795	0.866	0.929	0.960	0.978	0.987	0.993
5	0.000	0.214	0.365	0.477	0.563	0.631	0.685	0.729	0.822	0.906	0.948	0.970	0.983	0.990
6		0.000	0.193	0.335	0.444	0.530	0.599	0.655	0.774	0.880	0.933	0.962	0.978	0.987
7			0.000	0.176	0.312	0.418	0.503	0.573	0.720	0.851	0.918	0.953	0.973	0.984
8				0.000	0.164	0.293	0.397	0.482	0.660	0.820	0.900	0.943	0.967	0.981
9					0.000	0.154	0.279	0.380	0.593	0.784	0.880	0.932	0.961	0.977
10						0.000	0.147	0.266	0.519	0.745	0.858	0.919	0.954	0.973
11							0.000	0.140	0.436	0.701	0.834	0.906	0.946	0.969
12								0.000	0.344	0.652	0.807	0.890	0.937	0.963
15									0.000	0.470	0.706	0.833	0.904	0.944
20										0.000	0.445	0.685	0.819	0.895
25											0.000	0.432	0.673	0.810
30												0.000	0.424	0.666
35													0.000	0.420
40														0.000

Remaining Principal Balance Factors

For Mortgages with an Interest Rate of 11.00% and an Original Term of:

Age of Loan in Years	5 Years	6 Years	7 Years	8 Years	9 Years	10 Years	11 Years	12 Years	15 Years	20 Years	25 Years	30 Years	35 Years	40 Years
1	0.841	0.875	0.900	0.917	0.931	0.942	0.950	0.957	0.972	0.985	0.992	0.995	0.997	0.999
2	0.664	0.736	0.788	0.825	0.854	0.877	0.895	0.910	0.941	0.969	0.983	0.990	0.995	0.997
3	0.466	0.581	0.662	0.722	0.768	0.805	0.833	0.857	0.907	0.951	0.973	0.985	0.991	0.995
4	0.246	0.408	0.523	0.608	0.673	0.724	0.765	0.798	0.868	0.931	0.962	0.979	0.988	0.993
5	0.000	0.215	0.367	0.480	0.566	0.634	0.688	0.732	0.825	0.908	0.950	0.972	0.984	0.991
6		0.000	0.194	0.337	0.447	0.533	0.602	0.659	0.777	0.883	0.936	0.964	0.979	0.988
7			0.000	0.178	0.314	0.421	0.507	0.577	0.724	0.855	0.920	0.955	0.974	0.985
8				0.000	0.165	0.296	0.400	0.485	0.664	0.823	0.903	0.945	0.969	0.982
9					0.000	0.156	0.281	0.383	0.597	0.788	0.884	0.935	0.963	0.979
10						0.000	0.148	0.269	0.523	0.749	0.862	0.923	0.956	0.975
11							0.000	0.142	0.440	0.706	0.838	0.909	0.948	0.970
12								0.000	0.347	0.657	0.812	0.894	0.940	0.965
15									0.000	0.475	0.712	0.838	0.908	0.947
20										0.000	0.451	0.691	0.824	0.899
25											0.000	0.438	0.680	0.817
30												0.000	0.431	0.674
35													0.000	0.427
40														0.000

For Mortgages with an Interest Rate of 11.25% and an Original Term of:

Age of Loan in Years	5 Years	6 Years	7 Years	8 Years	9 Years	10 Years	11 Years	12 Years	15 Years	20 Years	25 Years	30 Years	35 Years	40 Years
1	0.842	0.876	0.900	0.918	0.932	0.943	0.951	0.958	0.973	0.986	0.992	0.996	0.998	0.999
2	0.666	0.738	0.789	0.827	0.856	0.878	0.897	0.911	0.942	0.970	0.984	0.991	0.995	0.997
3	0.468	0.583	0.664	0.725	0.770	0.807	0.836	0.859	0.909	0.952	0.974	0.986	0.992	0.995
4	0.247	0.410	0.525	0.610	0.675	0.726	0.767	0.801	0.871	0.933	0.963	0.980	0.989	0.994
5	0.000	0.217	0.369	0.482	0.569	0.636	0.691	0.735	0.828	0.911	0.951	0.973	0.985	0.991
6		0.000	0.195	0.339	0.449	0.536	0.605	0.662	0.780	0.886	0.938	0.966	0.981	.989
7			0.000	0.179	0.316	0.424	0.510	0.580	0.727	0.858	0.923	0.957	0.976	0.986
8				0.000	0.167	0.298	0.403	0.488	0.668	0.827	0.906	0.948	0.971	0.983
9					0.000	0.157	0.283	0.386	0.601	0.793	0.887	0.937	0.965	0.980
10						0.000	0.150	0.271	0.527	0.754	0.866	0.926	0.958	0.976
11							0.000	0.143	0.444	0.711	0.843	0.913	0.951	0.972
12								0.000	0.351	0.662	0.816	0.898	0.943	0.967
15									0.000	0.480	0.717	0.843	0.912	0.950
20										0.000	0.456	0.698	0.830	0.904
25											0.000	0.444	0.687	0.823
30												0.000	0.437	0.681
35													0.000	0.434
40														0.000

Remaining Principal Balance Factors

For Mortgages with an Interest Rate of 11.50% and an Original Term of:

Age of Loan in Years	5 Years	6 Years	7 Years	8 Years	9 Years	10 Years	11 Years	12 Years	15 Years	20 Years	25 Years	30 Years	35 Years	40 Years
1	0.843	0.877	0.901	0.919	0.933	0.943	0.952	0.959	0.973	0.986	0.993	0.996	0.998	0.999
2	0.667	0.739	0.791	0.828	0.857	0.880	0.898	0.913	0.944	0.971	0.984	0.991	0.995	0.997
3	0.470	0.585	0.666	0.727	0.773	0.809	0.838	0.861	0.910	0.954	0.975	0.986	0.992	0.996
4	0.248	0.412	0.527	0.612	0.678	0.729	0.770	0.803	0.873	0.935	0.965	0.981	0.989	0.994
5	0.000	0.218	0.371	0.485	0.571	0.639	0.694	0.738	0.831	0.913	0.953	0.974	0.986	0.992
6		0.000	0.196	0.341	0.452	0.539	0.609	0.665	0.784	0.889	0.940	0.967	0.982	0.990
7			0.000	0.180	0.318	0.426	0.513	0.584	0.731	0.861	0.925	0.959	0.977	0.987
8				0.000	0.168	0.300	0.406	0.492	0.672	0.831	0.909	0.950	0.972	0.984
9					0.000	0.159	0.286	0.389	0.606	0.797	0.891	0.940	0.967	0.981
10						0.000	0.151	0.274	0.531	0.759	0.870	0.929	0.960	0.978
11							0.000	0.145	0.448	0.716	0.847	0.916	0.953	0.974
12								0.000	0.354	0.667	0.821	0.902	0.945	0.969
15									0.000	0.485	0.723	0.848	0.915	0.953
20										0.000	0.462	0.704	0.836	0.908
25											0.000	0.450	0.694	0.829
30												0.000	0.444	0.689
35													0.000	0.440
40														0.000

For Mortgages with an Interest Rate of 11.75% and an Original Term of:

Age of Loan in Years	5 Years	6 Years	7 Years	8 Years	9 Years	10 Years	11 Years	12 Years	15 Years	20 Years	25 Years	30 Years	35 Years	40 Years
1	0.844	0.878	0.902	0.920	0.933	0.944	0.953	0.960	0.974	0.987	0.993	0.996	0.998	0.999
2	0.668	0.741	0.792	0.830	0.859	0.881	0.899	0.914	0.945	0.972	0.985	0.992	0.996	0.998
3	0.471	0.587	0.668	0.729	0.775	0.811	0.840	0.863	0.912	0.955	0.976	0.987	0.993	0.996
4	0.249	0.414	0.529	0.615	0.680	0.731	0.772	0.806	0.875	0.936	0.966	0.982	0.990	0.994
5	0.000	0.219	0.373	0.487	0.574	0.642	0.697	0.741	0.834	0.915	0.955	0.975	0.987	0.993
6		0.000	0.197	0.343	0.455	0.542	0.612	0.669	0.787	0.891	0.942	0.969	0.983	0.990
7			0.000	0.182	0.320	0.429	0.516	0.587	0.735	0.865	0.928	0.961	0.978	0.988
8				0.000	0.170	0.302	0.409	0.495	0.676	0.835	0.912	0.952	0.974	0.985
9					0.000	0.160	0.288	0.392	0.610	0.801	0.894	0.942	0.968	0.982
10						0.000	0.152	0.276	0.535	0.763	0.874	0.931	0.962	0.979
11							0.000	0.146	0.452	0.720	0.851	0.919	0.956	0.975
12								0.000	0.358	0.672	0.826	0.905	0.948	0.971
15									0.000	0.490	0.729	0.852	0.919	0.955
20										0.000	0.468	0.711	0.841	0.912
25											0.000	0.456	0.701	0.835
30												0.000	0.450	0.696
35													0.000	0.447
40														0.000

Remaining Principal Balance Factors

For Mortgages with an Interest Rate of 12.00% and an Original Term of:

Age of Loan in Years	5 Years	6 Years	7 Years	8 Years	9 Years	10 Years	11 Years	12 Years	15 Years	20 Years	25 Years	30 Years	35 Years	40 Years
1	0.845	0.879	0.903	0.921	0.934	0.945	0.953	0.960	0.975	0.987	0.993	0.996	0.998	0.999
2	0.670	0.742	0.794	0.831	0.860	0.883	0.901	0.915	0.946	0.973	0.986	0.992	0.996	0.998
3	0.473	0.589	0.670	0.731	0.777	0.813	0.842	0.865	0.914	0.956	0.977	0.988	0.993	0.996
4	0.250	0.415	0.531	0.617	0.683	0.734	0.775	0.808	0.877	0.938	0.967	0.982	0.990	0.995
5	0.000	0.220	0.375	0.489	0.577	0.645	0.700	0.744	0.837	0.917	0.957	0.977	0.987	0.993
6		0.000	0.199	0.345	0.457	0.545	0.615	0.672	0.790	0.894	0.944	0.970	0.984	0.991
7			0.000	0.183	0.323	0.432	0.519	0.590	0.738	0.868	0.930	0.963	0.980	0.989
8				0.000	0.171	0.305	0.412	0.499	0.680	0.838	0.915	0.954	0.975	0.986
9					0.000	0.161	0.291	0.395	0.614	0.805	0.897	0.945	0.970	0.984
10						0.000	0.154	0.279	0.540	0.767	0.878	0.934	0.964	0.980
11							0.000	0.148	0.456	0.725	0.855	0.922	0.958	0.977
12								0.000	0.361	0.677	0.830	0.909	0.950	0.973
15									0.000	0.495	0.734	0.857	0.922	0.958
20										0.000	0.473	0.717	0.846	0.916
25											0.000	0.462	0.708	0.840
30												0.000	0.457	0.703
35													0.000	0.453
40														0.000

For Mortgages with an Interest Rate of 12.25% and an Original Term of:

Age of Loan in Years	5 Years	6 Years	7 Years	8 Years	9 Years	10 Years	11 Years	12 Years	15 Years	20 Years	25 Years	30 Years	35 Years	40 Years
1	0.846	0.880	0.904	0.922	0.935	0.946	0.954	0.961	0.975	0.988	0.994	0.997	0.998	0.999
2	0.671	0.744	0.795	0.833	0.862	0.884	0.902	0.917	0.947	0.974	0.986	0.993	0.996	0.998
3	0.474	0.590	0.672	0.733	0.779	0.815	0.844	0.867	0.915	0.958	0.978	0.988	0.994	0.997
4	0.251	0.417	0.534	0.620	0.685	0.736	0.777	0.811	0.880	0.940	0.969	0.983	0.991	0.995
5	0.000	0.221	0.377	0.492	0.579	0.648	0.703	0.747	0.839	0.920	0.958	0.978	0.988	0.994
6		0.000	0.200	0.347	0.460	0.548	0.618	0.675	0.794	0.897	0.946	0.971	0.985	0.992
7			0.000	0.184	0.325	0.435	0.523	0.594	0.742	0.871	0.933	0.964	0.981	0.990
8				0.000	0.172	0.307	0.415	0.502	0.684	0.842	0.918	0.956	0.976	0.987
9					0.000	0.163	0.293	0.399	0.618	0.809	0.901	0.947	0.972	0.985
10						0.000	0.155	0.282	0.544	0.772	0.881	0.937	0.966	0.982
11							0.000	0.149	0.460	0.730	0.859	0.925	0.960	0.978
12								0.000	0.365	0.682	0.835	0.912	0.953	0.974
15									0.000	0.500	0.740	0.862	0.926	0.960
20										0.000	0.479	0.723	0.851	0.920
25											0.000	0.468	0.714	0.846
30												0.000	0.463	0.710
35													0.000	0.460
40														0.000

Remaining Principal Balance Factors

For Mortgages with an Interest Rate of 12.50% and an Original Term of:

Age of Loan in Years	5 Years	6 Years	7 Years	8 Years	9 Years	10 Years	11 Years	12 Years	15 Years	20 Years	25 Years	30 Years	35 Years	40 Years
1	0.846	0.881	0.905	0.922	0.936	0.946	0.955	0.962	0.976	0.988	0.994	0.997	0.998	0.999
2	0.673	0.745	0.797	0.834	0.863	0.886	0.904	0.918	0.948	0.974	0.987	0.993	0.996	0.998
3	0.476	0.592	0.674	0.735	0.781	0.817	0.846	0.869	0.917	0.959	0.979	0.989	0.994	0.997
4	0.253	0.419	0.536	0.622	0.688	0.739	0.780	0.813	0.882	0.942	0.970	0.984	0.992	0.996
5	0.000	0.222	0.379	0.494	0.582	0.651	0.705	0.750	0.842	0.922	0.960	0.979	0.989	0.994
6		0.000	0.201	0.349	0.462	0.551	0.621	0.678	0.797	0.899	0.948	0.973	0.986	0.992
7			0.000	0.186	0.327	0.438	0.526	0.597	0.746	0.874	0.935	0.966	0.982	0.990
8				0.000	0.174	0.309	0.418	0.506	0.688	0.845	0.920	0.958	0.978	0.988
9					0.000	0.164	0.295	0.402	0.622	0.813	0.904	0.949	0.973	0.986
10						0.000	0.157	0.284	0.548	0.776	0.885	0.939	0.968	0.983
11							0.000	0.151	0.464	0.735	0.863	0.928	0.962	0.980
12								0.000	0.368	0.687	0.839	0.915	0.955	0.976
15									0.000	0.505	0.745	0.866	0.929	0.962
20										0.000	0.485	0.729	0.856	0.923
25											0.000	0.474	0.721	0.851
30												0.000	0.469	0.717
35													0.000	0.466
40														0.000

For Mortgages with an Interest Rate of 12.75% and an Original Term of:

Age of Loan in Years	5 Years	6 Years	7 Years	8 Years	9 Years	10 Years	11 Years	12 Years	15 Years	20 Years	25 Years	30 Years	35 Years	40 Years
1	0.847	0.881	0.905	0.923	0.937	0.947	0.955	0.962	0.976	0.988	0.994	0.997	0.998	0.999
2	0.674	0.747	0.798	0.836	0.865	0.887	0.905	0.919	0.949	0.975	0.987	0.993	0.997	0.998
3	0.477	0.594	0.676	0.737	0.783	0.819	0.847	0.871	0.919	0.960	0.980	0.989	0.994	0.997
4	0.254	0.421	0.538	0.624	0.690	0.741	0.782	0.815	0.884	0.943	0.971	0.985	0.992	0.996
5	0.000	0.224	0.381	0.496	0.585	0.653	0.708	0.753	0.845	0.924	0.961	0.980	0.989	0.994
6		0.000	0.202	0.351	0.465	0.554	0.624	0.682	0.800	0.902	0.950	0.974	0.986	0.993
7			0.000	0.187	0.329	0.440	0.529	0.601	0.749	0.877	0.937	0.967	0.983	0.991
8				0.000	0.175	0.312	0.421	0.509	0.692	0.849	0.923	0.960	0.979	0.989
9					0.000	0.166	0.298	0.405	0.626	0.817	0.907	0.951	0.975	0.987
10						0.000	0.158	0.287	0.552	0.780	0.888	0.942	0.969	0.984
11							0.000	0.152	0.468	0.739	0.867	0.931	0.964	0.981
12								0.000	0.372	0.692	0.843	0.918	0.957	0.977
15									0.000	0.510	0.750	0.870	0.932	0.964
20										0.000	0.490	0.735	0.861	0.927
25											0.000	0.480	0.727	0.856
30												0.000	0.475	0.723
35													0.000	0.473
40														0.000

Remaining Principal Balance Factors

For Mortgages with an Interest Rate of 13.00% and an Original Term of:

Age of Loan in Years	5 Years	6 Years	7 Years	8 Years	9 Years	10 Years	11 Years	12 Years	15 Years	20 Years	25 Years	30 Years	35 Years	40 Years
1	0.848	0.882	0.906	0.924	0.937	0.948	0.956	0.963	0.977	0.989	0.994	0.997	0.998	0.999
2	0.675	0.748	0.800	0.837	0.866	0.888	0.906	0.921	0.950	0.976	0.988	0.994	0.997	0.998
3	0.479	0.596	0.678	0.739	0.785	0.821	0.849	0.873	0.920	0.961	0.981	0.990	0.995	0.997
4	0.255	0.422	0.540	0.626	0.692	0.744	0.785	0.818	0.886	0.945	0.972	0.986	0.993	0.996
5	0.000	0.225	0.383	0.499	0.587	0.656	0.711	0.756	0.847	0.926	0.963	0.981	0.990	0.995
6		0.000	0.204	0.354	0.468	0.557	0.627	0.685	0.803	0.905	0.952	0.975	0.987	0.993
7			0.000	0.188	0.331	0.443	0.532	0.604	0.753	0.880	0.940	0.969	0.984	0.992
8				0.000	0.176	0.314	0.424	0.512	0.695	0.852	0.926	0.962	0.980	0.990
9					0.000	0.167	0.300	0.408	0.630	0.821	0.910	0.954	0.976	0.987
10						0.000	0.160	0.289	0.556	0.785	0.891	0.944	0.971	0.985
11							0.000	0.154	0.472	0.744	0.871	0.934	0.966	0.982
12								0.000	0.376	0.697	0.847	0.922	0.959	0.979
15									0.000	0.515	0.755	0.874	0.935	0.966
20										0.000	0.496	0.741	0.866	0.930
25											0.000	0.486	0.733	0.861
30												0.000	0.481	0.730
35													0.000	0.479
40														0.000

For Mortgages with an Interest Rate of 13.25% and an Original Term of:

Age of Loan in Years	5 Years	6 Years	7 Years	8 Years	9 Years	10 Years	11 Years	12 Years	15 Years	20 Years	25 Years	30 Years	35 Years	40 Years
1	0.849	0.883	0.907	0.925	0.938	0.949	0.957	0.964	0.977	0.989	0.995	0.997	0.999	0.999
2	0.677	0.750	0.801	0.839	0.867	0.890	0.908	0.922	0.952	0.977	0.988	0.994	0.997	0.998
3	0.480	0.598	0.680	0.741	0.787	0.823	0.851	0.874	0.922	0.963	0.981	0.991	0.995	0.997
4	0.256	0.424	0.542	0.629	0.695	0.746	0.787	0.820	0.888	0.946	0.973	0.986	0.993	0.996
5	0.000	0.226	0.385	0.501	0.590	0.659	0.714	0.758	0.850	0.928	0.964	0.982	0.991	0.995
6		0.000	0.205	0.356	0.470	0.559	0.631	0.688	0.806	0.907	0.954	0.976	0.988	0.994
7			0.000	0.189	0.334	0.446	0.535	0.608	0.756	0.883	0.942	0.970	0.985	0.992
8				0.000	0.178	0.316	0.427	0.516	0.699	0.856	0.928	0.963	0.981	0.990
9					0.000	0.169	0.303	0.411	0.634	0.824	0.912	0.956	0.977	0.988
10						0.000	0.161	0.292	0.560	0.789	0.895	0.946	0.973	0.986
11							0.000	0.155	0.476	0.748	0.874	0.936	0.967	0.983
12								0.000	0.379	0.702	0.851	0.924	0.961	0.980
15									0.000	0.520	0.760	0.878	0.938	0.968
20										0.000	0.501	0.747	0.870	0.933
25											0.000	0.492	0.740	0.866
30												0.000	0.487	0.736
35													0.000	0.485
40														0.000

Remaining Principal Balance Factors

For Mortgages with an Interest Rate of 13.50% and an Original Term of:

Age of Loan in Years	5 Years	6 Years	7 Years	8 Years	9 Years	10 Years	11 Years	12 Years	15 Years	20 Years	25 Years	30 Years	35 Years	40 Years
1	0.850	0.884	0.908	0.925	0.939	0.949	0.957	0.964	0.978	0.989	0.995	0.997	0.999	0.999
2	0.678	0.751	0.802	0.840	0.869	0.891	0.909	0.923	0.953	0.977	0.989	0.994	0.997	0.999
3	0.482	0.599	0.682	0.743	0.789	0.825	0.853	0.876	0.924	0.964	0.982	0.991	0.995	0.998
4	0.257	0.426	0.544	0.631	0.697	0.749	0.790	0.823	0.890	0.948	0.974	0.987	0.993	0.997
5	0.000	0.227	0.386	0.504	0.592	0.662	0.717	0.761	0.853	0.930	0.965	0.983	0.991	0.996
6		0.000	0.206	0.358	0.473	0.562	0.634	0.691	0.809	0.909	0.955	0.978	0.989	0.994
7			0.000	0.191	0.336	0.449	0.538	0.611	0.760	0.886	0.944	0.972	0.986	0.993
8				0.000	0.179	0.319	0.430	0.519	0.703	0.859	0.930	0.965	0.982	0.991
9					0.000	0.170	0.305	0.414	0.638	0.828	0.915	0.957	0.978	0.989
10						0.000	0.163	0.294	0.564	0.793	0.898	0.949	0.974	0.987
11							0.000	0.157	0.480	0.753	0.878	0.939	0.969	0.984
12								0.000	0.383	0.707	0.855	0.927	0.963	0.981
15									0.000	0.525	0.765	0.882	0.940	0.970
20										0.000	0.507	0.752	0.874	0.936
25											0.000	0.498	0.746	0.871
30												0.000	0.493	0.742
35													0.000	0.491
40														0.000

For Mortgages with an Interest Rate of 13.75% and an Original Term of:

Age of Loan in Years	5 Years	6 Years	7 Years	8 Years	9 Years	10 Years	11 Years	12 Years	15 Years	20 Years	25 Years	30 Years	35 Years	40 Years
1	0.851	0.885	0.909	0.926	0.940	0.950	0.958	0.965	0.978	0.990	0.995	0.998	0.999	0.999
2	0.679	0.753	0.804	0.842	0.870	0.892	0.910	0.924	0.954	0.978	0.989	0.995	0.997	0.999
3	0.483	0.601	0.684	0.745	0.791	0.827	0.855	0.878	0.925	0.965	0.983	0.991	0.996	0.998
4	0.258	0.427	0.546	0.633	0.700	0.751	0.792	0.825	0.893	0.949	0.975	0.988	0.994	0.997
5	0.000	0.228	0.388	0.506	0.595	0.665	0.720	0.764	0.855	0.932	0.967	0.983	0.992	0.996
6		0.000	0.207	0.360	0.475	0.565	0.637	0.694	0.812	0.912	0.957	0.979	0.989	0.995
7			0.000	0.192	0.338	0.452	0.542	0.614	0.763	0.889	0.946	0.973	0.986	0.993
8				0.000	0.181	0.321	0.433	0.523	0.707	0.862	0.933	0.967	0.983	0.992
9					0.000	0.171	0.308	0.417	0.642	0.832	0.918	0.959	0.980	0.990
10						0.000	0.164	0.297	0.568	0.797	0.901	0.951	0.975	0.988
11							0.000	0.159	0.483	0.757	0.881	0.941	0.971	0.985
12								0.000	0.386	0.711	0.859	0.930	0.965	0.982
15									0.000	0.530	0.770	0.886	0.943	0.971
20										0.000	0.512	0.758	0.879	0.939
25											0.000	0.504	0.751	0.875
30												0.000	0.499	0.748
35													0.000	0.497
40														0.000

Remaining Principal Balance Factors

For Mortgages with an Interest Rate of 14.00% and an Original Term of:

Age of Loan in Years	5 Years	6 Years	7 Years	8 Years	9 Years	10 Years	11 Years	12 Years	15 Years	20 Years	25 Years	30 Years	35 Years	40 Years
1	0.851	0.886	0.909	0.927	0.940	0.951	0.959	0.965	0.979	0.990	0.995	0.998	0.999	0.999
2	0.681	0.754	0.805	0.843	0.872	0.894	0.911	0.926	0.955	0.979	0.990	0.995	0.998	0.999
3	0.485	0.603	0.686	0.747	0.793	0.829	0.857	0.880	0.927	0.966	0.984	0.992	0.996	0.998
4	0.259	0.429	0.548	0.636	0.702	0.754	0.794	0.827	0.895	0.951	0.976	0.988	0.994	0.997
5	0.000	0.229	0.390	0.508	0.598	0.667	0.722	0.767	0.858	0.934	0.968	0.984	0.992	0.996
6		0.000	0.209	0.362	0.478	0.568	0.640	0.697	0.815	0.914	0.959	0.980	0.990	0.995
7			0.000	0.193	0.340	0.454	0.545	0.618	0.767	0.891	0.948	0.974	0.987	0.994
8				0.000	0.182	0.323	0.436	0.526	0.711	0.865	0.935	0.968	0.984	0.992
9					0.000	0.173	0.310	0.420	0.646	0.835	0.921	0.961	0.981	0.990
10						0.000	0.166	0.299	0.572	0.801	0.904	0.953	0.977	0.988
11							0.000	0.160	0.487	0.761	0.885	0.943	0.972	0.986
12								0.000	0.390	0.716	0.863	0.933	0.967	0.983
15									0.000	0.534	0.775	0.890	0.945	0.973
20										0.000	0.517	0.763	0.883	0.942
25											0.000	0.509	0.757	0.879
30												0.000	0.505	0.754
35													0.000	0.503
40														0.000

For Mortgages with an Interest Rate of 14.25% and an Original Term of:

Age of Loan in Years	5 Years	6 Years	7 Years	8 Years	9 Years	10 Years	11 Years	12 Years	15 Years	20 Years	25 Years	30 Years	35 Years	40 Years
1	0.852	0.886	0.910	0.928	0.941	0.951	0.959	0.966	0.979	0.990	0.995	0.998	0.999	0.999
2	0.682	0.755	0.807	0.844	0.873	0.895	0.913	0.927	0.956	0.980	0.990	0.995	0.998	0.999
3	0.486	0.605	0.688	0.749	0.795	0.830	0.859	0.882	0.928	0.967	0.984	0.992	0.996	0.998
4	0.260	0.431	0.550	0.638	0.704	0.756	0.797	0.830	0.897	0.952	0.977	0.989	0.995	0.997
5	0.000	0.231	0.392	0.511	0.600	0.670	0.725	0.770	0.860	0.936	0.969	0.985	0.993	0.996
6		0.000	0.210	0.364	0.480	0.571	0.643	0.701	0.818	0.916	0.960	0.981	0.991	0.995
7			0.000	0.195	0.342	0.457	0.548	0.621	0.770	0.894	0.949	0.975	0.988	0.994
8				0.000	0.183	0.326	0.439	0.529	0.714	0.868	0.937	0.970	0.985	0.993
9					0.000	0.174	0.313	0.424	0.650	0.839	0.923	0.963	0.982	0.991
10						0.000	0.167	0.302	0.576	0.805	0.907	0.955	0.978	0.989
11							0.000	0.162	0.491	0.766	0.888	0.946	0.973	0.987
12								0.000	0.393	0.720	0.867	0.935	0.968	0.984
15									0.000	0.539	0.780	0.893	0.948	0.974
20										0.000	0.523	0.768	0.887	0.944
25											0.000	0.515	0.763	0.884
30												0.000	0.511	0.760
35													0.000	0.509
40														0.000

Remaining Principal Balance Factors

For Mortgages with an Interest Rate of 14.50% and an Original Term of:

Age of Loan in Years	5 Years	6 Years	7 Years	8 Years	9 Years	10 Years	11 Years	12 Years	15 Years	20 Years	25 Years	30 Years	35 Years	40 Years
1	0.853	0.887	0.911	0.928	0.942	0.952	0.960	0.967	0.980	0.991	0.996	0.998	0.999	1.000
2	0.684	0.757	0.808	0.846	0.874	0.896	0.914	0.928	0.957	0.980	0.991	0.996	0.998	0.999
3	0.488	0.606	0.690	0.750	0.797	0.832	0.861	0.883	0.930	0.968	0.985	0.993	0.996	0.998
4	0.261	0.433	0.552	0.640	0.707	0.758	0.799	0.832	0.899	0.954	0.978	0.990	0.995	0.998
5	0.000	0.232	0.394	0.513	0.603	0.673	0.728	0.772	0.863	0.937	0.970	0.986	0.993	0.997
6		0.000	0.211	0.366	0.483	0.574	0.646	0.704	0.821	0.918	0.962	0.982	0.991	0.996
7			0.000	0.196	0.345	0.460	0.551	0.624	0.773	0.897	0.951	0.977	0.989	0.995
8				0.000	0.185	0.328	0.441	0.533	0.718	0.871	0.939	0.971	0.986	0.993
9					0.000	0.176	0.315	0.427	0.654	0.842	0.926	0.964	0.983	0.992
10						0.000	0.169	0.304	0.580	0.809	0.910	0.957	0.979	0.990
11							0.000	0.163	0.495	0.770	0.891	0.948	0.975	0.988
12								0.000	0.397	0.725	0.870	0.938	0.970	0.985
15									0.000	0.544	0.785	0.897	0.950	0.976
20										0.000	0.528	0.774	0.891	0.947
25											0.000	0.520	0.768	0.888
30												0.000	0.517	0.766
35													0.000	0.515
40														0.000

For Mortgages with an Interest Rate of 14.75% and an Original Term of:

Age of Loan in Years	5 Years	6 Years	7 Years	8 Years	9 Years	10 Years	11 Years	12 Years	15 Years	20 Years	25 Years	30 Years	35 Years	40 Years
1	0.854	0.888	0.912	0.929	0.942	0.953	0.961	0.967	0.980	0.991	0.996	0.998	0.999	1.000
2	0.685	0.758	0.810	0.847	0.876	0.898	0.915	0.929	0.957	0.981	0.991	0.996	0.998	0.999
3	0.489	0.608	0.691	0.752	0.798	0.834	0.862	0.885	0.931	0.969	0.985	0.993	0.997	0.998
4	0.262	0.434	0.555	0.643	0.709	0.761	0.801	0.834	0.901	0.955	0.979	0.990	0.995	0.998
5	0.000	0.233	0.396	0.515	0.606	0.675	0.731	0.775	0.865	0.939	0.972	0.987	0.994	0.997
6		0.000	0.213	0.368	0.486	0.577	0.649	0.707	0.824	0.921	0.963	0.982	0.992	0.996
7			0.000	0.197	0.347	0.463	0.554	0.628	0.777	0.899	0.953	0.978	0.989	0.995
8				0.000	0.186	0.330	0.444	0.536	0.722	0.874	0.941	0.972	0.987	0.994
9					0.000	0.177	0.317	0.430	0.658	0.846	0.928	0.966	0.984	0.992
10						0.000	0.170	0.307	0.584	0.812	0.912	0.959	0.980	0.991
11							0.000	0.165	0.499	0.774	0.894	0.950	0.976	0.989
12								0.000	0.400	0.729	0.874	0.940	0.971	0.986
15									0.000	0.549	0.789	0.900	0.952	0.977
20										0.000	0.533	0.779	0.894	0.949
25											0.000	0.526	0.774	0.892
30												0.000	0.523	0.771
35													0.000	0.521
40														0.000

Remaining Principal Balance Factors

For Mortgages with an Interest Rate of 15.00% and an Original Term of:

Age of Loan in Years	5 Years	6 Years	7 Years	8 Years	9 Years	10 Years	11 Years	12 Years	15 Years	20 Years	25 Years	30 Years	35 Years	40 Years
1	0.855	0.889	0.913	0.930	0.943	0.953	0.961	0.968	0.981	0.991	0.996	0.998	0.999	1.000
2	0.686	0.760	0.811	0.849	0.877	0.899	0.916	0.930	0.958	0.981	0.991	0.996	0.998	0.999
3	0.491	0.610	0.693	0.754	0.800	0.836	0.864	0.887	0.933	0.970	0.986	0.993	0.997	0.999
4	0.264	0.436	0.557	0.645	0.711	0.763	0.804	0.836	0.902	0.956	0.980	0.991	0.996	0.998
5	0.000	0.234	0.398	0.518	0.608	0.678	0.733	0.778	0.868	0.941	0.973	0.987	0.994	0.997
6		0.000	0.214	0.370	0.488	0.580	0.652	0.710	0.827	0.923	0.964	0.983	0.992	0.996
7			0.000	0.199	0.349	0.465	0.557	0.631	0.780	0.902	0.955	0.979	0.990	0.995
8				0.000	0.188	0.333	0.447	0.539	0.725	0.877	0.943	0.973	0.987	0.994
9					0.000	0.179	0.320	0.433	0.662	0.849	0.930	0.967	0.985	0.993
10						0.000	0.172	0.310	0.588	0.816	0.915	0.960	0.981	0.991
11							0.000	0.166	0.503	0.778	0.898	0.952	0.977	0.989
12								0.000	0.404	0.734	0.877	0.942	0.973	0.987
15									0.000	0.554	0.794	0.903	0.954	0.978
20										0.000	0.538	0.784	0.898	0.952
25											0.000	0.532	0.779	0.895
30												0.000	0.528	0.777
35													0.000	0.527
40														0.000

For Mortgages with an Interest Rate of 15.25% and an Original Term of:

Age of Loan in Years	5 Years	6 Years	7 Years	8 Years	9 Years	10 Years	11 Years	12 Years	15 Years	20 Years	25 Years	30 Years	35 Years	40 Years
1	0.856	0.890	0.913	0.931	0.944	0.954	0.962	0.968	0.981	0.992	0.996	0.998	0.999	1.000
2	0.688	0.761	0.813	0.850	0.878	0.900	0.918	0.931	0.959	0.982	0.992	0.996	0.998	0.999
3	0.492	0.612	0.695	0.756	0.802	0.838	0.866	0.889	0.934	0.971	0.987	0.994	0.997	0.999
4	0.265	0.438	0.559	0.647	0.714	0.765	0.806	0.839	0.904	0.958	0.981	0.991	0.996	0.998
5	0.000	0.235	0.400	0.520	0.611	0.681	0.736	0.780	0.870	0.943	0.974	0.988	0.994	0.997
6		0.000	0.215	0.372	0.491	0.583	0.655	0.713	0.830	0.925	0.966	0.984	0.993	0.997
7			0.000	0.200	0.351	0.468	0.560	0.634	0.783	0.904	0.956	0.980	0.991	0.996
8				0.000	0.189	0.335	0.450	0.543	0.729	0.880	0.945	0.975	0.988	0.994
9					0.000	0.180	0.322	0.436	0.666	0.852	0.933	0.969	0.985	0.993
10						0.000	0.173	0.312	0.592	0.820	0.918	0.962	0.982	0.992
11							0.000	0.168	0.507	0.782	0.901	0.954	0.979	0.990
12								0.000	0.407	0.738	0.880	0.945	0.974	0.988
15									0.000	0.558	0.798	0.907	0.956	0.980
20										0.000	0.544	0.789	0.901	0.954
25											0.000	0.537	0.784	0.899
30												0.000	0.534	0.782
35													0.000	0.532
40														0.000

Remaining Principal Balance Factors

For Mortgages with an Interest Rate of 15.50% and an Original Term of:

Age of Loan in Years	5 Years	6 Years	7 Years	8 Years	9 Years	10 Years	11 Years	12 Years	15 Years	20 Years	25 Years	30 Years	35 Years	40 Years
1	0.856	0.890	0.914	0.931	0.944	0.955	0.963	0.969	0.982	0.992	0.996	0.998	0.999	1.000
2	0.689	0.763	0.814	0.851	0.880	0.902	0.919	0.933	0.960	0.983	0.992	0.996	0.998	0.999
3	0.494	0.613	0.697	0.758	0.804	0.840	0.868	0.890	0.935	0.972	0.987	0.994	0.997	0.999
4	0.266	0.440	0.561	0.649	0.716	0.768	0.808	0.841	0.906	0.959	0.981	0.992	0.996	0.998
5	0.000	0.237	0.402	0.522	0.613	0.684	0.739	0.783	0.872	0.944	0.975	0.988	0.995	0.998
6		0.000	0.216	0.374	0.493	0.585	0.658	0.716	0.833	0.927	0.967	0.985	0.993	0.997
7			0.000	0.202	0.353	0.471	0.563	0.637	0.786	0.907	0.958	0.981	0.991	0.996
8				0.000	0.190	0.337	0.453	0.546	0.732	0.883	0.947	0.976	0.989	0.995
9					0.000	0.182	0.325	0.439	0.670	0.856	0.935	0.970	0.986	0.994
10						0.000	0.175	0.315	0.596	0.823	0.920	0.964	0.983	0.992
11							0.000	0.169	0.511	0.786	0.903	0.956	0.980	0.991
12								0.000	0.411	0.742	0.884	0.947	0.975	0.989
15									0.000	0.563	0.803	0.910	0.958	0.981
20										0.000	0.549	0.793	0.905	0.956
25											0.000	0.542	0.789	0.903
30												0.000	0.539	0.787
35													0.000	0.538
40														0.000

For Mortgages with an Interest Rate of 15.75% and an Original Term of:

Age of Loan in Years	5 Years	6 Years	7 Years	8 Years	9 Years	10 Years	11 Years	12 Years	15 Years	20 Years	25 Years	30 Years	35 Years	40 Years
1	0.857	0.891	0.915	0.932	0.945	0.955	0.963	0.969	0.982	0.992	0.997	0.998	0.999	1.000
2	0.690	0.764	0.815	0.853	0.881	0.903	0.920	0.934	0.961	0.983	0.992	0.997	0.998	0.999
3	0.495	0.615	0.699	0.760	0.806	0.842	0.870	0.892	0.937	0.973	0.988	0.994	0.997	0.999
4	0.267	0.441	0.563	0.652	0.718	0.770	0.811	0.843	0.908	0.960	0.982	0.992	0.996	0.998
5	0.000	0.238	0.404	0.525	0.616	0.686	0.742	0.786	0.875	0.946	0.976	0.989	0.995	0.998
6		0.000	0.218	0.376	0.496	0.588	0.661	0.719	0.835	0.929	0.968	0.986	0.993	0.997
7			0.000	0.203	0.356	0.474	0.567	0.641	0.790	0.909	0.959	0.982	0.992	0.996
8				0.000	0.192	0.340	0.456	0.549	0.736	0.886	0.949	0.977	0.990	0.995
9					0.000	0.183	0.327	0.442	0.673	0.859	0.937	0.971	0.987	0.994
10						0.000	0.176	0.317	0.600	0.827	0.923	0.965	0.984	0.993
11							0.000	0.171	0.514	0.790	0.906	0.958	0.981	0.991
12								0.000	0.414	0.747	0.887	0.949	0.977	0.989
15									0.000	0.568	0.807	0.913	0.960	0.982
20										0.000	0.554	0.798	0.908	0.958
25											0.000	0.548	0.794	0.906
30												0.000	0.545	0.792
35													0.000	0.544
40														0.000

Remaining Principal Balance Factors

For Mortgages with an Interest Rate of 16.00% and an Original Term of:

Age of Loan in Years	5 Years	6 Years	7 Years	8 Years	9 Years	10 Years	11 Years	12 Years	15 Years	20 Years	25 Years	30 Years	35 Years	40 Years
1	0.858	0.892	0.916	0.933	0.946	0.956	0.964	0.970	0.983	0.993	0.997	0.999	0.999	1.000
2	0.692	0.765	0.817	0.854	0.882	0.904	0.921	0.935	0.962	0.984	0.993	0.997	0.999	0.999
3	0.497	0.617	0.701	0.762	0.808	0.843	0.871	0.893	0.938	0.973	0.988	0.995	0.998	0.999
4	0.268	0.443	0.565	0.654	0.721	0.772	0.813	0.845	0.910	0.961	0.983	0.992	0.997	0.998
5	0.000	0.239	0.406	0.527	0.618	0.689	0.744	0.788	0.877	0.947	0.977	0.990	0.995	0.998
6		0.000	0.219	0.378	0.498	0.591	0.664	0.722	0.838	0.931	0.969	0.986	0.994	0.997
7			0.000	0.204	0.358	0.476	0.570	0.644	0.793	0.911	0.961	0.983	0.992	0.996
8				0.000	0.193	0.342	0.459	0.553	0.739	0.889	0.951	0.978	0.990	0.996
9					0.000	0.185	0.330	0.445	0.677	0.862	0.939	0.973	0.988	0.994
10						0.000	0.178	0.320	0.604	0.831	0.925	0.967	0.985	0.993
11							0.000	0.173	0.518	0.794	0.909	0.959	0.982	0.992
12								0.000	0.418	0.751	0.890	0.951	0.978	0.990
15									0.000	0.572	0.811	0.916	0.962	0.983
20										0.000	0.559	0.803	0.911	0.960
25											0.000	0.553	0.799	0.909
30												0.000	0.550	0.797
35													0.000	0.549
40														0.000

For Mortgages with an Interest Rate of 16.25% and an Original Term of:

Age of Loan in Years	5 Years	6 Years	7 Years	8 Years	9 Years	10 Years	11 Years	12 Years	15 Years	20 Years	25 Years	30 Years	35 Years	40 Years
1	0.859	0.893	0.916	0.934	0.947	0.956	0.964	0.970	0.983	0.993	0.997	0.999	0.999	1.000
2	0.693	0.767	0.818	0.856	0.884	0.905	0.922	0.936	0.963	0.984	0.993	0.997	0.999	0.999
3	0.498	0.619	0.703	0.764	0.810	0.845	0.873	0.895	0.939	0.974	0.989	0.995	0.998	0.999
4	0.269	0.445	0.567	0.656	0.723	0.775	0.815	0.847	0.912	0.963	0.984	0.993	0.997	0.999
5	0.000	0.240	0.408	0.529	0.621	0.691	0.747	0.791	0.879	0.949	0.978	0.990	0.996	0.998
6		0.000	0.220	0.381	0.501	0.594	0.667	0.725	0.841	0.933	0.971	0.987	0.994	0.997
7			0.000	0.206	0.360	0.479	0.573	0.647	0.796	0.914	0.962	0.983	0.993	0.997
8				0.000	0.195	0.344	0.462	0.556	0.743	0.891	0.953	0.979	0.991	0.996
9					0.000	0.186	0.332	0.448	0.681	0.865	0.941	0.974	0.988	0.995
10						0.000	0.179	0.322	0.608	0.834	0.928	0.968	0.986	0.994
11							0.000	0.174	0.522	0.798	0.912	0.961	0.983	0.992
12								0.000	0.421	0.755	0.893	0.953	0.979	0.991
15									0.000	0.577	0.815	0.918	0.964	0.984
20										0.000	0.564	0.807	0.914	0.962
25											0.000	0.558	0.804	0.913
30												0.000	0.556	0.802
35													0.000	0.555
40														0.000

Remaining Principal Balance Factors

For Mortgages with an Interest Rate of 16.50% and an Original Term of:

Age of Loan in Years	5 Years	6 Years	7 Years	8 Years	9 Years	10 Years	11 Years	12 Years	15 Years	20 Years	25 Years	30 Years	35 Years	40 Years
1	0.860	0.894	0.917	0.934	0.947	0.957	0.965	0.971	0.983	0.993	0.997	0.999	0.999	1.000
2	0.694	0.768	0.820	0.857	0.885	0.907	0.923	0.937	0.964	0.985	0.993	0.997	0.999	0.999
3	0.500	0.620	0.705	0.766	0.812	0.847	0.875	0.897	0.941	0.975	0.989	0.995	0.998	0.999
4	0.270	0.446	0.569	0.658	0.725	0.777	0.817	0.849	0.913	0.964	0.984	0.993	0.997	0.999
5	0.000	0.241	0.409	0.532	0.623	0.694	0.749	0.793	0.881	0.950	0.979	0.991	0.996	0.998
6		0.000	0.221	0.383	0.504	0.597	0.670	0.728	0.843	0.934	0.972	0.988	0.995	0.998
7			0.000	0.207	0.362	0.482	0.576	0.650	0.799	0.916	0.964	0.984	0.993	0.997
8				0.000	0.196	0.347	0.465	0.559	0.746	0.894	0.954	0.980	0.991	0.996
9					0.000	0.188	0.335	0.452	0.684	0.868	0.943	0.975	0.989	0.995
10						0.000	0.181	0.325	0.612	0.837	0.930	0.969	0.987	0.994
11							0.000	0.176	0.526	0.801	0.914	0.963	0.984	0.993
12								0.000	0.425	0.759	0.896	0.955	0.980	0.991
15									0.000	0.581	0.819	0.921	0.965	0.985
20										0.000	0.569	0.812	0.917	0.964
25											0.000	0.563	0.808	0.916
30												0.000	0.561	0.807
35													0.000	0.560
40														0.000

For Mortgages with an Interest Rate of 16.75% and an Original Term of:

Age of Loan in Years	5 Years	6 Years	7 Years	8 Years	9 Years	10 Years	11 Years	12 Years	15 Years	20 Years	25 Years	30 Years	35 Years	40 Years
1	0.860	0.894	0.918	0.935	0.948	0.958	0.965	0.972	0.984	0.993	0.997	0.999	0.999	1.000
2	0.696	0.770	0.821	0.858	0.886	0.908	0.925	0.938	0.965	0.985	0.994	0.997	0.999	0.999
3	0.501	0.622	0.706	0.768	0.813	0.849	0.876	0.898	0.942	0.976	0.990	0.996	0.998	0.999
4	0.271	0.448	0.571	0.660	0.727	0.779	0.819	0.851	0.915	0.965	0.985	0.994	0.997	0.999
5	0.000	0.243	0.411	0.534	0.626	0.697	0.752	0.796	0.883	0.952	0.979	0.991	0.996	0.998
6		0.000	0.223	0.385	0.506	0.600	0.673	0.731	0.846	0.936	0.973	0.988	0.995	0.998
7			0.000	0.208	0.365	0.485	0.579	0.653	0.802	0.918	0.965	0.985	0.993	0.997
8				0.000	0.197	0.349	0.468	0.562	0.750	0.896	0.956	0.981	0.992	0.996
9					0.000	0.189	0.337	0.455	0.688	0.871	0.945	0.976	0.990	0.996
10						0.000	0.183	0.327	0.615	0.841	0.932	0.971	0.987	0.994
11							0.000	0.177	0.530	0.805	0.917	0.964	0.984	0.993
12								0.000	0.428	0.763	0.899	0.956	0.981	0.992
15									0.000	0.586	0.823	0.924	0.967	0.986
20										0.000	0.574	0.816	0.920	0.965
25											0.000	0.569	0.813	0.919
30												0.000	0.566	0.812
35													0.000	0.565
40														0.000

Remaining Principal Balance Factors

For Mortgages with an Interest Rate of 17.00% and an Original Term of:

Age of Loan in Years	5 Years	6 Years	7 Years	8 Years	9 Years	10 Years	11 Years	12 Years	15 Years	20 Years	25 Years	30 Years	35 Years	40 Years
1	0.861	0.895	0.919	0.936	0.948	0.958	0.966	0.972	0.984	0.993	0.997	0.999	0.999	1.000
2	0.697	0.771	0.822	0.860	0.887	0.909	0.926	0.939	0.965	0.986	0.994	0.997	0.999	1.000
3	0.503	0.624	0.708	0.769	0.815	0.850	0.878	0.900	0.943	0.977	0.990	0.996	0.998	0.999
4	0.272	0.450	0.573	0.663	0.730	0.781	0.822	0.853	0.917	0.966	0.986	0.994	0.997	0.999
5	0.000	0.244	0.413	0.536	0.629	0.699	0.755	0.799	0.886	0.953	0.980	0.992	0.996	0.998
6		0.000	0.224	0.387	0.509	0.602	0.676	0.734	0.849	0.938	0.974	0.989	0.995	0.998
7			0.000	0.210	0.367	0.487	0.582	0.657	0.805	0.920	0.966	0.986	0.994	0.997
8				0.000	0.199	0.352	0.471	0.566	0.753	0.899	0.957	0.982	0.992	0.997
9					0.000	0.191	0.340	0.458	0.692	0.874	0.947	0.977	0.990	0.996
10						0.000	0.184	0.330	0.619	0.844	0.934	0.972	0.988	0.995
11							0.000	0.179	0.533	0.809	0.919	0.966	0.985	0.994
12								0.000	0.432	0.767	0.902	0.958	0.982	0.992
15									0.000	0.590	0.827	0.926	0.968	0.986
20										0.000	0.579	0.820	0.923	0.967
25											0.000	0.574	0.817	0.922
30												0.000	0.572	0.816
35													0.000	0.571
40														0.000

For Mortgages with an Interest Rate of 17.25% and an Original Term of:

Age of Loan in Years	5 Years	6 Years	7 Years	8 Years	9 Years	10 Years	11 Years	12 Years	15 Years	20 Years	25 Years	30 Years	35 Years	40 Years
1	0.862	0.896	0.919	0.936	0.949	0.959	0.967	0.973	0.985	0.994	0.997	0.999	1.000	1.000
2	0.698	0.772	0.824	0.861	0.889	0.910	0.927	0.940	0.966	0.986	0.994	0.998	0.999	1.000
3	0.504	0.626	0.710	0.771	0.817	0.852	0.880	0.901	0.944	0.977	0.991	0.996	0.998	0.999
4	0.274	0.452	0.575	0.665	0.732	0.783	0.824	0.855	0.918	0.967	0.986	0.994	0.998	0.999
5	0.000	0.245	0.415	0.539	0.631	0.702	0.757	0.801	0.888	0.954	0.981	0.992	0.997	0.999
6		0.000	0.225	0.389	0.511	0.605	0.678	0.736	0.851	0.940	0.975	0.989	0.996	0.998
7			0.000	0.211	0.369	0.490	0.585	0.660	0.808	0.922	0.968	0.986	0.994	0.998
8				0.000	0.200	0.354	0.474	0.569	0.756	0.901	0.959	0.983	0.993	0.997
9					0.000	0.192	0.342	0.461	0.695	0.877	0.949	0.978	0.991	0.996
10						0.000	0.186	0.333	0.623	0.847	0.936	0.973	0.989	0.995
11							0.000	0.181	0.537	0.812	0.922	0.967	0.986	0.994
12								0.000	0.435	0.771	0.905	0.960	0.983	0.993
15									0.000	0.595	0.831	0.929	0.970	0.987
20										0.000	0.583	0.824	0.926	0.968
25											0.000	0.579	0.822	0.924
30												0.000	0.577	0.820
35													0.000	0.576
40														0.000

Remaining Principal Balance Factors

For Mortgages with an Interest Rate of 17.50% and an Original Term of:

Age of Loan in Years	5 Years	6 Years	7 Years	8 Years	9 Years	10 Years	11 Years	12 Years	15 Years	20 Years	25 Years	30 Years	35 Years	40 Years
1	0.863	0.897	0.920	0.937	0.950	0.959	0.967	0.973	0.985	0.994	0.998	0.999	1.000	1.000
2	0.700	0.774	0.825	0.862	0.890	0.911	0.928	0.941	0.967	0.987	0.995	0.998	0.999	1.000
3	0.506	0.627	0.712	0.773	0.819	0.854	0.881	0.903	0.945	0.978	0.991	0.996	0.998	0.999
4	0.275	0.453	0.577	0.667	0.734	0.786	0.826	0.858	0.920	0.968	0.987	0.995	0.998	0.999
5	0.000	0.246	0.417	0.541	0.634	0.704	0.760	0.804	0.890	0.956	0.982	0.992	0.997	0.999
6		0.000	0.227	0.391	0.514	0.608	0.681	0.739	0.854	0.941	0.976	0.990	0.996	0.998
7			0.000	0.212	0.371	0.493	0.588	0.663	0.811	0.924	0.969	0.987	0.995	0.998
8				0.000	0.202	0.356	0.477	0.572	0.760	0.904	0.960	0.983	0.993	0.997
9					0.000	0.194	0.344	0.464	0.699	0.879	0.950	0.979	0.991	0.996
10						0.000	0.187	0.335	0.627	0.850	0.938	0.974	0.989	0.996
11							0.000	0.182	0.541	0.816	0.924	0.968	0.987	0.994
12								0.000	0.439	0.775	0.907	0.961	0.984	0.993
15									0.000	0.599	0.835	0.931	0.971	0.988
20										0.000	0.588	0.829	0.928	0.970
25											0.000	0.584	0.826	0.927
30												0.000	0.582	0.825
35													0.000	0.581
40														0.000

For Mortgages with an Interest Rate of 17.75% and an Original Term of:

Age of Loan in Years	5 Years	6 Years	7 Years	8 Years	9 Years	10 Years	11 Years	12 Years	15 Years	20 Years	25 Years	30 Years	35 Years	40 Years
1	0.864	0.897	0.921	0.938	0.950	0.960	0.968	0.974	0.985	0.994	0.998	0.999	1.000	1.000
2	0.701	0.775	0.826	0.863	0.891	0.912	0.929	0.942	0.968	0.987	0.995	0.998	0.999	1.000
3	0.507	0.629	0.714	0.775	0.821	0.856	0.883	0.904	0.947	0.979	0.991	0.996	0.999	0.999
4	0.276	0.455	0.579	0.669	0.736	0.788	0.828	0.860	0.922	0.969	0.987	0.995	0.998	0.999
5	0.000	0.248	0.419	0.543	0.636	0.707	0.762	0.806	0.892	0.957	0.983	0.993	0.997	0.999
6		0.000	0.228	0.393	0.516	0.611	0.684	0.742	0.856	0.943	0.977	0.990	0.996	0.998
7			0.000	0.214	0.373	0.496	0.591	0.666	0.814	0.926	0.970	0.988	0.995	0.998
8				0.000	0.203	0.359	0.480	0.575	0.763	0.906	0.962	0.984	0.993	0.997
9					0.000	0.195	0.347	0.467	0.703	0.882	0.952	0.980	0.992	0.997
10						0.000	0.189	0.338	0.630	0.853	0.940	0.975	0.990	0.996
11							0.000	0.184	0.545	0.819	0.926	0.970	0.988	0.995
12								0.000	0.442	0.779	0.910	0.963	0.985	0.994
15									0.000	0.603	0.839	0.934	0.973	0.989
20										0.000	0.593	0.833	0.931	0.971
25											0.000	0.589	0.830	0.930
30												0.000	0.587	0.829
35													0.000	0.586
40														0.000

Glossary

abstract of title (abstract) History of a parcel of real estate, compiled from public records, listing transfers of ownership and claims against the property

acceleration clause Provision in a mortgage document stating that if a payment is missed or any other provision violated the whole debt becomes immediately due and payable

acknowledgment Formal declaration before a public official that one has signed a document

acre Land measure equal to 43,560 square feet

adjustable rate mortgage (ARM) Loan whose interest rate is changed periodically to keep pace with current levels

adjusted basis Original cost of property plus any later improvements and minus a figure for depreciation claimed

adjusted sales price Sale price minus commissions, legal fees and other costs of selling

agent Person authorized to act on behalf of another in dealings with third parties

agreement of sale (purchase agreement, sales agreement, contract to purchase) Written contract detailing terms under which buyer agrees to buy and seller agrees to sell

alienation clause (due-on-sale, nonassumption) Provision in a mortgage document stating that the loan must be paid in full if ownership is transferred, sometimes contingent upon other occurrences

amortization Gradual payment of a debt through regular installments that cover both interest and principal

appraisal Estimate of value of real estate, presumably by an expert

appreciation Increase in value or worth of property

"as is" Present condition of property being transferred, with no guaranty or warranty provided by the seller

assessed valuation Value placed on property as a basis for levying property taxes; not identical with appraised or market value

assignment Transfer of a contract from one party to another

assumable mortgage Loan that may be passed to the next owner of the property

assumption Takeover of a loan by any qualified buyer (available for FHA and VA loans)

automatic renewal clause Provision that allows a listing contract to be renewed indefinitely unless canceled by the property owner

balloon loan Mortgage in which the remaining balance becomes fully due and payable at a predetermined time

balloon payment Final payment on a balloon loan

bill of sale Written document transferring personal property

binder Preliminary agreement of sale, usually accompanied by earnest money (term also used with property insurance)

bond Roughly the same as *promissory note*, a written promise to repay a loan, often with an accompanying mortgage that pledges real estate as security

broker Person licensed by the state to represent another for a fee in real estate transactions

building code Regulations of local government stipulating requirements and standards for building and construction

buydown The payment of additional points to a mortgage lender in return for a lower interest rate on the loan

buyer's broker Agent who takes the buyer as client, is obligated to put the buyer's interests above all others, and owes specific fiduciary duties to the buyer

buyers' market Situation in which supply of homes for sale exceeds demand

cap Limit (typically about two percent) by which an adjustable mortgage rate might be raised at any one time

capital gain Taxable profit on the sale of an appreciated asset

caveat emptor Let the buyer beware

ceiling Also known as *lifetime cap,* limit beyond which an adjustable mortgage rate may never be raised

certificate of occupancy Document issued by local governmental agency stating that property meets standards for occupancy

chattel Personal property

client The broker's principal, to whom fiduciary duties are owed

closing (settlement, escrow, passing papers) Conclusion of a real estate sale, at which time title is transferred and necessary funds change hands

closing costs One-time charges paid by buyer and seller on the day property changes hands

closing statement Statement prepared for buyer and seller listing debits and credits, completed by the person in charge of the closing

cloud (on title) Outstanding claim or encumbrance that challenges the owner's clear title

commission Fee paid (usually by a seller) for a broker's services in securing a buyer for property; commonly a percentage of sales price

commitment (letter) Written promise to grant a mortgage loan

common elements Parts of a condominium development in which each owner holds an interest (swimming pool, etc.)

comparable Recently sold similar property, used to estimate market value

comparative market analysis Method of valuing homes using study of comparables, property that failed to sell, and other property currently on the market

conditional commitment Lender's promise to make a loan subject to the fulfillment of specified conditions

conditional offer Purchase offer in which the buyer proposes to purchase only after certain occurrences (sale of another home, securing of financing, etc.)

condominium Type of ownership involving individual ownership of dwelling units and common ownership of shared areas

consideration Anything of value given to induce another to enter into a contract

contingency Condition (inserted into the contract) which must be satisfied before the buyer purchases a house

contract Legally enforceable agreement to do (or not to do) a particular thing

contract for deed (land contract) Method of selling whereby the buyer receives possession but the seller retains title

conventional mortgage Loan arranged between lender and borrower with no governmental guarantee or insurance

cost basis Accounting figure that includes original cost of property plus certain expenses to purchase, money spent on permanent improvements and other costs, minus any depreciation claimed on tax returns over the years

curtesy In some states, rights a widower obtains to a portion of his deceased wife's real property

customer Typically, the buyer, as opposed to the principal (seller)

days on market (DOM) Number of days between the time a house is put on the market and the date of a firm sale contract

deed Formal written document transferring title to real estate; a new deed is used for each transfer

deed of trust Document by which title to property is held by a neutral third party until a debt is paid; used instead of a mortgage in some states

deed restriction (restrictive covenant) Provision placed in a deed to control use and occupancy of the property by future owners

default Failure to make mortgage payment

deferred maintenance Needed repairs that have been put off

deficiency judgment Personal claim against the debtor, when foreclosed property does not yield enough at sale to pay off loans against it

delivery Legal transfer of a deed to the new property owner, the moment at which transfer of title occurs

depreciation Decrease in value of property because of deterioration or obsolescence; sometimes, an artificial bookkeeping concept valuable as a tax shelter

direct endorsement Complete processing of an FHA mortgage application by an authorized local lender

documentary tax stamp Charge levied by state or local governments when real estate is transferred or mortgaged

dower In some states, the rights of a widow to a portion of her deceased husband's property

down payment Cash to be paid by the buyer at closing

DVA Department of Veterans Affairs. Formerly VA, Veterans Administration

earnest money Buyer's "good faith" deposit accompanying purchase offer.

easement A permanent right to use another's property (telephone lines, common driveway, footpath, etc.)

encroachment Unauthorized intrusion of a building or improvement onto another's land

encumbrance Claim against another's real estate (unpaid tax, mortgage, easement, etc.)

equity The money realized when property is sold and all the claims against it are paid; commonly, sales price minus present mortgage

escrow   Funds given to a third party to be held pending some occurrence; may refer to earnest money, funds collected by a lender for the payment of taxes and insurance charges, funds withheld at closing to insure uncompleted repairs, or in some states the entire process of closing

exclusive agency   Listing agreement under which only the listing office can sell the property and keep the commission except if the owner sells the house, in which case no commission is paid

exclusive right-to-sell   Listing agreement under which the owner promises to pay a commission if the property is sold during the listing period by anyone, even the owner

fair market value   see **market value**

FHA   Federal Housing Administration (HUD), which insures mortgages to protect the lending institution in case of default

FHA mortgage   Loan made by a local lending institution and insured by the FHA, with the borrower paying the premium

fee simple (absolute)   Highest possible degree of ownership of land

fiduciary   A person in a position of trust or responsibility with specific duties to act in the best interest of the client

first mortgage   Mortgage holding priority over the claims of subsequent lenders against the same property

fixture   Personal property that has become part of the real estate

foreclosure   Legal procedure for enforcing payment of a debt by seizing and selling the mortgaged property

front foot   Measurement of land along a street or waterfront—each front foot is one foot wide and extends to the depth of the lot

grantee   The buyer, who receives a deed

grantor   The seller, who gives a deed

guaranteed sale   Promise by the listing broker that if the property cannot be sold by a specific date, the broker will buy it, usually at a sharply discounted price

hazard insurance   insurance on a property against fire and similar risks

homeowner's policy   Policy which puts many kinds of insurance together into one package

improvements   Permanent additions that increase the value of a home

index   Benchmark measure of current interest levels, used to calculate periodic changes in rates charged on adjustable rate mortgages

joint tenancy   Ownership by two or more persons, each with an undivided ownership—if one dies, the property goes automatically to the survivor

junior mortgage   A mortgage subordinate to another

land contract   Type of layaway installment plan for buying a house; sought by a buyer who does not have enough down payment to qualify for a bank loan or to persuade the seller to turn over title

lien   A claim against property for the payment of a debt: mechanic's lien, mortgage, unpaid taxes, judgments

lis pendens   Notice that litigation is pending on property

listing agreement (listing)   Written employment agreement between a property owner and a real estate broker, authorizing the broker to find a buyer

listing presentation Proposal submitted orally or in writing by a real estate agent who seeks to put a prospective seller's property on the market

loan servicing Handling paperwork of collecting loan payments, checking property tax and insurance coverage, handling delinquencies

lock-in Guarantee that the borrower will receive the rate in effect at the time of loan application

maintenance fees Payments made by the unit owner of a condominium to the homeowners' association for expenses incurred in upkeep of the common areas

margin Percentage (typically about 2.5 percent) added to *index* to calculate mortgage rate adjustment

marketable title Title free of *liens, clouds* and *defects*; a title that will be freely accepted by a buyer

market value The most likely price a given property will bring if widely exposed on the market, assuming fully informed buyer and seller

mechanic's lien Claim placed against property by unpaid workers or suppliers

meeting of the minds Agreement by buyer and seller on the provisions of a contract

mortgage A *lien* or claim against real property given as security for a loan; the homeowner "gives" the mortgage; the lender "takes" it

mortgagee The lender

mortgagor The borrower

multiple-listing service (MLS) Arrangement by which brokers work together on the sale of each other's listed homes, with shared commissions

negative amortization Arrangement under which the shortfall in a mortgage payment is added to the amount borrowed; gradual raising of a debt

net listing Arrangement under which the seller receives a specific sum from the sale price and the agent keeps the rest as sales commission (open to abuses, illegal in most states)

note see **bond**

PITI Abbreviation for principal, interest, taxes and insurance, often lumped together in a monthly mortgage payment

plat A map or chart of a lot, subdivision or community, showing boundary lines, buildings and easements

PMI Private mortgage insurance

point (discount point) One percent of a new mortgage being placed, paid in a one-time lump sum to the lender

portfolio loans Loans made by a bank that keeps its mortgages as assets in its own portfolio (also called *nonconforming loans*)

prepayment Payment of a mortgage loan before its due date

prepayment penalty Charge levied by the lender for paying off a mortgage before its maturity date

principal The party (typically the seller) who hires and pays an agent

procuring cause Actions by a broker that bring about the desired results

prorations Expenses that are fairly divided between buyer and seller at closing

purchase-money mortgage Mortgage for the purchase of real property, commonly a mortgage "taken back" by the seller

quitclaim deed   Deed that completely transfers whatever ownership the grantor may have had, but makes no claim of ownership in the first place

real property   Land and the improvements on it

Realtist   Member of the National Association of Real Estate Brokers

REALTOR®   Registered name for a member of the National Association of REALTORS®

REALTOR-ASSOCIATE®   Salesperson associated with a broker who is a member of a Board of REALTORS®

redlining   The practice of refusing to provide loans or insurance in a certain neighborhood

RESPA   Real Estate Settlement Procedures Act, requiring advance disclosure to the borrower of information pertinent to the loan

restrictive covenant   See **deed restriction**

reverse mortgage   Arrangement under which an elderly homeowner, who does not need to meet income or credit requirements, can draw against the equity in the home with no immediate repayment

salesperson   Holder of an entry-level license who is allowed to assist a broker who is legally responsible for the salesperson's activities (synonymous in some areas with *agent*)

seller's broker   Agent who takes the seller as a client, is legally obligated to a set of fiduciary duties, and is required to put the seller's interests above all others'

sellers' market   Situation in which demand for homes exceeds the supply offered for sale

settlement   See **closing**

specific performance   Lawsuit requesting that a contract be exactly carried out, usually asking that the seller be ordered to convey the property as previously agreed

subagency   Legal process by which the seller who lists property for sale with a broker takes on the broker's associates and cooperating firms in a multiple listing system as agents

survey   Map made by a licensed surveyor who measures the land and charts its boundaries, improvements and relationship to the property surrounding it

time is of the essence   Legal phrase in a contract, requiring punctual performance of all obligations

title   Rights of ownership, control and possession of property

title insurance   Policy protecting the insured against loss or damage due to defects in title: the "owner's policy" protects the buyer, the "mortgagee's policy" protects the lender; paid with a one-time premium

title search   Check of the public records, usually at the local courthouse, to make sure that no adverse claims affect the value of the title

VA   Department of Veterans Affairs (formerly Veterans Administration), which guarantees a veteran's mortgage so that a lender is willing to make the loan with little or no down payment

vendee   The buyer

vendor   The seller

warranty deed   Most valuable type of deed, in which the grantor makes formal assurance of title

zoning   Laws of local government establishing building codes and regulations on usage of property

Index